Homegrown

HOMEGROWN

Guidance and Inspiration for Navigating
Your Homeschooling Journey

AMBER O'NEAL JOHNSTON, ED.

a division of Baker Publishing Group
Grand Rapids, Michigan

© 2025 by Amber O'Neal Johnston

Published by Revell
a division of Baker Publishing Group
Grand Rapids, Michigan
RevellBooks.com

Printed in the United States of America

All rights reserved. No part of this publication may be reproduced, stored in a retrieval system, or transmitted in any form or by any means—for example, electronic, photocopy, recording—without the prior written permission of the publisher. The only exception is brief quotations in printed reviews.

Library of Congress Cataloging-in-Publication Data
Names: Johnston, Amber O'Neal, editor.
Title: Homegrown : guidance and inspiration for navigating your homeschooling journey / Amber O'Neal Johnston, Ed.
Description: Grand Rapids, Michigan : Revell, a division of Baker Publishing Group, [2025] | Includes bibliographical references.
Identifiers: LCCN 2025001464 | ISBN 9780800746193 (paperback) | ISBN 9780800747138 (casebound) | ISBN 9781493450640 (ebook)
Subjects: LCSH: Home schooling. | Education—Parent participation. | Individualized instruction.
Classification: LCC LC40 .H643 2025 | DDC 371.04/2—dc23/eng/20250205
LC record available at https://lccn.loc.gov/2025001464

Unless otherwise indicated, Scripture quotations are from the Holy Bible, New International Version®, NIV®. Copyright © 1973, 1978, 1984, 2011 by Biblica, Inc.® Used by permission of Zondervan. All rights reserved worldwide. www.zondervan.com. The "NIV" and "New International Version" are trademarks registered in the United States Patent and Trademark Office by Biblica, Inc.®

Scripture quotations labeled ESV are from The Holy Bible, English Standard Version® (ESV®). Copyright © 2001 by Crossway, a publishing ministry of Good News Publishers. Used by permission. All rights reserved. ESV Text Edition: 2016

Scripture quotations labeled NASB are from the (NASB®) New American Standard Bible®. Copyright © 1960, 1971, 1977, 1995, 2020 by The Lockman Foundation. Used by permission. All rights reserved. www.lockman.org

Some names and details have been changed to protect the privacy of the individuals involved.

Cover design and illustration by Amy Cerra.

The author is represented by the literary agency of Write View, LLC.

Baker Publishing Group publications use paper produced from sustainable forestry practices and postconsumer waste whenever possible.

25 26 27 28 29 30 31   7 6 5 4 3 2 1

To the fiercely committed and tender guides
who have dedicated themselves to this wild and
wonderful journey of raising homegrown kids.

Contents

Introduction 9

1. THE BEAUTY WE FIND AT HOME

The Ecosystem of a Homeschool • *Ainsley Arment* 17

Cherishing the Journey • *Greta Eskridge* 27

How Do You Know Homeschooling Is Right for You? • *Julie Bogart* 37

Finding Freedom on the Path Less Traveled • *Amber O'Neal Johnston* 46

2. THE ELEMENTS WE RELY ON MOST

Mother Nature Is a Reliable Homeschool Helper • *Ginny Yurich* 57

Slowing Down and Preparing for Challenges • *Leslie M. Martino* 66

Beyond the Classroom: Lessons Learned at Home • *Yvette Henry* 76

The Power of Good Habits • *Sonya Shafer* 85

3. THE ROADMAP FOR FORGING OUR WAY

The Enduring Wonder of a Living Education • *Leah Boden* 97

The Transformative Power of Literature in the Home • *Rea Berg* 107

Nurturing Wonder, Formation, and Belonging in the Home • *Alberta Stevens* 116

The Scenic Route That Is Homeschooling Middle School • *Trisha Vuong* 126

Preparing to Launch: Navigating the High School Years • *Susan Seay* 134

Contents

4. THE RELATIONSHIPS THAT CARRY US THROUGH

Cultivating Relationships Through Mentoring • *Sally Clarkson* 145

The Gift of Allohomeschooling • *Delina Pryce McPhaull* 154

Aristotle Smiles: The Gift of Together Schooling • *Erin Loechner* 161

I Wasn't Supposed to Homeschool: A Father's Journey • *Richard M. Smith, PhD* 168

Heartstrings and Hugs: Cultivating Connection with Our Children • *Jennifer Pepito* 176

5. THE BELONGING WE CRAVE

The Story of What Matters • *Rachel Devenish Ford* 187

Finding Home • *Mandy Davis* 196

Revolutionary and Restorative: Getting Back to the Village • *Jason B. Esters* 204

Honoring Our Home Field Advantage • *Elsie Iudicello* 213

6. THE ENCOURAGEMENT THAT SPURS US AHEAD

Connecting Through the Unexpected • *Alisha Roth* 225

Navigating Life's Wildfires • *Torrie Oglesby* 233

Joy Comes in the Morning • *Erika Alicea* 240

When Homeschooling Heals • *Brytni McNeil* 250

7. THE VISION INSPIRING OUR DAYS

Engaging Imagination and Creativity Through Vision • *Nicole Cottrell* 261

We Are Uniquely Equipped • *Brenaea Fairchild* 270

Taking Your Thoughts Captive • *Julie H. Ross* 280

The Holy Audacity of an Unhurried Mama • *Min Hwang* 289

Conclusion 299

Notes 303

About the Editor 309

Introduction

When I began homeschooling over a decade ago, I quickly realized that finding information was easy, but I longed for something more substantial. Google searches provided quick answers, but my real growth came from sitting in the homes of other homeschooling moms, a cup of tea in hand, absorbing their wisdom and seeing for myself what made their homes and, therefore, their home*schools* tick. I needed to understand what fueled families to educate at home and how lifestyle, relationships, culture, and vision shaped their decisions. I wanted to hear about navigating through divorce, miscarriage, financial hardship, and health crises, and the roles spouses, friends, and communities played in each homeschooling journey. I sought to see how culture, heritage, history, and legacy seamlessly intertwined with academics within various homes.

Homegrown is birthed from these long-held desires. My prayer is that you'll feel seen and supported in the pages to come. In this one-of-a-kind anthology are intertwined perspectives from thirty of today's most encouraging and influential homeschoolers. Our goal is to provide you with faith-filled reassurance and comfort, whether you sit and soak it all in at once, or linger, exploring each idea slowly. The curated voices will speak to you as friends, and once they have, you, dear reader, will be inspired and motivated as you forge ahead.

These essays are not just stories but testimonies of perseverance, creativity, and unwavering commitment to providing a nurturing educational environment for our children. We offer a rich tapestry of perspectives on the homeschooling journey, highlighting the beauty and challenges of this unique path. Unprecedented in its diversity, this project features contributors from all walks of life, each with their own inspiring tale of dedication and perseverance.

We Are the Storytellers

You'll hear from grandmothers like Rea Berg, Julie Bogart, and Sally Clarkson, whose children have graduated and started families of their own, as well as from moms like Alisha Roth, who recently gave birth to a sweet baby who will soon join her older siblings for read-alouds and nature walks. We have dads like Richard Smith sharing their often overlooked insights, and second-generation homeschoolers like Greta Eskridge reflecting on her decades of experience from both sides of the table. While most of our contributors are based in the United States, we also have voices from jet-setting worldschoolers like Nicole Cottrell and families living across the pond, including Leah Boden and Alberta Stevens.

Throughout *Homegrown*, you'll encounter parents like Delina Pryce McPhaull, who has embraced homeschooling from the beginning, those who transitioned from public or private schools, and others who are constantly renewing their commitment to homeschool despite the uphill battles. Each narrative is a testament to the adaptability and determination that homeschooling requires. Whether it's a family living on a bustling homestead with chickens and goats or an apartment-dwelling brood finding beauty amid city life, these essays illustrate that homeschooling is not confined to a specific setting or lifestyle.

We have moms of many like Susan Seay, Brytni McNeil, and Jennifer Pepito writing alongside Erika Alicea, mom to one remarkable girl, each sharing how homeschooling has shaped their families. You'll find parents celebrating various milestones in their personal lives—whether commemorating years of marriage, navigating life after divorce or the loss of a spouse, or forging new paths with teens and young adults.

We represent a wide range of racial and cultural backgrounds, including multiracial, White, Black, Latino, and Asian parents, managing homes bustling with biological kids, adopted children, and bonus kiddos too. We live cross-denominationally with different approaches to homemaking and education but share a fierce desire to love our families well while raising children in the way they should go. Our diversity of thought, culture, and experience ensures that every reader will find a voice that resonates with their own experience while growing exponentially through the ideas and priorities of homeschooling they may never have encountered elsewhere.

Homegrown is for parents in every season of homeschooling: the early years and seasons of survival, the core years and seasons of maintenance, and the twilight years and seasons of growth and expansion. It represents the true, the good, and the beautiful, mixed with the joys and devastations this earthly voyage brings. I hope you'll appreciate the breadth of perspective and authenticity found in our essays, as this plethora of inspired homeschooling ideas from a robust collection of trusted parents in a single space is a rare jewel. Harmonizing our voices through this collection is our gift to you as we humbly offer the treasure we all wish we'd had at one point or another.

Reflections from the Field

In the opening essays of chapter 1, readers will understand why many families feel called to educate their children at home. Ainsley Arment eloquently describes the ecosystem of a homeschool as we highlight the essence of "home" and the emotions accompanying learning and living as a family. We'll discuss the responsibility of leading our children well and establish that home education is much more than teaching a body of information; it's an entire lifestyle that informs many aspects of our days and years.

Homeschoolers often prioritize other areas of child development alongside traditional subject-based learning. They see home education as an opportunity to approach learning holistically, emphasizing creativity, freedom, and exploration. Chapter 2 details how essential extras, like Ginny Yurich's time spent in nature, Sonya Shafer's good habits, and Leslie M. Martino's slower pace of life, are seamlessly woven into homeschooling days. Yvette Henry describes the rocky process of blending the roles of "mom" and "teacher" with a much-needed dose of honesty to validate our toughest days.

While home education extends far beyond lesson planning, schedules, and curriculum, these elements are still foundational underpinnings of many home learning environments. The third chapter provides detailed notes on how literature, living ideas, and a medley of morning pursuits pave the path for homeschooling through the years, including middle and high school. The essays use humor and heart as Trisha Vuong and others shine a light on daunting tasks and game-changing methods, inspiring parents to listen closely to the ins and outs of establishing a life-giving cadence.

Community and connection are crucial for long-term homeschooling success. The writers in chapter 4 delve into the emotional and relational dynamics that come with this educational choice. The relationships that develop between parents and children and the broader community are essential. You'll read how Erin Loechner's family and others build strong support networks, including extended family, friends, and community members who contribute to their children's education and well-being. We'll highlight how homeschooling dads are becoming more involved as invested thought partners, teachers, and mentors while exploring the many opportunities for connection homeschooling uniquely provides.

The face of homeschooling is expanding rapidly, with record numbers of families joining the ranks. Chapter 5 provides insight into the hearts of varied families, showcasing how they incorporate their unique locales, cultural traditions, and diverse needs into homeschooling while creating havens of belonging within their homes. Rachel Devenish Ford is a Canadian mom raising biracial teens in the mountains of northern Thailand. Mandy Davis, a former principal and Korean adoptee, longs for her children to be deeply seen. Jason B. Esters is a Black father who has found purpose within and beyond his own children's education. Cuban mama Elsie Iudicello ensures that everyone on her son's team sees him as a born person, fully deserving of all the beauty life has to offer.

Though this collection of homeschooling ideas and anecdotes is delightful, we don't sugarcoat our experiences. In chapter 6, you'll connect with homeschooling families facing everything from small, everyday obstacles to significant, life-altering events. The resilience and resourcefulness displayed by these families are inspiring. Through intimate personal reflections, Torrie Oglesby and other contributors share how they navigate these difficulties, offering readers a sense of solidarity and encouragement.

Home education doesn't come with a roadmap or one-size-fits-all guidelines. Experience builds confidence, and hopes, dreams, and aspirations carry us forward. The final chapter explains how homeschoolers like Min Hwang, Brenaea Fairchild, and Julie Ross carve paths through uncharted territory and remain committed while making critical decisions. Their stories illuminate the tenacity and creativity required to navigate this journey, offering inspiration and practical wisdom. By sharing their strategies, these women provide a beacon for those who follow, ensuring that each family's unique approach to home education is honored and supported.

Engaging, insightful, and brimming with hope, *Homegrown* will touch your heart and inspire your mind, evoking laughter and maybe even tears as you reflect deeply on bringing or keeping your children home. This book encapsulates the essence of homeschooling, blending diverse perspectives into a rich tapestry of wisdom. As you turn these pages, you'll gain renewed confidence and vision, drawing from some of the most celebrated and emerging voices in the homeschooling community. Prepare to be uplifted and empowered, gaining a deeper trust in the transformative potential of educating your children at home.

Amber O'Neal Johnston
curator and editor of *Homegrown*

1

The Beauty We Find at Home

The Ecosystem of a Homeschool
Ainsley Arment

I'm officially "the older mom." My eldest son is in college. My seventeen-year-old son is nearly a foot taller than I am, and my fourteen-year-old son is responsible for lifting any and all heavy objects in the house.

So when I take my eight- and eleven-year-old daughters to our homeschool co-op on Thursday mornings, the other mothers stare at me like I'm the eighth wonder of the world. They have young children the same ages as my girls, but they don't have crow's feet around their eyes that could tell a thousand stories or college bills to pay.

I coo at their babies and watch with amusement as they breastfeed their infants on the floor while trying to tame a spirited two-year-old with a stash of crackers and the mere tone of their voice. I feel like I'm getting one of those coveted "do-overs" in life. My younger mama-friends ask my opinion on curriculum choices, sibling dynamics, and what it must be like for us to have built-in babysitters after fifteen dateless years. But mostly, they want assurances that they're not doing this wrong.

There are tremendous stakes when you pull your children out of school and bring them home to educate them. The audacity of it is inspiring—until it's daunting. The freedom of it is thrilling—until it's terrifying.

For me, homeschooling followed the pattern of my motherhood journey. It has been one of unraveling and rebirth, of stripping away preconceptions and rebuilding a life that fosters, well, life. It has been a painful process at times—altogether beautiful and brutal, wholly nuanced and necessary. It's an invitation of acceptance and awakening, grief and growth. An invitation of awareness.

Despite what I used to think and what many people still believe, homeschooling is not an administrative activity. It's not about choosing the best curriculum, preparing for standardized testing, ensuring our children's socialization, and keeping up with the public school system. It has very little to do with any of those things at all.

Homeschooling is an ecosystem of factors that produces the kind of children we raise—some of which are entirely in our control and many of which are not. Four factors in particular come to mind.

1. The Habitat of Attachment

I recently overheard my two daughters playing with their Calico Critters. Mama Wolf was caring for orphaned Baby Mole. They were happy and loved each other very much, but like any good story, the plot thickened, and Baby Mole got adopted by Mama Bear. As the critters drove away with the baby in their tiny blue car, tears rolled down my eight-year-old daughter's cheeks.

Several weeks later—the story continuing to unfold—a car arrived at Mama Wolf's home. When she opened the door, Baby Mole was standing there on the doorstep. My daughter sobbed again.

Children are born in need of attachment. This sacred connection with another human being gives them a sense of security and identity in the world. Without it, they go through their lives feeling insecure, swept every which way by alternative caregivers.

Their natural point of orientation is meant to be you and me—their parents. Our children are hardwired to depend on us. They need us even when they don't think they need us—long before they're aware we're separate people and long after they push us away for fear of embarrassing them in public.

For centuries, society was structured to support mothers and fathers as this central point of orientation. Grandparents were like planets, orbiting around the family unit, and uncles, aunts, and cousins were like moons and stars in this synchronous solar system of connection. All other points of orientation—whether peers, teachers, or family friends—were introduced to them by way of the original family structure, which provided a safe and reliable way to expand this network of nurturing relationships. It kept the next generation from drifting out into the world without a solid identity.

I think about my youngest son, Cody, who, for the first year of his life, was laid down for his nap most afternoons by his grandmother who loved him so very much. My mother would sit in the brown tweed rocker in his nursery and hold him on her chest while she sang "Baa, Baa, Black Sheep" until he dozed off into dreamland. Every time Cody saw my mother, he cooed "Baa, baa" because he knew what was coming. His first word was not "Mom" or "Dad" or "Ball" but the words of a black sheep.

In Cody's second year of life, my mother was diagnosed with a brain tumor and passed away quite suddenly, which severed this important point of orientation for my son. Thankfully, he still had his mother and father, his brothers, and his aunt and uncle. But the loss of a significant attachment figure can leave an indelible mark that is difficult for us to fully understand.

These bonds of attachment are so strong that they affect how our brains are wired, how we feel about ourselves, and how we perceive the world. A strong parent-child attachment develops a child in ways that no curriculum, program, or self-help tactic could.

Our children need us.
For the long haul.
Through the ups and downs.
For as long as it takes.

I must confess: my eight-year-old comes to sleep in my bed more nights than not, and despite the furrowed brows I can imagine this statement might evoke, I'm not mad about it. I know the result of secure attachments throughout childhood is an adult with healthy self-esteem, age-appropriate independence, and confidence to navigate this world. From a strong foundation, they are able to create appropriate boundaries, express empathy, and value their own self-worth, not to mention have the ability to experience meaningful relationships later in life.

The stronger the attachment our children share with us, the more trusting they become. Unlike birds, we don't push our children out of the nest to help them fly. This safety net of secure attachment allows them to test their independence and spread their wings in this world.

Our culture has put such an emphasis on independence that we have lost sight of what childhood is really about. But dependence leads to independence. Closeness creates safety in separation. And connection fosters confidence.

2. The Ecology of Creativity

If you walked into my kitchen on any given day, you would not see any wall hangings from Hobby Lobby declaring "Bless This Mess" or "Sticky Floors, Dirty Ovens, Happy Kids"—but based on the condition of my home, there would be no doubt that I wholeheartedly embrace these sentiments (if not the decor). The proof is everywhere.

I recently stumbled upon an old photo from when we were a quaint family of four. I marveled at how clean our house looked. The floors were swept, the shelves were organized, and the counters were spotless. A longing for these days of order rose up in me as I glanced at our kitchen table covered in art supplies, marked with dents, splattered with paint, and stripped of stain from years of use.

I'm not saying that organization and cleanliness aren't important to me. But I've surrendered the notion of a "clutter-free" house in favor of children who have turned our domicile into their creative workshop. Model rockets are stacked along the hearth. Paintings and sketches are strewn about the kitchen table. Miniature cannons with leftover metal scraps are scattered across the coffee table—just to name a few.

Each one of my children desires to have a personal workshop of their own (a smithing shed, an art studio, a recording studio) and reminds me of this regularly. But until their goals are realized, our home serves as an all-in-one studio for their dreams, passions, and creative endeavors. And I wholeheartedly embrace it. For this too shall pass.

The other week, my eleven-year-old daughter stumbled upon a tutorial for how to draw lifelike eyes—including the shading, the eyelashes, and even the reflective glint in the corner of the iris. She set to work with a determination that only my Annie could harness, practicing her craft, drawing eye after eye until she perfected the technique, leaving hundreds of eyeballs in her wake.

I can no longer find my kitchen table.
The eyes have it.

Being free to express themselves through creative endeavors has taught my children more about the learning process than I could ever have hoped to achieve in their twelve years of formal education. In truth, learning is a creative endeavor—a messy, hands-on experience—from art to science, reading to writing, mathematics to engineering. And let's not forget about nature. Nature is the best classroom because the creativity never ceases. From exploring to excavating, climbing to crafting, nature is the *real* dirty work.

Much to my younger self's chagrin, home education does not look Pinterest-worthy. A homeschool adventure is a life in the making. As the documentarian of the one wild and precious life my children each have, I choose to behold the beauty of their stories unfolding.

Just pay no mind to the mud tracked across my kitchen floor.

3. The Realm of Imagination

While we were driving home from dinner last week, my eight-year-old asked me a surprising question.

"Mom, how does the moon know where we live?"

"What do you mean, honey?" I asked.

I saw her straining to look at the night sky from her window's view in the back seat. "It's been following us home."

In the 1991 film *Hook*, Robin Williams plays Peter Banning, a corporate lawyer and workaholic who has lost his appreciation for childhood and all its wonder. There's a scene where Peter's son Jack is angry with him and bounces his baseball against the ceiling of the airplane. After several failed attempts to get him to stop, Peter exclaims, "What's the matter with you? When are you going to stop acting like a child?"

Jack simply replies, "I *am* a child."[1]

Out of the mouths of babes.

It takes returning to Neverland and visiting the Lost Boys to reawaken Peter's imagination and enable him to delight in childhood again.

Our children's imaginations are still wild and untamed, so pure they make our insides ache with our own forgotten imaginings. Cotton candy skies and strawberry moons awaken this feeling in me, as does the sound of swirling autumn leaves or the crisp, woodsy smell of snow. For all I know, I could still be five years old.

I've reached midlife, but my childhood calls out when I forget it. It keeps me wise to wonder and awakens my awareness. It keeps me open, appreciative, and expansive to the magical ways of children. Our children don't need us to be purveyors of their imagination but nurturers of it.

They need us to love their wild.

Loving their wild is appreciating their imagination.
Loving their wild is choosing to see magic in the messy days.
Loving their wild is wondering without answers along with them.
Loving their wild is choosing curiosity instead of jumping to conclusions.
Loving their wild is remembering this process of growing and learning takes time.

In *A Tree Grows in Brooklyn*, Betty Smith writes,

> Because the child must have a valuable thing which is called imagination. The child must have a secret world in which live things that never were. It is necessary that she *believe*. She must start out believing in things not of this world. Then when the world becomes too ugly for living in, the child can reach back and live in her imagination.[2]

My imagination rescued me on many occasions as a child. When I couldn't make sense of the world's pain or life's confusing parts, when I felt sad or angry, when I was tired and undone, I turned the lock on a secret door inside myself. I found refuge in a world that was not altogether safe but was a safe haven all the same because it was mine, and I could imagine every scenario and outcome.

A child's imagination does not exist merely to help them escape reality but rather to make sense of it. In short, imagination is an essential language of childhood. Let's not expect our children to stop acting like children just yet. And while we're at it, neither should we.

4. The Refuge of Relationship

One of my favorite quips about homeschooling comes from my dear friend Leah Boden—Modern Miss Mason herself—who once said to me, "We are all entirely bonkers. We have chosen to be with our offspring 24/7."

No one prepared me for this. Like you, I choose to be with my offspring because I enjoy their company. I love them. Even more, I *like* them. And I believe that home is the best place for them to spend their quiet, growing years. But no one prepared me for the sheer intensity of living together.

All the time.
Every day.
From sunrise until sunset.

There's a lot of life lived between those bookends. Some are breathtakingly beautiful, and others are, quite simply, terrible, no-good, very bad days. Before we were parents, we got the movie poster version of parenthood, but we didn't see how the story unfolded with its unexplained mysteries, character arcs, and plot twists.

Motherhood began for me as a milky haze of smiles and snuggles and sleepy dream feeds. It was fears and tears and falling asleep with one engorged boob exposed to any and all passersby. It was joy and exhaustion like I'd never known before. It was perfection and living completely upside down.

But motherhood didn't remain this way. It has aged and changed me along with my children, leaving all of us never the same. Over the years, I have been many different mothers to the same five children, and they have been many different children to me. That's the gift of sharing life with these precious souls.

Parenthood is a beautiful dichotomy.
A tortured symphony of loving and becoming.

Growing up feels a lot like this too. Kids pull us close one moment and push us away the next. *Help me. I can do it myself. Comfort me. Go away. I love you. I hate you.* We hold these relationships in our keeping, and the safety we give our children to navigate these contradictions becomes a refuge.

Home is the place where our children learn to try out their own personalities, to see what sticks in the world. It's more sanctifying than satisfying at times. But they learn to live in relationship. We all do.

This is why math drills, science experiments, and term papers don't matter quite as much. They have their place, of course, but they aren't worthy of the import we give them—at least not at the expense of sunshine and smiles, delight and discipline, cuddling and conversations.

Home is where our kids bask in the revelry and reverie of childhood. It's a place to practice the fundamentals of relationship, and some days it Wears. Us. Out. The bickering, the forgiving, the crying and trying, the lashing out and loving again. Home is the laboratory where they prepare for the world.

Benediction

Homeschooling is an extension of parenting, and we cannot partition life from learning when we choose this path. Some nights I walk barefoot through the neighborhood and talk to the moon. But most nights, I walk softly down the hall to my children's bedrooms and whisper prayers over their sleeping heads. In the darkness, I feel the gravity of gratitude for their perfection, and my petitions to the Maker for their potential rise up in me like a chorus. In these moments, motherhood is beyond my own capabilities.

There are times when reality and the supernatural are so intertwined that it feels like I am living a dream. In these moments, I am never doing anything extraordinary but rather very, very ordinary. Listening to my baby sigh in her sleep. Watching a mourning dove gently land on the fence and *coo-woo-woo*. Holding a sleep-heavy child with croup on my chest in the dark of night. Feeling the warm morning breeze on the first day of summer or the rain-soaked stones in the garden with my bare toes.

It doesn't happen every time. But once in a while, like a divine appointment, I step outside myself into another dimension. And for just a moment, heaven and earth stand still simply for me to experience it.

A holy hush.

Ainsley Arment is the founder of Wild + Free and host of the *Wild + Free* podcast. She is the author of *The Call of the Wild + Free* and *The Wild + Free Family*, a call for families to forge their own path to a life full of wonder, adventure, and connection. She shares her passion for home education and curates monthly content for mothers at BeWildAndFree.org. Ainsley lives with her husband, Ben, and their five children in Virginia Beach, Virginia. | @ainsl3y

Cherishing the Journey
Greta Eskridge

My parents began homeschooling my brother and me in the 1980s. We didn't start off as a homeschooling family. In fact, my mom would tell you that homeschooling was never on her radar. My brother and I were enrolled in a small private Christian school, and we loved it. My parents chose private school because my older siblings had been through the public school system in our small town, and my parents weren't thrilled with the experience. They saw my brother and sister suffer adverse effects—academically, socially, emotionally, and even spiritually—during their time in public school. So eight years later, when they had a new set of kids to educate, they decided to try something different.

I fondly remember my first few years at St. Steven Lutheran School, and it was wonderful. It felt like family for all of us. We loved the teachers, the principal, the students, and their parents. Then our family encountered financial trouble, and my dad's small business hardly stayed afloat. Keeping us enrolled in private school became less important than keeping a roof over our heads. My parents were at a crossroads, feeling sure they wanted an alternative educational experience for us but not knowing how it would be possible. Then they heard about homeschooling.

That's when my life changed forever.

That might sound exaggerated, but I assure you, it's not. Homeschooling was a massive shift for our whole family. But far beyond the change to our routine and manner of education, homeschooling changed the trajectory of my life and even the lives of the children I'd one day have.

Neither of my parents had heard of homeschooling until one morning, when my mom was listening to Christian radio and heard an interview with Dr. Raymond Moore, considered by many the father of the modern-day homeschool movement in America. He talked about his book on homeschooling, *Better Late Than Early*, and his ideas for educating children in a way that involved more than just academics but also included things like faith, family, work, and service.

My mom was intrigued, but just by the idea of homeschooling. *Not for our family*, she thought. However, when she casually mentioned the interview to my dad, he was immediately all in. "This is the answer we've been looking for!" he said. "We're doing this!" It took some time, prayer, and convincing my mom that she really could homeschool us, but by the time the next school year began, we were homeschoolers.

Despite their conviction that this was the right choice for their family, my parents would be the first to tell you that homeschooling at that time was a lonely path. There were few resources available. In fact, when they first considered it, they weren't even entirely sure it was legal. (It was.) We didn't know anyone else who homeschooled. Hardest of all, though, were the reactions from family members, friends, people at the school we were leaving, and even strangers. They responded with everything from disbelief to suspicion, concern, or even anger. Because neither of my parents possessed teaching credentials or even college degrees, most people assumed they were unqualified to teach their children. Plenty of people told them they were making a big mistake with their children's lives.

And, as many had predicted, that first year was hard. It was a radical adjustment for all of us. There was an instant and significant loss in relationships as we no longer saw friends at school and knew almost no other homeschoolers. My mom went from a full-time stay-at-home mom to a full-time homeschooling mom. She now had two full-time jobs, and the transition was challenging and lonely.

School was different too. There was a new curriculum, a new teacher who was also our mom, a new schedule, and a new routine. In the earliest days of that first year, we'd start the morning at the kitchen table with our big pile of schoolbooks. Even though there was no flag, we'd stand and say the Pledge of Allegiance. That was how the day began at school (after prayer, anyway), so that was what we did at home. But it didn't last because it felt silly, and we all knew it. It wasn't long before my brother and I started asking when we could return to school.

In time, though, we found our way. I remember some hard and incredibly lonely parts of that first year and even the second; by year three, we had settled into homeschooling, which was a good fit. It grew into a very good fit.

Those are the memories of homeschooling that fill my heart to this day. Cups of tea and reading the newspaper in bed with my mom at the start of the day replaced standing for the pledge. I loved walking to the library and filling up my backpack with books I'd sail through in a matter of days. My mom read aloud so many books to us on the oversized brown couch: *Anne of Green Gables*, *The Yearling*, *Where the Red Fern Grows*, and *Beezus and Ramona*.

During the Christmas season, we worked for our dad and learned about running a small business. I joined 4-H and volunteered at the library. We made new friends as our local homeschool group grew.

Some of my favorite moments were when my mom let me do my schoolwork in our tree house, on my bed, on the back patio with the dog resting at my feet, or, my favorite, on a blanket spread out on fresh spring grass, with the blue sky overhead and wildflowers dancing in the wind all around me. Why would I ever want to return to a staid and boring traditional classroom when my new classrooms were so varied, comfortable, and beautiful? I didn't want to go back. I loved homeschooling.

I was an independent and self-motivated learner. As such, my mom gave me a lot of freedom. As long as I got my schoolwork done, she didn't seem to care where I did it or when. She knew I thrived in that atmosphere. I say I was self-motivated, but really, my biggest motivation to get my schoolwork done was to allow plenty of time to read and babysit. Both were my passions, and I worked my school schedule around them.

By age thirteen, I began taking a few classes, like history and sign language, at a local community college with my older sister and a mom I babysat for. By sixteen, I was ready to graduate, so my parents held a sweet graduation party in our backyard. I spent the following summer in Hungary helping to build an orphanage and then came home to start community college full-time. Just like that, my homeschool days were over.

They weren't truly over, though. Homeschooling was in my blood, and even more, in my heart. My days as a homeschool student were done, but the rest of my homeschool journey was just beginning.

● ● ●

I graduated from college with a degree in English and creative writing and went on to get my teaching credential. At the tender age of twenty-two, I stepped into a public school for the first time as a ninth- and twelfth-grade English teacher. In the five years that I taught, I learned a few critical things: I loved high school students, I loved teaching, and I would definitely homeschool my kids whenever they came along. I also learned what pot smelled like, how to break up a fight, and how to help kids who hadn't read a book since *Cat in the Hat* in kindergarten learn to love reading again. But that is an essay for another day.

What stood out to me repeatedly was that I could not meet the educational and emotional needs of my 150 students in the fifty minutes I saw them each day. There was not enough of me to go around. I wanted to meet those needs. I wanted to desperately. But we were all stuck in a system that wasn't built for a personalized, individualized educational experience. Instead, it was a model of pushing all learners through the same round hole, no matter the size or shape of their learning needs.

Years later, I read the book *Dumbing Us Down* by John Taylor Gotto, and he describes it this way: "What's gotten in the way of education in the United States is a theory of social engineering that says there is one right way to proceed with growing up."[3] I couldn't help but compare his description to my educational experience, which perfectly suited my needs as a learner and person. An education that was full of the things that I loved, that delighted me and brought me joy. I knew I wanted to offer my children that kind of educational experience. So, when I became pregnant with our first child, I made the difficult decision to quit the public school teaching job I loved and pursue a new career as a homeschooler.

I felt more than prepared for my new role. After all, I had experience as a homeschool student and as a classroom teacher. All that remained was to find a group of fellow homeschoolers to join, and I'd be ready to embark on this new journey as a homeschooling mom. My son was only an infant, but I could hardly contain my excitement as I thought of the years of learning together that lie ahead for us both.

I imagined making learning beautiful, fun, and rich for him. As I stepped back into the world of homeschooling, I realized it had changed so much since my mom homeschooled me. She used the order form in the back of a thin homeschool catalog and mailed in her check to get a box of books from the two or three kinds of curriculum available. Now, there were so many curricula to choose from, plus many books about homeschool philosophies and methods. I dove in headfirst, ready to learn about them all.

After reading the seminal tome on classical education, *The Well-Trained Mind* by Jessi Wise and Susan Wise Bauer, I decided this was our educational path. At this point I had two sons, ages three and one, and we hadn't started any kind of formal homeschooling, but I just knew this style of learning would be the perfect fit.

What I didn't realize was that I was attracted to the classical education method for the wrong reasons.

As I read about first graders studying Latin, middle schoolers learning the trivium (I had to look that up), and high schoolers who were more academically advanced than most college students, I thought, *I want that to be my kids*. If I had finished that thought honestly, it would have been, *to prove to everyone that homeschooling worked for me and it's working for my kids. Homeschooling works!*

The temptation to choose an educational method because I had something to prove was powerful. There was a part of me that wanted to show all the people who had doubted my parents and me that homeschooling did, indeed, work. That it was, in fact, awesome! But doing so would have meant missing out on one of the greatest parts of homeschooling: teaching the whole child based on their needs and the things that lit them up.

Thankfully, I also read some other books that showed me what I longed for. I didn't really want kids whose elementary school Latin skills I could show off to make myself feel better. I wanted kids who loved to learn, were curious, and enjoyed our family life. I read *Educating the Wholehearted Child* by Clay and Sally Clarkson, *For the Children's Sake* by Susan Schaeffer Macaulay, and *Honey for a Child's Heart* by Gladys Hunt, and

I felt like those authors were speaking to my heart. I learned from homeschool veteran Carol Joy Seid and was introduced to the educational philosophies of Charlotte Mason. I began to have a bigger and more beautiful vision for homeschooling.

I thought back to the things I'd loved most as a homeschool student: lots of reading, lots of time in nature; freedom to work at my own pace; incorporating my passions, interests, and faith as part of my schooling; and an emphasis on relationships. Those were the things I wanted to include as I homeschooled my kids. I especially longed to cultivate relationships not just among our family but also with fellow homeschool families. I wanted a community for my kids and for myself. This desire led me to one of the very best parts of my homeschool journey: creating our homeschool group, which we call Adventure Club.

Since I was a teen, I'd known that I wanted to homeschool my own kids, and teaching public high school only confirmed it. That confidence made me feel sure all the details, including finding a homeschool group, would work out when I got there. It was upsetting, then, when I began to look for a group to join and couldn't find any that fit. There were groups in the city I lived in and in cities nearby. I visited a few and just read about others on their websites or Facebook pages. Some were decidedly not religious. Others only met for co-op classes, and others were made up of unschoolers who preferred entirely self-directed learning. Not one was a good fit for me and my kids. I began to feel discouraged and even sad and lonely. The reality did not match the vision I'd had in my head.

I tried recruiting friends to homeschool, but they'd put their kids in preschool because that is what most people do. My kids were doing preschool at home because I was already homeschooling. My conviction to homeschool hadn't changed, but I began feeling left out as all my friends and even my son's friends were part of a world that we weren't. Like my parents before me, I found that walking a different path can be lonely. But I didn't waver. I knew this was the path our family was supposed to be on, so I kept asking everyone I knew about homeschooling groups in our area and talking up homeschooling to all my friends and their friends. If I couldn't find a community to belong to, I'd create my own!

In the end, that's precisely what happened. I finally stumbled upon a group of families pursuing the kind of homeschooling I longed for: literature-led learning with lots of time for outdoor play and exploration. These parents were heavily influenced by the educational philosophies of Charlotte Mason and gathered monthly to read her books. I had not yet learned about Charlotte Mason, but I quickly discovered her ideas embodied the ones that most spoke to my heart as I'd begun to read homeschooling books a few years back. I knew I'd found a place to belong.

There were a few other mamas in the group who were ready to start weekly meetings with our kids in tow, so we began. We started at the playground, meeting every other week. It only took a few weeks for us to decide we wanted more time together and our natural surroundings to be more . . . untamed. So we abandoned the swings and slides for the nature trail and upped our meetings to every week. Mamas and children had never been happier.

Our kids made forts of tree branches and blankets, splashed in creeks, found bugs and lizards and frogs, and got delightfully dirty and tired. We read books together, recited poetry, and learned the names of the flowers, plants, and trees we saw on the hiking trail each week. As our kids grew, so did our confidence, and we began to explore new trails, longer trails, and trails farther from home.

When our group began meeting, my kids were five, three, and one. Now they're twenty, eighteen, sixteen, and there's one more in the mix who's thirteen. We've met out in nature with these same homeschooling friends every Tuesday for fifteen years! It's the legacy I dreamed of, hoped for, and worked hard to create and then keep.

All these years later, our homeschooling journey is equal parts sitting around the dining room table, eating snacks, reading good books together, and hiking miles of trails with our Adventure Club. It's meeting the challenge of teaching my dyslexic kids to navigate reading in a way that makes sense to their differently abled brains and celebrating when they win hard-fought battles. It's taking the day off to be outside because there is a wildflower superbloom and we can't miss it. It's seeing my kids are often "behind" their public school counterparts but believing it will all work out in the end. It's days at the tide pools, squealing with delight because we found starfish and an octopus. It's changing our math curriculum over and over again because math is hard for all of us. It's watching lifelong friendships flourish because homeschooled kids are socialized. It's watching kids dress up in costume for book club, and no one is embarrassed because books are cool and our community is even cooler. It's worrying if I've done enough to prepare them for life and then seeing them flourishing and trusting that I have. It's exhausting and exhilarating and mundane and magnificent and painful and precious, often all in the same day.

What stands out to me as I reflect on all these memories and years of homeschooling is that it's hard—and it's worth it. Not "homeschooling is hard *but* worth it." And. *And* worth it. Homeschooling is hard *and* worth it. Both of those things were true for my parents when they started this homeschool journey with me, and both of those things are true for me as I've continued the journey with my kids. Homeschooling is one of the best gifts my parents gave to me. Now I know the sacrifice it entailed. They'd be the first to tell you it was worth it. Just like I'd be the first to tell you homeschooling our four kids has been worth it. I would not trade this life and all the tears, worry, glory, and good it's been for any other. I'm incredibly grateful for homeschooling.

Greta Eskridge is a second-generation homeschooling mom to four. She is passionate about creating connection, preserving childhood, and chasing adventure. She is the host of the popular *Greta Eskridge Podcast* and author of *Adventuring Together* and *100 Days of Adventure*. | @maandpamodern

---

How Do You Know Homeschooling Is Right for You?
Julie Bogart

I could never homeschool. My kids and I would fight all day."

"I'm not a teacher. If my kids need to learn a subject I'm not good at, how will they learn it?"

"What if my kids don't make friends and are sad they missed school traditions like football games and prom?"

"My partner and I want to homeschool, but my family is against it. I worry about how my parents will treat my kids compared with their cousins who are in school."

"What if I'm not good at homeschooling? What if I fail my children?"

I got these kinds of comments while on soccer fields, at piano recitals, and in dentist chairs. Predictably, whenever I told another parent my kids were being homeschooled, they would either defend their child's school experience or criticize my homeschooling choice. I've learned in the last forty years that talking about homeschooling is like a Rorschach inkblot test for parenting. When a homeschool parent declares that they gladly spend twenty-four hours a day, seven days a week with their children *and* have the confidence to solely provide for their children's education, other parents feel just a *teensy-weensy* bit judged, and maybe a tad guilty too.

Some of today's parents are obsessed with giving their children the best possible childhood of all time, forever and amen. That means that any choice these parents make must be the top choice, which is *a lot* of pressure. Homeschooling, then, is either the best choice ever or the worst possible option. Very little room exists in the current cultural Zeitgeist for homeschooling to be an "ordinary" educational path. And yet, if we get right down to it, that's exactly what homeschooling is—one educational choice among many, each of which has strengths and weaknesses.

You get to decide whether home education is a good fit for your family right now and whether to keep going as each year goes by. You get to make this decision free of the responsibility to ensure that it is the *only and best* schooling strategy for every and any child, for every and all years. The happy functioning of your family is your responsibility—no one else's. In short, you get to decide whether homeschooling is right for you!

So, with this understanding in mind, let's talk about homeschooling as one of many educational options you might choose for your family. You don't get extra brownie points or gold stars for homeschooling. No one but your family will truly appreciate how hard you work, how tirelessly you give, or how incompetent you often feel. No one can fully appreciate how thrilling it is to see a child learn to read in *your* lap. No one else will celebrate the year your thirteen-year-old broke through in algebra the way you will. These experiences are yours and yours alone. But let me tell you right up front—as someone who made that choice for my five children—I've never regretted it.

What makes homeschooling unique among educational options is this: as a learning strategy, it's less about school and more about home. The home becomes the key place where learning, love, and living happen all day, every day. Today's classrooms often attempt to mimic aspects of home—they import sofas, create reading nooks, or invite kids to break into small groups to collaborate on projects. But no matter how cozy the environment, kids in school are not at ease the way they are at home.

A home education allows kids to be relaxed and curious. They can put their entire energy into finishing a puzzle or handwriting the letter *b* without worry that a bell will ring to cut them short or, conversely, that they'll have to sit and wait patiently for everyone else to finish. Home can be an optimal place for children to be the natural learners they are born to be!

So, how do you know if your home is where the learning ought to happen? That's the subject of this essay, so grab a mug of your favorite hot beverage and settle in. I've got you covered.

Three Reasons *Not* to Homeschool

Before I extol the wonders of home education, there are good reasons *not* to homeschool. See if any of these are yours:

1. **You don't want to.** That's a good enough reason. You don't have to defend your choice. If you choose to homeschool, some part of you should *want* to be home with your kids, providing for their education. Homeschooling because you think you *should* rather than because you *want to* is not a great reason. Why? Because homeschooling is demanding. For all its wonderful benefits, it is time-consuming and weighty with responsibility. If you begin with a feeling that you don't even want to be there, it will be harder to put in that effort when the going gets tough. And that's okay. Millions of children are educated in traditional schools. Put your heart and energy into a school until you feel differently.

2. **Both parents work full-time.** Kids deserve invested educators. It's unrealistic to expect children to self-educate while the adults in the house are busy elsewhere during the main hours of the day. Some families tag team their work schedules. They find a way to homeschool while swapping who works and when. Under these conditions, the key is to ensure that children are not expected to sit quietly at a table, working through a textbook alone, waiting for a parent to emerge from the car or an upstairs office. The central part of a child's day should have a parent/adult available for conversation and academic support.
3. **You're depressed, stressed, or ill.** Homeschooling thrives when life at home is (on balance) filled with optimism, curiosity, and time to indulge various interests. There may be a season in your life when you're recovering from grief at the loss of a loved one. Perhaps you're uncovering trauma from your childhood or are struggling with postpartum depression. Maybe you've gotten a cancer diagnosis and are about to start chemotherapy. If you need to take good care of yourself and homeschooling feels like too tall an order, it's okay to simply step back and attend to your needs until you feel buoyed and ready to return to a lifestyle of learning with your children.

Eight Reasons *to* Homeschool

There are many more reasons to homeschool than not, however. See if any of these spark a feeling of *That would be a wonderful experience to have with my family!* If so, you may be an excellent fit for this incredible life of shared learning.

1. **You want to.** Go for it! Perhaps you've seen other families homeschool, and you're tempted to try. Shoot

your shot! Dive in. One of the unwitting benefits of the COVID lockdowns is that many parents who *wanted* to try homeschooling were afforded a chance to test the waters without risk. We learned from that experience that parents who had a hunch homeschooling would be good for their children usually discovered they were right! You can take that to the bank. If you want to try it, by all means—jump in. If it doesn't work out, your kids can return to traditional school the following year. Promise!

2. **You want your kids to love learning.** A popular reason for homeschooling is that parents wish they could see their children light up when learning about the big, beautiful world we inhabit. Too many kids get caught on the treadmill of standardized testing and assessment. They lose touch with the surprise of a baking soda volcano or the joy of skip counting while tossing a Frisbee. The delight-based learning that comes so easily to your toddler can be transformed into a vibrant, pulsating energy for school-age kids when they learn at home. Homeschooling allows children to follow their passions, stick with a particular activity for as long as they're interested, and easily create connections between subject areas.

3. **You want to tailor the education to the child.** Today's neurodiverse families find homeschooling to be a true balm after trying to fit into standardized school settings. Homeschooling allows your child to be at a fifth-grade level in science, a second-grade level in math, and a seventh-grade level in reading. Each child gets to move at the individual pace that is right for them. The content of the subject areas can be suited to a child's particular interests and tastes! Truly, tailor-made education is one of the best reasons to homeschool.

4. **You want your children to form powerful bonds in your family.** Amazingly, homeschooling provides a cohesive family culture. As your children spend time together, they create shared memories that last a lifetime. They discover that their family story is uniquely theirs. Through years of negotiating their relationships, they often discover real friendship as adults and create bonds that help them feel supported and connected. This is the report of many, many homeschool families with adult kids.

5. **Your children have time-consuming passions.** Some kids are destined to be Olympic skiers or gymnasts. Others act on Broadway. Still other children and teens love horses, writing music, quilting, or 4-H. Kids who have these kinds of passions need time to do them. School demands a specific set of hours in a particular location. Homeschooling is flexible. It can fit around sports schedules and theater tech weeks. Homeschooling allows your kids to specialize early, if that's what serves them best.

6. **You want to give your children a particular education.** Some families homeschool because they have a set of preferences—religious, political, humanities emphasis, STEM. There are additional parents who are interested in cultivating critical thinkers. They want to teach kids *how* to think rather than relying on school to teach kids *what* to think. Still others feel that the schools where they live unfairly discriminate against their children. And finally, homeschooling allows some families to take learning on the road! Traveling to other countries or choosing to homeschool while driving around the United States in a camper is one of the remarkable benefits of learning outside the classroom.

7. **Your child is bullied.** One of the most poignant reasons kids are pulled out of school is the rise in bullying—whether on the playground or through cyberbullying attacks. Homeschooling helps to protect children from unsupervised attacks by other students. The long-term effects of bullying on children are real and serious. Bringing children home so that they can feel safe and loved is a perfectly valid and important reason to embark on the project of home education.
8. **Safety.** Enough said. Today's brick-and-mortar buildings are not enough to prevent horrific, unprovoked attacks on our children. Many parents choose homeschooling for that reason alone.

What I loved most about homeschooling was that it took my family on a shared learning adventure. Each night, as we sat to eat dinner, we'd discuss a topic that had been a part of the day. We might talk about a documentary we watched or which birds showed up at the feeder. One of the kids might read a poem they wrote, or we would discuss our opinions about the American Revolution. Even though plenty of families have enjoyable conversations at mealtime regardless of where their kids go to school, homeschooling creates a family story of *shared* learning.

Our insights and ideas build on each other's. What we learned during the day together shows up at bath time, on drives to the dentist, and over dinners on the deck in the summer. Why? Because when you homeschool, learning happens all the time. It all counts. Children see their education as indistinguishable from the rest of their lives—all of it flows together.

Certainly, there's a learning curve for the homeschooling parent too. In the first year, it's easy to assume that your job is to replicate what your children might learn at school. You may be tempted to line up the workbooks or do each subject for a set time each day. You may even assume that testing is an essential tool for measuring progress. But as you lean in to the unique experience of guiding your young learners, a strange thing happens to you too.

You discover the *heart* of what it means to learn.

Where education and schooling used to mean mastery of facts for tests, homeschooling reveals that learning is an ongoing conversation about any subject that ranges over a variety of sources—from comic books to movies to museums to dress-up clothes to arts and crafts to cooking. The story of learning becomes intertwined with the joy of spending time with your favorite people. Just as you loved watching your baby roll over, sit up, and eventually walk, now you get to see your child learn to handwrite, read, and code. The day your child spontaneously shows you a poem they've written or the base-12 times table they developed purely because they were curious is an incredible day!

The real question to ask yourself is this: How would it feel to wake up with your children each morning, tumble down the stairs in your jammies, and know that today, you all get to go on an adventure of learning together? Picture a curiosity-guided, tailor-made education designed to awaken your senses so you appreciate this big, bold, beautiful world together. What might that be like? Do you dare dream you could have that life together? If so, hop on board! There are millions of us here to help you. As I said at the top of this essay, it's one choice I made for my family that I've never regretted. I wish that for you too.

Julie Bogart is known for her commonsense parenting and education advice. She's the author of the beloved book *The Brave Learner*, which has brought joy and freedom to countless home educators. Her newest book, *Raising Critical Thinkers*, offers parents a lifeline in navigating the complex digital world our kids are confronting. Julie's also the creator of the award-winning, innovative online writing program called Brave Writer, now twenty-four years old and serving 191 countries. She home-educated her five children, who are globe-trotting adults. Today, Julie lives in Cincinnati, Ohio, and can be found sipping a cup of tea while planning her next visit to one of her lifelong learning kids. | @juliebravewriter

Finding Freedom on the Path Less Traveled
Amber O'Neal Johnston

When my husband, Scott, first approached me about homeschooling, I quickly laughed it off as one of his corny pranks. He tried numerous times to gauge my reaction to his preposterous idea, and with each effort, I offered him only a giggle and a roll of my eyes. It wasn't until he took my hand across the table during a rare date night and told me sincerely that he was not joking that I straightened up and listened to what he had to say.

As he explained his rationale and asked if I'd be willing to give home education a try, my muffled giggles quickly morphed into stifled tears as I tried to imagine my new life. I envisioned old-school memory drills washed down with dull textbooks and hours of worksheets, quizzes, and multiple-choice exams. No matter how much vision Scott tried to give me, at that moment I couldn't see past my own education. And I couldn't accept that I would be the purveyor of boredom for my spunky, vivacious daughter.

We'd spent her early years living vibrantly. Our days were filled with scrumptious stories read on cozy blankets in the park and visits to a tiny history museum that hid Etta the Mouse in various displays for children to spy while visiting. We drank hot apple cider with cinnamon whipped cream at the local coffee shop and visited the fire station up the street from our home. We hiked tree-lined trails with friends, took classes in the basement of the art museum, and snagged great seats for our town's best theater performances.

Before it was time for "real" school, our growing family would run away to the mountains or the beach, depending on our mood, and walk around small towns together as we experienced slices of Americana that my schoolbooks had never spoken of. Sometimes, our mini road trips turned into epic drives to other regions of the country as we slipped into the daily rhythms of life far from Georgia. Scott and I were already planning to take our adventures abroad when time and money allowed so we could show our kids as much of the world as possible.

Our lives were full of adventure, and homeschooling felt like the end of all that. Even a quick search online pulled up flash cards, online classes, and boring books that reminded me why I'd always wanted school to be over. How could I honor my husband's request if it meant losing a massive piece of what made me tick? I wanted my children to have an excellent education, but I didn't want to sign up for a life of the mundane. It felt like an impossible dilemma.

As I explained my feelings to Scott, he threw me a lifeline.

"How about if you commit to one year? If you don't enjoy homeschooling and don't feel like it's right for our family after that year, we'll stick with our original plan, and I'll never ask you about it again."

I took that deal and ran with it. I knew that I'd hate being stuck in the house and that our daughter, Nina, would buck under the pressure of "school at home," so I figured his suggestion was the best way out. I'd show him that we weren't meant to be stifled and that maintaining an exuberant home that would give our daughter a break from the drag of schoolwork would be a better effort than trying to combine the two.

And so, our homeschooling journey began.

• • •

With a toddler in tow and a bun in the oven, I shifted my intention from that of a stay-at-home mom with littles to that of a homeschooling mom of a school-age child, not knowing that my identity wouldn't change nearly as much as I'd expected. I began researching various methods for educating children, and much to my surprise, I found that though the education I'd received was still considered standard, there was an entire world of people who were reimagining what learning could be. The more I read, the more curious I became, and I began to feel tiny bits of excitement welling up inside me.

A living education. That term came up repeatedly across various materials. The idea of a living education spoke to me so completely that I found it hard to consider anything else. Knowing I could step away from the most traditional path to help my children form their own unique relationships with people (past and present), places, things, and ideas inspired me to no end.

I started to envision our home as a nucleus of learning from which life would burst forth rather than a finite place housing desks, chairs, and a directive to do things the way they'd always been done. When I stepped back to evaluate this "new" view of education, I was quickly reminded (by my wise mama) that what I saw as new was actually an updated version of an older way of life. A life where parents confidently knew what their kids needed to learn and facilitated that learning through interactions with the community, well-written books, engaging discussions, beautiful ideas, valuable experiences, and their natural intuition.

This renewed and updated nostalgia was something I believed in and wanted to get behind, but pulling my big-picture ideas into an actionable plan for our days wasn't easy. Still, through the hard days and long nights, I found joy tucked inside each crack. The deeper we dug into the rich soil of the "homeschool life," the more our family bloomed. I knew that, despite the weeds and stones, we were rooted in the perfect spot. As a home educator, I relished the freedom and ability to move within our family's natural waves and rhythms. At the end of the first year, Scott asked how I felt about continuing. The answer was easy, and we both knew it. I claimed freedom as my reason for homeschooling, and that freedom has fueled our path ever since.

Freedom to Change Plans

From the beginning, I've relied on the freedom to change plans. My husband's vision for homeschooling was that we would accelerate our daughter through formal schooling. He felt that Nina was precocious and was being held back from developing to her full potential by a fatally "late" birthday. He knew she was ready to start school in the fall, but our local schools had a strict policy about age cutoff dates. His theory was that we could homeschool her for a couple of years and then enroll her in school when it was obvious that she shouldn't be held back.

I wasn't sure about his plan, but I noticed that Nina seemed more at home with older children and had already reached the goals our chosen pre-K program shared during the open house we attended. (Little did I know that many new parents feel the same about their firstborns.) I didn't want her to be held back by the calendar, so I officially started her in "school"—in our kitchen—that fall. All was going well during the day, but each night, when I settled in to read essays and books from various education philosophers and writers, I noticed that even when they disagreed about the paths for older children, they all found consensus on one thing: a slow childhood is a gift.

I wasn't prepared to hear that. I didn't even know what *slow childhood* meant. On the one hand, I couldn't understand why we wouldn't take every opportunity to move our girl along as quickly as possible. And on the other hand, I felt drawn to the idea of meandering down the lane of childhood. I wondered what removing our kids from the race altogether would be like. Would they fall behind? And if so, who would they be behind, and what would that matter when they were sixteen, twenty-four, or forty? And what if the opposite were true? What if slowing down now meant they'd develop a stronger foundation to live well later?

I mulled these ideas over with Scott, and we became convinced that we wanted to not only backpedal on our initial homeschooling motivations but do a complete U-turn. At the end of that first school year, I sat Nina down and said, "Congratulations on completing your first year! Yay! And now that you've finished kindergarten A, you get to do kindergarten B!" She started cheering and jumping up and down. We ate ice cream and played with her bucket of consignment sale My Little Ponies to celebrate. And that was that. We settled into another full year of play, stories, exploration, and natural learning, and it was one of the best decisions we've ever made.

That's when I learned that the freedom to change plans is a superpower, and I've called upon that power many times in the ensuing years. With home education, there is no bureaucracy or red tape to wade through when you want to shift direction. When you know better, you do better, and you can start any time. Knowing that we don't have to live forever with every decision we make helps prevent analysis paralysis, allowing us to take measured risks and experiment in ways that aren't possible within the confines of community-based schooling. The freedom to change my mind is a gift, and I treasure it.

Freedom to Prioritize Free Time

When my kids were little, it was easy to maintain a comfortable pace of life by managing our family calendar well. I tried to steer clear of weekly commitments, and we had plenty of time to rest, play, learn, and spontaneously set out on adventures. But as the kids grew, their personalities firmly led them down different paths, and they wanted to delve into various activities outside the house. Initially, we said each child could pick one activity, but at times, even that moderate approach threatened to consume the margin we'd so carefully protected.

There was a constant flow of opportunities to learn new things and have fun experiences within our community and friend groups, and I wanted to say yes to all of them. Yes, I want my children to play an instrument and sing in the chorus! Yes, I want them to be on the swim team, dance in *The Nutcracker*, and learn to play soccer! Yes, we wanted in on book club, scouting, musical theater, and coding class! Yes to nature club, Little League, club volleyball, and 4-H! I didn't want my kids to miss out on any of these great activities, and though I resisted and often said no, we slowly slipped into the land of the Very Full Calendar.

I kept telling myself that when such-and-such ended, we wouldn't sign up for anything new, and I mostly kept that promise. But then, rather than the kids being pulled into a new activity, I would join a committee, a women's group, or a volunteer project. And my husband would say yes to being on one board and then another. The merry-go-round kept spinning, and I couldn't figure out how to undo what we'd done. Everything snuck up on us so quietly and innocently. Life continued this way for nearly a year, and ultimately, travel saved us.

We were planning a big trip overseas, and since we'd be gone for several months, we didn't sign up for many things and stepped away from what we'd already been doing. When we boarded the plane we had a clean slate, and though I'd assumed we'd come back and pick up where we'd left off, those three months away changed me.

While we were gone, I studied my children and myself and carefully noticed how we maneuvered when outside activities weren't dictating our time. I saw when we went to bed, how our mornings flowed, what we did during the day, and how peaceful life felt. I also witnessed incredible bursts of discovery and insight in my kids. They weren't just reading and playing more but thinking more. Thinking about the things they saw and the conversations we had. They were leaning in to relationships and growing from them as they gave of themselves. Each child engaged in exciting projects, and adventuring became second nature again.

None of this was new to me. I wasn't uncovering something I'd never known was there. Instead, I was reclaiming the life we'd lived before I'd gotten swept up in the fervor of wanting to give my kids the best of everything all at once and before I'd been stricken with a "disease to please" that held such a tight grip I lost the ability to say no to anyone I cared for or respected.

After experiencing those months of freedom, I returned home with a resolve to never again allow our free time to be sucked up, even with tantalizing "must-haves." Since then, we've all learned to protect space in our family. We value our ability to come and go, to pick and choose, and to pursue a life of adventure. After years of this approach, even my teenager will say, "I'd love to try that, but I'm going to wait until something else ends because I don't want to give up my free time." Whenever I hear that, I know we're on the right path.

Freedom to Read Expansively

In recent years, we haven't been able to turn on the news without hearing about national debates over student curricula. Some of the disagreement is more of what's always been—well-meaning and passionate educators wanting to improve how and what kids are taught in the classroom for the sake of the children. But not all of what's happening is so benign.

Books and curricula, particularly history lessons, have become politicized, and things have gotten ugly. The more I learn about banned book lists, and the strict lesson parameters and directives, much of which are meant to muzzle mouths seeking to share the rich history of people who look like my children and me, the more thankful I am for the freedom my children have to read expansively.

This freedom is most apparent in history reading, where my family digs in deeply to try our best to touch the times we're studying. We can explore competing and controversial viewpoints while accepting that human nature dictates that people can simultaneously pursue outstanding achievements while committing evil deeds and knowing that any accurate survey of history will necessitate a discussion of both.

In our home, no books are off-limits according to someone else's agenda. Our children can read deeply in every direction, and I love it. Years ago, while reading *When Children Love to Learn*, I came across this vision for holistically studying history: "The child is to come away having seen the sights; tasted the foods; experienced the struggles; appreciated the culture, life, and times of the real people of history."[4] My goodness. I want that for my children and, honestly, for myself too.

The freedom to read and study a varied, broad feast of books doesn't stop with history. The same applies to our shelves of tall tales, coming-of-age stories, fairy tales, mysteries, historical fiction, folktales, biographies, sci-fi, fables, poetry, essays, mythology, and fantasy picture books and novels explored through the years. My kids enjoy traditional classics in an informed manner while swimming in rich cultural texts reflecting our own background and others' without anyone's fears, preferences, or ignorance determining their learning path. This is one of the greatest freedoms that home education has afforded us. So much so that I wrote *Soul School*, an entire "book of books" to share the beauty of Black American children's literature with families everywhere.

Our homeschooling path has taken many turns as we've traversed over mountains and through valleys. I've changed my mind myriad times and spent many days celebrating wins while humbly learning from my mistakes. But one thing has not faltered: freedom attracted me to home education, and freedom is why my family still starts our days reading, singing, and laughing at the kitchen table over a hot breakfast and a big pot of tea. I have many years of homeschooling left, and I plan to soak up all I can as we learn to live well together.

Amber O'Neal Johnston is an author, speaker, and worldschooling mama who blends life-giving books and a culturally rich environment for her four children and others seeking to do the same. She recommends we offer children opportunities to see themselves and others reflected in their lessons, especially throughout their books, and she's known for sharing literary "mirrors and windows" on HeritageMom.com and @heritagemomblog. Amber is the author of *A Place to Belong*, a guide for families of all backgrounds to raise kids to celebrate their heritage, community, and the world, and *Soul School*, a work of masterfully curated booklists, sorted by age, for diving into the fullness of the Black American cultural experience.

2

The Elements We Rely on Most

Mother Nature Is a Reliable Homeschool Helper
Ginny Yurich

I thought—I was convinced, even—that I was going to be a fantastic mother. It was my plan. I'd read all the books, babysat (very little, but still), and liked kids. Right before we had our first child, a brief but frantic thought floated through my mind: *What exactly are we going to do all day?*

I had lived a life where all my days were filled, from start to finish, and even during the summer I seemed to have little open space. There was summer school to teach, prep for the fall start of classes, house projects, and relationships that had waned during the school year and needed an extra injection of time and effort. My minutes had mostly been accounted for, but what loomed ahead was open-ended time. And I had no idea what I was supposed to do with it.

Most of my friends already had kids, and many of them had a schedule. The schedule went something like eat, do an activity, then sleep—in two-hour increments. That seemed easy enough, so I mapped it out.

The 8:00 a.m. time slot was slated for eating, reading, and then sleeping. The 10:00 a.m. time slot was set aside for eating, a short walk outside, and then again, sleeping. I was on a roll! I also planned an activity for myself during each time slot, which would be what I would accomplish during the "sleeping" portion. My ideas included exercise, laundry, cleaning, and cooking from scratch—maybe even grabbing a little catnap for myself. I was set and ready, locked and loaded. The Mother-of-the-Year award would be arriving shortly.

And then he arrived, our precious firstborn son.

I taught high school math before becoming a mom—right up until the very end. My last day in the school system was on a Friday. All weekend long, I glamorously collected every drop of my pee in an orange jug. On Monday, upon delivery of my jug to the doctor, some crucial numbers were extracted from my urine that indicated I would need an induction for medical reasons.

That orange pee jug should've been my warning sign. It was my message in a bottle, shouting, "This is not going to go how you think it's going to go!" And lo and behold, my baby, though he was just wee hours, days, and weeks old, communicated clearly that this schedule thing was not his thing.

We returned home from a Monday-to-Friday stay at the hospital, and the following Monday (that would be two days later), my husband, Josh, went back to work. Despite an induction, IVs, magnesium sulfate, high bilirubin levels, and a failure-to-progress C-section (none of which were in my beautifully printed birth plan), I still held out hope for my schedule. I was ready for that 8:00 a.m. time block. The board books were stacked, and I was prepared. But then our sweet little one got up for the day at 4:00 a.m. and never went back to bed—seemingly ever. He wouldn't do the sleeping part. He just ate the whole time.

When I was in the hospital, the lactation consultant came in for a visit and remarked, "Wow, he's a voracious eater." I wondered how she could even know that. He was just a few hours old. But she turned out to be entirely correct. He gained one pound weekly for the first three months of his life. By six months, he had blown through every bit of clothing we had gotten from baby showers, and he was taller than me by the time he was ten.

From the very beginning—even before the very beginning—I struggled with adjusting to being a mom. It's a good thing we had another baby fifteen months later and still another one seventeen months after that. But whether it was one child or three kids under age three, I felt as though I was drowning and, as comedian Jim Gaffigan says, "someone handed me a baby"[1] (or three of them). I struggled during those early years of motherhood, and it was disappointing because I wanted so desperately to love it. But I didn't. I just floundered and stumbled my way through.

I signed up for different child-focused programs because everyone else seemed to be doing that. We'd go to the library or swim class, and no matter where we were headed, it was just so much work. I had to pack up three different-sized diapers and extra outfits (also in three sizes), plus snacks, wipes, toys, and the library bag.

It all had to be transported to the car—plus the children (who let me know they didn't really like to be transported)—and then came the circus act of trying to get them all buckled. Cue the crying. And cue some additional crying that ensued when one of them didn't want to listen to the story at story hour or one of them wanted to swim while it wasn't her turn but the one who was in the pool didn't want to be in the pool, and so forth. This was my life.

I would return home from that day's child-focused program (some of which I had handed out cold, hard cash for) utterly exhausted. Spent. I would glance at the clock. 11:00 a.m. Only eight more hours to go until Josh got home.

I joined MOPS during those years (now called MomCo International) and loved the moms at my table. I made some enduring friendships at MOPS. It was so thoughtful that it included two hours of childcare—however, my kids were the kids who were always crying and would often be brought back to me.

One day, I was sitting at my table with my crying baby and crying toddlers, and a friend who had been doing some educational research told me, "Charlotte Mason says kids should be outside for four to six hours a day whenever the weather is tolerable."

That sounded like a punishment. Four to six hours at one time? Everything we'd done never lasted more than forty minutes. The homemade playdough (handcrafted with wildflower petals and essential oils) didn't even last that long, and most of it ended up all over the floor. The sensory bin I made with multicolored chickpeas and dried pasta? Basically, I just stepped on bits of it for several years straight.

Honestly, what would a child do for four to six hours outside? And to make matters worse, this friend didn't tell me that Mason was from the 1800s. That seems like an important detail, doesn't it? I was under the impression that she was some modern-day parenting guru.

While my mind reeled against this preposterous advice, and I tried to keep a straight face and be kind because I desperately wanted friends, an awful thing happened.

My friend asked me, "Will you try it with me?"

My mind screamed, *Absolutely not!* but my body reacted differently. Answering my clamoring desire for friendship, my mouth smiled and said, "Okay."

In September 2011, I had a three-year-old, a one-year-old, and a six-month-old. My friend had three children roughly the same age, and we made plans to go to a park from nine in the morning until one in the afternoon. I knew emphatically that this was not going to go well. When my friend threw in the kicker that I wasn't supposed to bring anything but a large blanket and lunch, I knew we were doomed. What about toys? Crafts? Books? Sensory bins? A train table?

We're showing up with nothing to do? With young kids? For four hours?

But I had committed to a friend, so I arrived at our meeting spot on that crisp fall day—a park in Farmington Hills, Michigan. While I wasn't aware of the distinction then, I learned there is a difference between a park and a playground. This was a park without a playground. Translation: grass. As in a field of grass. There were also some trees and a shallow creek meandering through. And that's all. Here's what happened:

The kids played.

What I thought would crash and burn turned out to be the best day of my life because it was the first good day I had as a mom. The first one! And I had been a mom for over three years. My blood pressure dropped as the kids played and engaged in these simple surroundings. For the first time, I could truly exhale and let it all go. I got to have an entire conversation with a friend, one where we finished most of our sentences. The kids came and went, getting snacks or their lunch, and our babies slept, nursed, grabbed for the grass, or watched the vibrantly colored leaves swaying in the autumn breeze.

It was the first time that we all felt good after an outing, even me. When we headed home at the end of those four hours, all the kids fell asleep in the car. It was a miracle. And just like that, it was 4:00 p.m. I'd survived most of the day—and not just survived but thrived.

What had looked to be a day of nothing—or worse, a day of wailing and gnashing of teeth—drastically changed how we were living our lives. At first, I made the change primarily for myself. I figured being a more present and peaceful mother would be better for our family. But I quickly noticed that our kids were thriving too. They were eating better, sleeping better, feeling happier, getting along better, and more.

My observations of our children led me to learn more about what happens when we take our kids outside. I realized it helps them in every facet of their development: cognitive, physical, emotional, and social. And it helps us adults too. What an amazing thing.

Time in nature became a foundational element of our family's homeschooling, and we relied on it for everything from cognitive growth to relationship building to emotional respite. Over a decade later, it continues to be all that and more.

In the early 2010s, the National Wildlife Federation stated the average American child spent around four to seven minutes a day in free play but four to seven hours on a screen. Sadly, this has affected child development and quality of life.[2] There are more benefits to spending time in nature than could ever be covered in one section of a book and, indeed, more than could be covered in volumes and volumes of books, yet more benefits continue to surface. This holds true for all of us: you can do less and gain more with simple nature time.

When considering cognition, it's imperative to know that complex movements enhance and protect brain function. You can learn while sitting but do not have to sit at a desk to learn. Dr. Carla Hannaford wrote one of my favorite books, *Smart Moves: Why Learning Is Not All in Your Head*. She is currently in her eighties, and she often talks about how she didn't learn to read until she was ten. She remarks that it didn't matter back when she was a kid.

One of the many fascinating things she writes about is how moving in complex ways increases the function of our brain relative to our neural wiring. She references a statistic that states that elderly people who dance regularly decrease their risk of dementia and Alzheimer's by 76 percent. Those who play a musical instrument decrease the risk by 69 percent.[3] These are some substantial numbers, and it all has to do with complex movements.

When kids are given the time and the space, what do they naturally do? They engage in complex movements spurred on by their own bodies. I noticed it right away. Our time outside included an often-sung chorus of "Watch me, Mom!" As kids get older, the complex movements they attempt change, but teens and preteens still pursue them if, once again, they are granted the time and space. It may look like shooting hoops, riding a bike without holding the handlebars, riding a skateboard, or playing disc golf.

Time spent outside is excellent for cognition and also helps with social skills. Another of my favorite books is *Simplicity Parenting* by Kim John Payne and Lisa M. Ross. Payne says the primary predictor of success and happiness is how well we get along with others.[4]

What happens when we go outside? Since kids are intrinsically motivated to play, they learn to get along with others because they want to keep playing. The playground is where kids learn how to negotiate, compromise, be creative, and create something out of nothing. It is phenomenal to witness the intricacies of play when you stop and observe.

Research also shows that kids rarely get injured playing pickup games.[5] When I was a kid, we had a little ragtag baseball field near our home. We would show up, and there'd sometimes be six kids there to play and other times ten. No matter how many kids were there, we'd have to figure out all the logistics. Who is going to be the pitcher? How are we going to manage the outfield? Is someone going to switch on and off if the teams are uneven? We would have to come up with an elaborate set of rules.

If one child leaves because they've gotten hurt, all that hard work is gone. Poof! Vanished! So if the eight-year-old slams into the five-year-old running into second base and the younger child cries and goes home, all that work the kids put into figuring out the rules is over and done with. Because of this, there are hardly ever any major injuries in pickup sports; kids are intrinsically motivated to keep playing.

In environments of play, especially mixed-age play, kids learn so much. Can you see how play experiences would translate to a boardroom? You can't be overbearing, but you also can't stand back in the shadows too much. You have to be able to learn where, how, and when to use your voice. Kids are learning a vast set of skills during free play.

When your kids play, they learn those things. When you get together with your group of friends, and you've got kids of all ages, they will all benefit in ways that will extend into adulthood.

• • •

And yet, alongside all these cognitive, physical, emotional, and social benefits that appear simply because we've stepped outdoors, we also weave together a foundation of memories that we all share as a family. Whenever you have a novel experience, it expands your sense of time. And that's what nature gives—one novel experience after another.

We are making memories, celebrating real life, enhancing our homeschool, and teaching our children that hands-on moments are a worthy use of time. We have the obligation to pass on what analog experiences feel like. Homeschooling can get overwhelming at times, yet nature is always there, ready to relieve us of our burdens and enhance our lives. Extraordinary moments happen on ordinary paths.

See you outside!

Ginny Yurich is a Michigan homeschooling mother of five and the founder of 1000 Hours Outside, a global movement, media company, and lifestyle brand meant to bring back balance between virtual life and real life, reclaim childhood, and reconnect families. She is also the host and producer of the extremely popular *1000 Hours Outside Podcast*, a keynote speaker, and a bestselling author. Ginny holds a master's degree in education from the University of Michigan, and she loves growing zinnias. | @1000hoursoutside

Slowing Down and Preparing for Challenges
Leslie M. Martino

One day, my children and I were watching birds out of the back window of our home like we always do. That's when my son spotted a little thrush in the distance, nestled into a bush. It was perched on a branch and barely moving. "Is it sick?" he asked. Another child grabbed the binoculars and peered through them for a closer look. "No," she replied. "I think it's molting."

That little bird was doing something physically demanding that birds all over the world do in many different ways at different times of the year. It was in the process of replacing feathers that had become worn or damaged. Whether the new feathers are vibrant plumage or more subdued in color, birds need a great deal of energy to molt, which requires them to time it when they can best meet that demand.[6] Our resident bird nerd (a.k.a. my daughter) told us all about it.

The casual conversation continued as one child said to the others, "Birds sure do have to go through a lot to get their beautiful feathers." At that moment, I remember thinking that this was a great example of how new growth often results from challenging experiences.

Aside from bird-watching, my four children, my husband, and I have spent the last fourteen years exploring the many ways we can cultivate the imagination, develop interests, and build a deep understanding of ideas right at home. We've made each person's growth a priority, and as a result, so, too, is the kind of environment where we can know our children fully and offer them tools for meeting authentic challenges.

Our Hopes for Education

I have discovered that to know my children better and to understand who they are as learners, workers, and thinkers, I need to see them engaged with a variety of materials, under mixed circumstances, for many different reasons, over long stretches that allow for their strengths to be revealed. That means we've had to create routines that dedicate portions of the day to building knowledge through the pursuit of personal interests. In our home, we have what we affectionately call Project Time, during which, essentially, we empower our children to make choices about how they will spend their time or design parts of their day.

We encounter authentic challenges by tackling traditional subjects too. It's possible when, through inquiry, attention, risk-taking, and discovery, we seek to uncover the possibilities that the various disciplines hold for our questions and work. No matter what we are studying or doing, we attempt to use the mind well.

When I consider all the ways my children create meaning or use their minds to attempt to know something, I recognize that using the mind well is not achieved overnight. When my daughter was studying geometry, she had to apply what she already knew about spatial relationships to new areas of thinking. To find out what she understood, I needed to observe her work closely and hear her explain what was happening in her head—and I also needed to observe repeatedly. This was the case whether she was writing geometric proofs, calculating translations, or using her mind in other ways.

As an artist herself, my daughter was horrified one day when she learned of a company that made reproductions of famous art pieces. Her biggest objection was that the pieces the company was selling were not even geometrically similar to the originals. (In geometry, two figures are "similar" if they preserve the same corresponding angles and the corresponding sides are proportionally scaled by a specific scale factor.) I kept pushing the conversation and questioned whether it mattered that geometry and art intersected in this way. As soon as she began her emotionally charged rant, I realized I was witnessing yet another example of how she was honing her mind around geometry ideas.

No matter our approach to how learning should happen or what educational philosophy we embrace, when we consider the purpose that education serves, many of us conclude that we want to help our children develop the type of resilience and habits of mind that will serve them in the long run. In my book *The Joy of Slow*, I phrased it like this:

> Lifelong learning is not just something you do after a formal education. It's developing in a way that serves you over and over for the rest of your life, whether you're eight or eighty-eight. It's having ideas, engaging with the world around you, developing skills, adapting to change, and making your own valuable contributions. It's trying, failing, celebrating, and overcoming, connecting to the emotions of whatever the experiences bring, growing, and repeating. It's also exercising and strengthening your ability to make sound choices that are grounded by personal ethics and values.[7]

The world is rapidly changing, and educating our children is largely about helping them develop tools for accessing information and thinking well and ensuring they are capable of embracing the unpredictability they are sure to face. Educator Deborah Meier, reflecting on the goals for a reimagined intellectual tradition, writes of the importance of "putting all our young people in a position to explore and act upon the fundamental intellectual and social issues of their times." She continues:

> If we agree that what we want are citizens with a lively curiosity—who ask, How come? and, Why? and, Is it truly so?—we'll have the start of a new definition of "well-educated." How about being closely *observant*, prepared to keep one's eyes and ears open for patterns, for details, for the unusual? Schooling should encourage *playfulness*—the capacity to imagine, to wonder, to put things together in new and interesting ways—as well as the possession of a *skeptical and open mind*. To be in the habit of *imagining how others think*, feel, and see the world—in the habit of stepping into the shoes of others—should surely be one of our new basics. . . . And of course we need to be *respectful of evidence*, to distinguish good data from bad, to hesitate before sounding off without any facts. I'd add *knowing how to communicate* carefully, persuasively, and powerfully in a variety of media—including the skilled use of written and spoken language. My definition would also put a high premium on *caring* enough about the world and one's fellow citizens to take a stand and defend it.[8]

Indeed, one cannot achieve this by being detached from what one is learning. This kind of wonder, reflection, and critical thinking come by way of one's own investment and hard work. If we are not helping our children to become more independent as they make choices and to maintain flexibility as they persist through difficult work that is meaningful to them, then these kinds of habits of the mind will be tough to achieve. Our hopes for education must be broader than just the academic disciplines we work so hard to present. I see my role as mentoring my children toward preparing for challenges. And I believe in slowing down to capture the best parts of the experience.

What We Learn from Success and Failure

Whenever I mention slowing down, some people assume I mean taking it easy. While I don't mean to detract from the importance of rest, freedom, and intentional space for creativity and spontaneity, "slow" is more like an approach that captures a paradox of balance in which things like leisure and hard work or success and failure exist in proximity. Slowing down is about intentionality, focusing on things we value, and paying better attention to the discrete elements of our children's learning experiences. It's the opposite of mindless productivity.

We are always calibrating our speed to adjust to the learners in our home and uncover the depths of intellectual activity beyond conventional school subjects. We're not simply there to help our children beat the challenges they encounter. We're guiding them as they use the valuable feedback they gain from these obstacles to make adjustments, grow, and get better. Both success and failure are constructive pieces of the learning process as we encounter new things. Slowing down also helps us find our strengths and learn new skills that help us prepare for how we'll confront challenges in the future.

In traditional school settings, failure is often the penalty students must pay for poor performance. But at home, we can create the potential for failure to be so much more. Let's take writing as an example. Brooke Nielson, a professor at the University of California at San Diego, found through research that when writers shifted from familiar or informal forms of expression to unfamiliar or formal types of writing, they made more mistakes due to their lack of skill.[9] As they lacked experience with formal writing, they didn't have the resources necessary to pull together writing they might have achieved with greater fluency in the mechanics involved. That makes sense, right? In describing this research, educator Mike Rose had this to say about how critical the writers' mistakes were:

Before we shake our heads at these errors, we should also consider the possibility that many such linguistic bungles are signs of growth, a stretching beyond what college freshmen can comfortably do with written language. In fact, we should *welcome* certain kinds of errors, make allowance for them in the curricula we develop, analyze rather than simply criticize them. Error marks the place where education begins.[10]

Of course, in our homes, our children should come across multiple opportunities to succeed. The confidence and self-awareness that come from accomplishing something personally significant are unmatched. However, equally important is what we learn when we don't succeed. In this place, researchers and psychologists like Tania Luna and LeeAnn Renninger say, we build resilience. The key is to create a pattern of struggle and success that uses the predictability of what struggles produce (tangible or emotional rewards) to build healthy expectations for the next challenge. We no longer have to fear struggles. First, we should set ourselves up to achieve small, easy wins. Then, we can welcome a new challenge at a greater level of difficulty before succeeding again.[11]

A few years ago, my son decided he wanted to make an elaborate 3D representation of a world map out of clay. He had recently become curious about the countries on each continent, and he did quite a bit of research to answer his most pressing questions. After deciding on the type of clay he wanted to use, my son made his first attempt at the model. He quickly realized the difficulties in the project he had undertaken. Things were not going well. The many questions he had yet to answer were affecting his current work. Was this going to be a raised relief map, or something else? Would his continents be created to scale? What would he do about land shapes that were difficult to render?

His clay started to dry out too soon and crack. Had he chosen the right material? How could he preserve the clay for work he would continue the next day when he couldn't exactly wrap this large creation in a towel or store it in a container? Did he have the patience to pull this off if it took longer than expected? Pretty soon, my son wanted to give up. I tried to help him by encouraging him to narrow his list of things gone wrong to just a few he wanted to focus on and improve. I knew he needed to tackle the challenges in smaller doses. He needed an experience of success to hold on to.

From that point on, my son began to address one problem at a time and worked hard to rectify what his errors revealed. This drove him to ask himself better questions about his work, like, What size map is manageable? What features of the geography am I really looking to show? Each problem also helped him better define the areas that still required research, even when it came to his chosen medium.

Somewhere in that process, through many conversations, I worked with him to pivot his attention from dwelling on what he saw as his failure to seeing the value of the negative experience and what he could still accomplish and become. This left room for so much possibility for more information, new skills, and better methods, while learning about himself along the way.

Even though it takes just as much energy to notice disadvantages over advantages, most of us resort to processing experiences by focusing on the former. But when we practice flexibility, we allow new things to emerge from uncertainty. We can move in a direction that might be different or new.

A Home Atmosphere That Supports Risk-Taking and Resilience Building

I'd love to say I have perfectly executed the conditions that make practicing flexibility and preparing for challenges possible—but I can't. I, too, have learned deeply from my many mistakes. However, I can confidently say that a solid family culture where children are sure of the support they'll receive makes things easier. With a nurturing environment to fall back on, our children are more apt to show vulnerability. They must see home as a haven in which they have the freedom to sort out their struggles.

When setbacks do happen, recovery can intensify when children are able to draw from the closeness and connection of the family. So, we work hard to maintain the emotional stability of healthy relationships. There are many studies in which psychologists have shown that learners can calmly focus and be open to learning when fear and anxiety are absent. In a positive atmosphere, high challenges are less likely to be seen as a threat. Who wouldn't want to practice difficult skills or take greater risks in the presence of safety? A loving atmosphere also encourages humility, which "frees us from the cycle of stress, performance, and competition."[12] It helps to set a tone where it's okay to recognize when we're wrong without feeling defensive about it.

As parents, we know we are to provide safety for our children. It's something many of us feel instinctively. However, occasionally it's difficult for us to explore what safety could mean. We feel safe when we are seen, known, and loved. Yet sometimes, when our children reveal their true feelings about something, we react as if it's a personal attack. Or they express great interest in something and we discount what they deem worthy of their time. Mostly, they need to know we will hold whatever they're showing us about themselves with love and respect.

Dependable home routines allow us to intentionally make love the guiding factor in organizing our days. They help us stay prudent and mindful of how we spend our time in ways that align with our values. They can support the nurturing environment we create when we've taken the time to build habits around meaningful goals and ideas. Routines create the certainty we desire to lean on when we encounter unpredictability.

Meaning and Perspective

I'd like to return to the bird story I told you about initially. The thrush my children were observing that day was an Eastern bluebird. Here's a fun fact about them (and other bluebirds): there's no such thing as blue feathers. Well, to the eye, yes, but the feathers are blue similar to how the sky is blue. It's not because of pigment, like in red feathers. We see the blue color because of how proteins in the feathers reflect the light as tiny air pockets scatter it.[13] The variations in the color of some bluebirds are because of the angle from which we view them. That bluebird would surely produce new feathers after its molt, but in a way, the beauty of the rich color would be a matter of perspective.

Our children will grow. They will undoubtedly overcome challenges to get there. Sometimes they will succeed; other times they will learn great lessons from failing as part of that overcoming. But like bluebird feathers, whether the growth or the growth process is beautiful is a matter of perspective—or how much light we allow to filter through our lens. Encountering struggles in a safe environment where our children have the confidence to fail produces a special kind of maturity. It is vastly different from struggling under stress and receiving no support. Our parental filter usually colors and shapes the meaning of these experiences. We can slow down and offer our children more.

Leslie M. Martino is the author of *The Joy of Slow: Restoring Balance and Wonder to Homeschool Learning*. She has over twenty years of experience teaching—as an elementary school teacher, a home educator, and an adjunct lecturer for graduate courses focused on the role of the teacher in supporting children's individual work preferences. She homeschools her four children and works as an educational consultant, writing curricula, training teachers, and coaching parents to approach learning in an interest-based and child-directed way. Leslie is a speaker on topics of education and motherhood and is also a contributing writer for the Wild + Free homeschooling community. She lives in sunny Florida with her husband and children. | @lesliemmartino

Beyond the Classroom: Lessons Learned at Home
Yvette Henry

"What do you want to be when you grow up?" This question often shapes our childhood dreams and aspirations. For me, the answer was always clear: I wanted to be a teacher—specifically, a high school math teacher and the director of the Associated Student Body. My journey took me from high school halls to college lecture rooms, driven by a passion that culminated in the exhilarating moment I received the keys to my very own classroom.

Teaching was more than just a profession; it was a calling. It offered the chance to ignite the spark of learning in young minds, foster meaningful connections, and inspire a love for mathematics. Each day, the thrill of lesson planning, the joy of witnessing aha moments, and the camaraderie shared with colleagues brought me a renewed sense of purpose and fulfillment.

However, amid the hustle and bustle of the classroom, a persistent ache tugged at my heart—a deep desire to be present for the moments that mattered most with my growing family. As my husband assumed the role of primary caregiver for our two young boys, I grappled with feelings of envy and an unrelenting longing for the precious moments I was missing. The birth of our daughter intensified this longing, stirring a fierce desire to leave the classroom and become the primary caregiver as my husband focused on our family business. I became a stay-at-home mom just in time for my oldest to begin preschool. With a leap of faith and a heart full of hope, I embarked on the uncharted journey of homeschooling.

Today, I'm immersed in the world of homeschooling, navigating the joys and challenges of raising four children. My eldest is in seventh grade, followed by his brother in sixth grade, while my two youngest are bringing up the rear in third grade and first grade. I cherish this precious time we spend learning and loving at home, and I wouldn't trade it for anything. Yet, some days, this season feels daunting and beyond my capabilities. Not long ago, I even considered alternative options, exploring charter schools and local private institutions.

Homeschooling was never part of the plan. In retrospect, I can say that my husband's conviction and the influence of other homeschooling families drew me in. It wasn't a path I had envisioned for myself or my children. Yet here we are. Amid whispers of doubt and uncertainty, amid the tension between tradition and innovation, I've found myself drawn to homeschooling's promise of freedom, flexibility, and familial connection. However, I don't always love it here.

As I confront the realities of homeschooling, I must acknowledge the discomfort of this unconventional path. It's a journey that starkly contrasts with the structured environment of the classroom that once shaped my identity. Yet, within the shadows of doubt and frustration are glimmers of light—moments of unexpected grace and resilience illuminating the path forward.

Here are five aspects of homeschooling that I find particularly challenging, each accompanied by a silver lining that affirms why God has me exactly where I am.

Challenge 1: Constant Physical Affection

Navigating physical touch within the homeschooling environment is a unique challenge, as it significantly differs from my upbringing and personal inclinations. Three of my four children frequently need hugs, often leaving me feeling "touched out" at the end of a long day. Balancing their need for affection with my own comfort requires constant effort and adjustment.

Physical touch wasn't prominent in my family growing up. While I'm sure hugs were exchanged, they weren't a regular occurrence, and I lack vivid memories of being nestled in my parents' embrace. It wasn't until my husband entered my life that I realized the absence of such displays of affection in my upbringing. His efforts to introduce them into our family dynamic initially felt unfamiliar and somewhat awkward for me.

Though I am not naturally inclined toward frequent displays of physical affection, my children have a different disposition. One in particular demonstrates an insatiable appetite for hugs. His desire for physical closeness manifests in a constant yearning for reassurance and comfort as he seeks hugs in moments of frustration, happiness, challenge, and pain.

When I asked my son how often he desired a hug, his response, "Every three minutes," was eye-opening and highlighted the depth of his craving for physical connection. To ensure a balance that respects both my emotional well-being and his need for affection, I've established limits he can count on, such as taking a break to hug every thirty minutes. Setting these boundaries is a positive step in effectively managing this aspect of our time together.

Amid the challenge lies a beautiful opportunity for growth and learning. By lovingly modeling the importance of respecting personal space, I create a safe environment for my child and teach valuable lessons on self-regulation and interpersonal boundaries. In a classroom setting, these opportunities for intimate connection and boundary setting might be missed, highlighting the unique advantages of homeschooling in addressing each child's holistic needs.

Challenge 2: Balancing Meal Preparation and Education

I often feel like the only homeschooling mom who hasn't mastered the art of including my children in beautifully curated learning experiences in the kitchen. Integrating them into our daily routines can be a struggle. Meal preparation, once a source of enjoyment, has become complex due to my children's dietary restrictions and picky eating habits. With two kids having extreme dietary limitations, meal planning is a delicate balancing act. Accommodating their needs while ensuring everyone receives a nutritious meal requires me to prepare multiple dishes at each mealtime, resulting in excessive time spent in the kitchen and added stress.

Balancing meal preparation with homeschooling presents its own set of unique challenges. The constant demands of educating my children mean that time is always at a premium. Planning and preparing meals requires careful scheduling to ensure it doesn't interfere with lesson times. Interruptions are frequent, as the kids need assistance with schoolwork or other activities, making it difficult to focus on cooking. This often leads to feeling stretched thin as I strive to meet my children's educational and nutritional needs.

Despite these challenges, I've embraced the opportunity to involve my children in cooking. As my oldest two boys express interest in learning culinary skills, I welcome them into the kitchen, recognizing these moments as valuable learning opportunities. Through cooking together, we bond over shared experiences, and I witness their growth as they experiment with ingredients, problem-solve, and develop essential life skills. While the kitchen may not be my preferred domain, I find fulfillment in providing my children with practical education beyond traditional classroom subjects.

Challenge 3: Differently Wired Kids

Over the past few years, I've faced significant challenges with one of my children, leading me to seek evaluations for autism. The results confirmed my suspicions, revealing that my child is indeed on the autism spectrum, along with other identified differences. While this revelation initially brought feelings of guilt and shame for not pursuing evaluations sooner and lament for the lack of readily available resources, it also opened the door to better understanding and support.

As a former public school educator, I'm familiar with the support systems for children with special needs, such as Individualized Education Plans (IEPs) and support staff. However, in our homeschooling environment, I am primarily responsible for addressing my child's unique needs, with limited resources and space to accommodate them effectively. Balancing the complexities of supporting a child with autism alongside the needs of three other children tests my patience and resolve daily. At times, I feel overwhelmed and inadequate, unsure if I can provide the level of support my child deserves.

Despite these challenges, embracing this journey wholeheartedly has led to unexpected growth and deeper connections. Through the trials, I've cultivated a deeper sense of empathy and understanding, forging stronger bonds with my children and appreciating their unique strengths. Although there are obstacles, I am committed to providing a nurturing and inclusive learning environment where each child feels supported and valued. This journey has not only strengthened our family but has also enriched our homeschooling experience.

Challenge 4: Teacher versus Mom

Transitioning from the structured environment of the public school classroom to homeschooling was a profound culture shock. In the classroom, I was known as "Mrs. Henry," a respected teacher students admired and sought out. However, at home, I'm simply "Mom"—a role that often feels worlds apart from my former identity as a teacher.

While my students at school revered "Mrs. Henry" and adhered to classroom rules and expectations, my children's behavior at home presents a stark contrast. They display typical childhood behaviors such as drawing on walls, resisting instruction, and testing boundaries. Adjusting to this dynamic and reconciling my roles as both mom and teacher have been a continual struggle.

Over time, I've realized that the strict separation between "mom" and "teacher" is unnecessary in our homeschooling environment. Instead, I embrace the unique opportunity to simultaneously be immersed in both roles. Homeschooling allows me to integrate learning seamlessly into our daily lives, blurring the lines between formal instruction and everyday experiences.

While structure and discipline are essential, I've learned to prioritize authenticity and vulnerability in our homeschooling journey. By embracing the fluidity of our dynamic, I've created an environment where learning extends beyond textbooks and permeates every aspect of our lives. I have the privilege of nurturing my children's education in a way that honors their individuality and fosters genuine connections, reminding me of the beauty and richness inherent in homeschooling.

Challenge 5: Letting Go of Traditional Measures

One of the most profound challenges I've encountered in homeschooling is addressing my children's gaps in learning. In the classroom, I often attributed such gaps to previous teachers. However, in homeschooling, I am the primary educator shaping my children's educational experiences, so perceived deficits or shortcomings feel more personal.

Surprisingly, this challenge has become my favorite aspect of homeschooling. It has compelled me to reassess my approach to measuring knowledge and progress. While I recognize the importance of benchmarks and standards, I've learned to embrace the understanding that each child learns differently and at their own pace.

Letting go of traditional measures of academic achievement has been liberating. Instead of comparing my children's progress to predetermined standards, I've witnessed their unique and individual growth and development. As I am their guide, my role is to cultivate their curiosity and love for learning rather than focusing solely on academic milestones.

Acknowledging my accountability in fostering their education, I've also come to appreciate that learning extends far beyond curricula and formal instruction. Homeschooling has shown me the intrinsic value of curiosity and the diverse ways learning manifests in our daily lives. This challenge has been a profound lesson in prioritizing what truly matters in education: nurturing a lifelong love for learning and fostering growth in all aspects of my children's lives.

In assuming the role of a homeschooling mom, I've realized that the teacher often learns the greatest lessons. Throughout this journey, I've grappled with the temptation to compare our homeschooling experience to the traditional system I once swam in, striving to replicate it within our home. Yet, the tension I've felt stemmed from attempting to fit a square peg into a round hole—a futile endeavor that only led to frustration and disillusionment.

Reflecting on these past couple of years, I recognize the need to continue uprooting old paradigms and cultivating a new approach that honors our family's unique needs and rhythms. It's time to create fertile ground where our family can flourish and learn in the most beautiful ways. By embracing the fluidity and flexibility of homeschooling, I trust in the growth and transformation that emerge as we navigate this journey together.

Yvette Henry, a former math teacher with seven years of public school experience, chose to stay home and homeschool her children after her daughter's birth. Since 2017, she has focused on fostering a lifelong love of learning in her children, redefining traditional education. Yvette aims to create an environment where her children can thrive, explore, and enjoy learning, all while being grounded in love and knowledge. Through their YouTube channel, Beleaf in Fatherhood, her family shares their authentic journey to inspire fathers, bring hope to mothers, and encourage children. Find Yvette online at YvetteHenry.com and @mrsmelanin.

The Power of Good Habits
Sonya Shafer

As Anne headed to the kitchen to prepare breakfast, she paused at each bedroom door along the hall. "Good morning," she greeted her children. Eight-year-old Josh, her early riser, was already dressed for the day, sitting on his neatly made bed and working on his math. His older brother, Joey, ten next month, had just sat up in his bed and was rubbing the sleep out of his eyes. In the next room, six-year-old Sophia stood on the tips of her toes at the dresser, rummaging through the clothes in the top drawer.

Twenty minutes later, Anne rang the chime that hung beside the kitchen table, and everyone gathered to eat. Some ate faster than others, but all stayed in their places until Anne picked up the Scripture Memory Box and led them in five minutes of recitation and review. After a prayer, each child cleared their dishes from the table and deposited them on the kitchen counter beside the sink. Josh opened the dishwasher; it was his turn to do breakfast dishes this week. Anne smiled and said, "Thank you, Josh," then checked the chore chart, making a mental note: Joey would be doing lunch dishes, and Sophia would be helping Anne with supper dishes.

Next, Anne headed to the bookshelf. She opened her lesson plans and glanced at the lineup for the day. While Joey and Sophia made their beds and brushed their teeth, Anne pulled the books she would need for the morning's lessons from the shelf. She stacked them in order and set them beside her place at the table. Then she selected the morning playlist, cranked up the volume, and went to make her bed. As the last notes of the final song played, everyone came to their places at the table. It was time for school. Another Monday had begun.

Does that description sound idealistic? Perhaps it is, yet that doesn't mean it's unobtainable. In fact, that scenario describes hundreds of typical mornings in our homeschool. But they don't happen by chance. The smoothness of such a morning is the result of intentional work: the work of habit training.

Habits are the stepping stones we lay in place to reach our ideals. We all want cooperative children, steady lessons, and a smooth-running home. No parent ever asks, "How can I get my children to ignore me, neglect their schoolwork, and forget their chores more often?" Of course not!

If smooth days are what we all want, why don't we all have them? In his bestselling book *Atomic Habits*, James Clear revealed the reason: we don't rise to the level of our ideals; we sink to the level of our habits.[14] We may have a great desire for a clean kitchen, but if no one in the family has the habit of clearing the table and doing the dishes after meals, that desire will never become a reality. The same holds true for making the bed, listening with full attention, or putting schoolbooks on the shelf.

Good habits play a vital role in achieving our vision of success in our homes and, even more so, in our homeschools. When good habits are in place, we can spend less time and energy arguing about household tasks and more on educating. But they don't just happen; we must be deliberate about instilling good habits.

Focus on One

The place to start is, of course, to decide which habit we will work on. In Anne's morning described above, we can discern habits of orderliness, initiative, cleanliness, courtesy, mental effort, attention, respect, and thankfulness. The temptation is to dive in and attempt to make all of those happen at once. However, working on multiple habits can set us up for failure. We can get distracted, overwhelmed, and end up discouraged because we don't feel like we've made progress. One successful business executive summed up the problem this way: "Most people take one step in twenty directions instead of twenty steps in one direction."[15] We can set ourselves up for success by focusing on one habit at a time, moving in that one direction, and making good progress with it.

Let's say we decide to work on putting things where they belong (orderliness). That's a useful habit to have in a homeschool. If things are where they should be, we won't waste lesson time searching for them. Once the habit category is chosen, it helps to take it a little further and picture the specifics: What will "putting things where they belong" look like for each child in this home? It's going to look different for a two-year-old than for a twelve-year-old. For the two-year-old, the goal might be that he would help you pick up the toys and put them in the toy basket before lunch and before bedtime every day. For the twelve-year-old, the goal might be that she would have everything put away in her room before bedtime every evening.

Imagination can help us picture what that habit will look like. The more vividly we can picture each child's habit focus, the easier it will be to cultivate it, for it is a fact of life that we move toward what we focus on. And therein lies an important tip: it's better to focus on good habits to instill rather than bad habits to break. For every bad habit, there is an opposite good habit. For example, in the case of a child who hits, we can work on the opposite good habit of self-control. If a child dawdles over grammar lessons, we could work on the good habit of attention. It's better to focus on where we want to go rather than what we want to avoid.

When our family lived near Chicago, my husband, John, rode his bike on the roads that led out of our suburb into relatively undeveloped countryside. The upside of those roads was less traffic; the downside was their narrow shoulders. Only about twelve inches of blacktop lay between the outside paint line and the edge of the road, where the asphalt dropped off to a ditch.

That narrow shoulder wasn't an issue most of the time, but every once in a while, John would hear the rumble of a big dump truck fast approaching from behind. He learned very quickly that if he was going to keep his bike (and himself) out of harm's way, he had to fasten his eyes on his front tire and keep it on that twelve-inch strip of pavement. If he looked over his shoulder to see where the truck was, he would inevitably veer into its lane. If he kept his eyes on the ditch he was trying to stay out of, he would be hard-pressed not to tumble into it.

We move toward what we focus on. The same is true for habits. Rather than focus on the bad habit we want to break, we can pick the good habit to cultivate, picture it as vividly as possible, and hold on to that mental image.

It can work well with a teenager if we choose a neutral time (not in the heat of battle) to have a short chat. We can tell him the one habit we have in mind, describe what we think it would look like for him, and—this is very important—include how that habit will benefit him. However, we must also be open to his ideas and invite them into the conversation. This joint effort is important in helping him transition to cultivating his own habits as an adult. We want to work together if possible. Some habits may be nonnegotiable in our households; that's fine. But a wise parent will try to alternate those types of habits with some of the young adult's ideas too.

Make It Obvious

Once we know what we want the habit to look like for each child, we can set ourselves up for success by making the new habit obvious—both to our children and to ourselves.

It should go without saying, but let's say it anyway: we need to clearly communicate our expectations to each child. For example, if we expect Sophia to put her schoolbooks on the shelf when she is done using them, we need to let her know that—to walk her through it, tell her and show her exactly what is expected, and help her practice it, if needed. Sometimes, our children don't do what we want them to because of childishness or forgetfulness, but other times it's because we haven't made our expectations crystal clear to them. We can make our path a lot smoother if we make sure each child knows exactly what they should work on and what success in that habit looks like.

The other way to make the habit obvious is to set up visual reminders we can't help but notice during the day. We all get busy, and it's easy to forget about new habits we're working on amid the hustle and bustle of daily life. For parents, an obvious reminder—whether on our phones, written into the margin of our lesson plans, or attached to our wrists—can help us remember the habit each child is working on throughout the day and achieve success sooner.

Reminders are also important for our children, but we need to make sure they get to the point where they aren't relying on us to be that reminder. A habit is not a habit until it is done without supervision. We can know that a child has grasped a habit when they do it without our prompting.

In some situations, especially with young children, we will most likely need to start by giving a verbal cue. For example, suppose a child is working on the habit of giving her best effort during a handwriting lesson or perhaps sitting properly on his chair during a meal. In that case, we might give a quick verbal reminder before that lesson or that meal begins. But we must be careful not to allow a child to depend on our cues long-term. As soon as possible (depending on the child's age and capabilities), we can move toward phasing out our reminders and transferring to the child the responsibility to remember.

At that point, we might post a picture in a conspicuous place that will remind children of what they are working on and what is expected during the coming weeks. Anne's chore chart, outlining which child was responsible for which meal's dishes that week, is one example, but the visual reminder could also take the form of colorful sticky notes, labeled craft sticks in a jar, or a fun poster. With teenagers, we can work together and help them brainstorm ideas that will remind them of their habit focus. The key is to do all we can to help each child successfully take responsibility for remembering. Getting there may take some baby steps, but that is the ultimate goal.

Practice and Inspire

After we have a clear picture of what each child is working on, we've communicated those expectations clearly, and we've set up some obvious reminders, we have only to practice the new habit every day. The more often a person repeats an action, the more quickly it becomes a habit; and the longer that action is repeated, the stronger that habit grows.

Here's how it works. Certain neurons in our brains fire in a particular path whenever we perform a specific action. The more often we perform that action, the more vividly that neuron path becomes ingrained in our brains. Once it is ingrained deeply enough, the neurons fire in that path automatically. We don't have to think about it; it has become a habit.

Repetition is the key. The more often our children repeat an action, the more quickly that action will become a habit. Science tells us that we will most likely be able to get that neuron path up and running in six to eight weeks.

Eight weeks. Two months may sound like a long time to work on a habit, but think of the possibilities. If we can instill one good habit in two months, that is six habits in a year! Take a moment and imagine what your home would look like if you and your children had six new good habits by this time next year. It can be done! One at a time, repeating it as often as possible for six to eight weeks.

During those weeks, we can help everyone stay motivated by inspiring them with stories, poems, real-life examples, and poignant quotations related to our selected habit. These don't have to be specific stories about each child's particular habit focus. For instance, if one child is working on doing the dishes, we don't have to go looking for inspiring quotes about scrubbing pots and pans. Stories about orderliness or cleanliness in general could go a long way toward encouraging everyone in their related habit. Just once or twice a week, gather the family together and share one of those inspiring selections or review the benefits the new habit will bring to all of you. This little touch every few days takes a short time, but it can have a large impact in keeping everyone on the same page and feeling positive about forming good habits.

Track the Progress

A habits journal can also help us as parents remain positive about habit training. At the end of those eight weeks, taking a few minutes to jot down some notes can be very motivating. Record what habit the family focused on (i.e., orderliness) and what specific habit each child worked on (putting schoolbooks away or cleaning up their room). Describe what obvious reminders were used and how well they worked. Most importantly, note the growth observed in each child over the weeks. We most likely won't see perfection; none of us are perfect. But we will see growth if we are consistent in communicating, practicing, and inspiring. It may be smaller than we had hoped—or exceed our wildest dreams. Either way, write it down.

As we take time to look at how family members have grown in their good habits, we will be encouraged to keep going and to continue working on those fledgling neuron paths even as we introduce new ones. Then we pick a different habit and go again: (1) picture how it will look for each child, (2) make it obvious through communication and reminders, (3) practice and inspire that action for six to eight weeks, and (4) track our progress. With each new habit we introduce, we keep an eye on those already formed. A habits journal will help and encourage us all along the way.

British educator Charlotte Mason offers this simple yet powerful insight: "The mother who takes pains to endow her children with good habits secures for herself smooth and easy days; while she who lets their habits take care of themselves has a weary life of endless friction with the children."[16] Our homes can be places of smooth and easy days or places of weary lives and endless friction. It all comes down to how intentional we are in cultivating good habits. We can sigh and say, "I wish" or "If only," or we can take hold of our ideals with both hands and start building the daily rhythms that will help us achieve those ideals. And we can start right now.

Mason also gives the vision: "A habit is a thing of *now*; it may be begun in a moment, formed in a month, confirmed in three months, become the character, the very man, in a year."[17] We can make the choice to work on a habit today. Yes, it will take weeks of focus and repeated action, but we don't have to do all the work all at once. We only have to think about what we're going to do at this moment. We only have to be faithful to practice that good habit this time, and then this time, and then this time—one *now* at a time, each *now* as it comes.

Sure, we might get distracted, but we can always refocus *now*. We might take two steps backward, but we can shift into forward gear and start gaining momentum again *now*. We might be tempted to become discouraged about that bad habit that has developed of its own accord over the years, but we can intentionally start cultivating the opposite good habit *now*.

Smoother and easier days are within reach. Our ideals can be achieved through the stepping stones of good habits, and we can take the first step *now*.

Sonya Shafer is a popular homeschool speaker and writer, specializing in the Charlotte Mason Method. She has been on an adventure for more than twenty-five years studying, researching, practicing, and teaching Charlotte's gentle and effective methods of education. Her passion for homeschooling her own four daughters grew into helping others and then into Simply Charlotte Mason, which publishes her many books and provides a place of practical encouragement to homeschoolers at SimplyCharlotteMason.com.

3

The Roadmap for Forging Our Way

The Enduring Wonder of a Living Education
Leah Boden

As a member of the last generation to recall life before the digital era, I navigate the ever-evolving technological landscape that our children are so familiar with while seeking simplicity and authenticity in the twenty-first century's rapid progress. Raised in Yorkshire, England, famed for its rugged coastlines and rolling hills immortalized in Brontë novels and James Herriot's veterinary tales, I had a childhood steeped in stories, woodland strolls, and the melodies of classical music that filled our book-brimming home. Though my parents were not esteemed academics, they recognized the profound impact of a well-rounded upbringing, laying the groundwork for a child's journey.

In my early years as a young mother researching home education, I stumbled upon the remarkable British educator Charlotte Mason. Her life and teachings resonated deeply with my upbringing and beliefs about children and education. Thus, when I began my journey as a home educator in the early 2000s, I fashioned my practices around her principles. While my children have now entered their teens and early adulthood, many of the methods we embraced at home continue to shape our lives. At the heart of our educational journey lies what Mason termed "living books" and the potent tool of narration—a method inviting children to articulate their understanding in their own words, internalizing and holding on to knowledge.

When brought together, living books and narration become the sturdy foundation stones of a child's learning adventure, stretching far beyond the schoolroom and staying with them into their adult years. These methods don't just make lessons interesting; they turn them into experiences that resonate deeply and stick throughout their lives. By diving into the rich stories found in living books and expressing their thoughts through narration, students aren't just memorizing facts—they're exploring, questioning, and making sense of the world around them.

Through the characters, cultures, and historical events encountered in these books, learners not only gain knowledge but also develop a broader perspective on life. And when they narrate these stories in their own words, something wonderful happens. They internalize the lessons in a way that's uniquely theirs, creating connections that last a lifetime. Living books and narration create a nurturing environment where curiosity thrives. Learners can grow into interested, compassionate adults and, hopefully, those who unashamedly ask good questions.

Understanding Living Books

> The children should have the joy of living in far lands, in other persons, in other times—a delightful double existence; and this joy they will find, for the most part, in their story-books.
>
> Charlotte Mason[1]

To grasp the essence of a living book, it's helpful to contrast it with the textbook—a common fixture in classrooms and educational settings. Textbooks typically convey information through words and images, presenting fragmented facts and lists tailored to specific subjects or areas of study. While textbooks serve a purpose, particularly in fields like medicine, engineering, or law, where memorizing standards and procedures is crucial, they often fall short in nurturing a child's holistic learning journey.

Our hope in using living books is to cultivate character and enrich the lives of our children. As students engage with and recount captivating biographies, narrative histories, and other compelling literary works, they encounter a multitude of characters spanning different periods. Moral growth stems from the connections formed with such a diverse array of individuals. These characters' struggles, triumphs, challenges, and decisions are not mere facts but possess vitality and significance. They evoke within children a sense of wonder, empathy, and a desire to explore both ideas and the moral landscape. Through the immersive experience of reading and narrating these vivid living books, we witness firsthand the profound impact on knowledge and understanding.

Living books offer a richer alternative to textbooks. They stay far from the confines of boxed-in information and instead entrust children with stories, poetry, and fables. These books become more than mere sources of knowledge; they serve as windows to imagination, empathy, and understanding. By immersing themselves in plays, prose, and heroic adventures, children not only learn about the world around them but also discover facets of themselves within the narratives.

For Charlotte Mason, living books were not just a recommendation but the cornerstone of education. They provided the foundation and inspired much of a child's educational experience. Mason's deliberate commitment to specific books within her ancient practice and programs for the Parents' National Education Union (PNEU) emphasized the importance of well-curated literature that could be revisited. She believed in the enduring value of certain texts and advocated for their repetition in children's education. For Mason, if a book was deemed rich enough to inspire ideas and foster growth, there was little need for constant change throughout the years.

Shakespeare's works were regularly included in her curriculum, offering timeless insights into human nature and language. Poetry, too, held a prominent place, with students often reciting and memorizing verses to internalize their beauty and significance. A diverse array of narrative-based books spanning various subjects were chosen, allowing children to explore different topics through engaging storytelling.

After reading these books individually or aloud as a group, Mason employed the method of narration, whereby children of different ages articulated their understanding of the story in their own words. This practice not only encouraged active engagement with the material but also fostered each child's unique perspective and interpretation, which we shall investigate further.

My family and I have built the foundations of our educational rhythms on living books and our ability and freedom to tell back what we've experienced from the stories we've read. From E. B. White's *Charlotte's Web* to *The Hiding Place* by Corrie ten Boom, living books have lined our shelves and enriched our lives. These narratives have imparted knowledge, sparked deep discussions, ignited imaginations, and cultivated empathy within our household. Classics such as Louisa May Alcott's *Little Women* and George Eliot's *Silas Marner* have transported us to different eras and landscapes, offering glimpses into the human condition and the complexities of life.

Exploring diverse perspectives through books like Malala Yousafzai's *I Am Malala* and N. H. Senzai's *Escape from Aleppo* has broadened our understanding of global issues and cultural diversity. Senzai's gripping narrative provides a window into the experiences of those living in conflict zones, fostering empathy and understanding across different backgrounds. *The Joy of Chemistry* by Cathy Cobb has made science come alive, fostering a fascination for the wonders of the natural world. *A Modern Plutarch: Comparisons of the Most Influential Modern Statesmen* has provided valuable insights into leadership, politics, and historical context, encouraging problem-solving, critical thinking, and analysis.

These living books have not only fostered a love of reading but have also instilled in us a lifelong thirst for knowledge. Our home is a sanctuary of learning where the pages of living books serve as windows to the world, inviting us to explore, empathize, and grow together.

The Power of Narration

> They must read the given pages and tell what they have read, they must perform, that is, what we may call the act of knowing.
>
> Charlotte Mason[2]

Narration, as Mason advocated, goes beyond simple recollection; it's a teaching philosophy deeply rooted in engaging students actively with their learning. Essentially, it's about students digesting information and expressing it in their own words. While it may seem like a straightforward exercise, there's more to it within the realm of education.

Mason believed that learning isn't passive but rather an interactive process of mental assimilation. By asking students to "tell back" what they've read, heard, or looked at, she aimed to foster a deeper connection with the material. This act of narration encourages students to internalize the information and present it in a way that makes sense to them.

Educators strive to minimize interruptions throughout the narration process, allowing students the space and time to articulate their thoughts freely. By encouraging originality and creativity, Mason empowered students to express their own perspectives and opinions rather than simply regurgitating information.

Narration cultivates a deeper understanding and connection with text, places, people, and objects. It enhances a child's ability to grasp, reflect upon, wonder, imagine, and evaluate, among other skills. Unlike conventional teaching methods such as specific questioning, worksheets, or rote memorization, narration fully engages a child's mind, comprehensively tapping into their cognitive abilities.

Mason emphasized the importance of focused attention. In today's world, distractions are abundant, making it essential to cultivate attentive listening and reading habits. By limiting repeated exposure to the material, she sought to tap into children's natural ability to concentrate and encourage active engagement.

Narration is not limited to oral retelling; it can take many forms, including written narration, drawing, acting, and other creative expressions. By embracing various techniques, educators can cater to their students' diverse learning styles and preferences, ensuring that everyone can show their understanding in a way that feels authentic to them.

Aside from its academic benefits, narration plays a significant role in language development. Mason aimed to improve students' communication skills by encouraging them to articulate their thoughts in their own words. Narration provides a platform for students to express themselves freely, fostering confidence and self-expression.

Ultimately, narration embodies the principles of active learning and independent thinking. Educators can empower students to take ownership of their learning journey by incorporating narration into teaching practices. Through narration, students gain knowledge and develop the skills and attitudes necessary for lifelong learning and personal growth.

Hand in Hand

> Narrating is an art, like poetry-making or painting, because it is there, in every child's mind, waiting to be discovered.
>
> Charlotte Mason[3]

Living books and the power of narration are essential aspects of Mason's educational philosophy, working together to create a rich learning environment that encourages engagement, understanding, and personal growth. At the heart of her approach are living books, which differ from traditional textbooks by immersing students in narratives that ignite their imagination and passion for learning. These books aren't just repositories of facts; they serve as gateways to diverse worlds, cultures, and experiences, spanning various genres from classic literature to biographies, historical tales, and scientific explorations.

Through exposure to living books, students deepen their grasp of academic subjects and develop empathy and a genuine enthusiasm for learning. As Mason wisely observed, "Give your child a single valuable idea, and you have done more for his education than if you had laid upon his mind the burden of bushels of information."[4] Immersing themselves in the stories and experiences within these books helps students forge meaningful connections between their own lives and the broader world. The wonder of living books lies in their ability to capture curiosity, encourage reflection, and inspire a lifelong pursuit of knowledge.

According to Mason, if we cannot narrate something, we do not truly comprehend it. She referred to narration as the pathway to genuine understanding. Narration goes beyond mere repetition; it embodies a profound process of understanding and expression. She rightly observed that true knowledge involves the ability to articulate it back. This deeper understanding, where a child engages with, absorbs, and articulates what they have read, possesses a transformative power that nurtures, enriches, and equips students for life.

Narration, a cornerstone of Mason's teaching method, complements the use of living books by encouraging active engagement with the material. Instead of passively absorbing information, students are prompted to digest and express it in their own words. This process not only shows their understanding of the content but also cultivates vital communication skills and nurtures confidence in their intellectual abilities.

Narration begins with careful reading or listening to a passage from a living book, followed by students articulating the material in their own words. This exercise encourages deep engagement, moving beyond rote memorization to genuine understanding and assimilation of knowledge. Narration adapts to different subjects and ages, allowing for flexible expression through oral, written, artistic, or dramatic means, catering to individual strengths and preferences.

When combined with living books, narration becomes a powerful tool for fostering a love of learning and cultivating intellectual interest. Engaging with living books through narration empowers students to participate in their education, laying the foundation for a lifetime of exploration.

The synergy between living books and narration exemplifies foundational elements of Mason's educational philosophy, offering a transformative approach to learning. By integrating these components into the educational experience, educators can create an enriching environment that deepens understanding and instills a lifelong appreciation of learning.

Through my many years of experience with my four children, I've witnessed the profound impact of integrating living books with narration into the daily rhythms of a Charlotte Mason–inspired home-educating environment. I purposefully focused on cultivating this method of learning in my children from an early age. This deliberate choice has ensured that even when faced with testing and exams (which they have encountered), they possess the skills to engage deeply with their studies and to pursue genuine, lasting learning.

Whether it's a few pages from a beloved book or an episode from history, the goal of narration is to present the material in a way that captivates the listener's attention and engages their imagination. By reading the passage only once, Charlotte aimed to reinforce the habit of attention, encouraging students to focus their minds on the task at hand.

Making It Stick

Research in educational psychology consistently highlights the efficacy of active learning methods, such as narration, in enhancing students' understanding and retention of information. By engaging students in the process of articulating their understanding through their own words, narration encourages deeper processing of the material, which leads to more robust memory formation. Using narrative-based materials, like living books, is shown to captivate students' interest and promote empathy. Such immersive experiences not only make learning more enjoyable but also facilitate the integration of new knowledge into students' existing mental frameworks, making it more likely to be kept in the long term. While specific studies may vary in methodologies and findings, the overarching consensus within educational research supports the idea that active engagement with rich, meaningful content fosters enduring learning outcomes.

By incorporating living books and narration into our children's learning journey, we cultivate an environment where learning becomes vibrant and purposeful. It goes beyond merely memorizing facts or excelling in tests; it fosters a genuine love for lifelong learning. Let's embrace this captivating educational experience, where books breathe life into our lessons and students' voices resonate with the depth of their knowledge and understanding.

Leah Boden is the wife of Dave, a mother to four teen and adult children, and a longtime home educator. She is the founder of Modern Miss Mason, an international initiative guiding parents and children to find their freedom within the Charlotte Mason philosophy. Leah is the author of *Modern Miss Mason*, advocating revolutionary ideas for a twenty-first-century approach to a Charlotte Mason education. She actively writes, speaks, podcasts, hosts coaching sessions, and manages the bestselling membership The Collective on Substack. | @modernmissmason

The Transformative Power of Literature in the Home

Rea Berg

Walking into the men's prison that first day, I involuntarily shuddered as three solid iron gates slammed behind me. The heavy metal locks clinked with an inescapable solidity. I understood for the first time the origin of the term "the slammer." The sound was unmistakable. I can hear it now, as I write.

Yet since that first experience, I have reentered those gates hundreds of times. I have spent a few thousand hours behind those barriers. Why would I, a busy writer, wife, business owner, and grandmother, venture into a men's prison regularly and joyfully? What has motivated me to do so? What path led me to that first moment? I believe it was the *power of story* that led me there.

When I was a young mother, I came across a little book—*For the Children's Sake*, by Susan Schaeffer Macaulay. Four decades on, I can look back and see how this book changed me. It set before me an enlarged perspective on life—a life informed by the best thoughts of men and women through the ages—what Macaulay referred to as "living books," in the terminology of Charlotte Mason. It set a vision before me of childhoods filled with living books, music, art, nature study, and lots of free, unstructured outdoor playtime. Playtime fueled by imaginations cultivated through literature.[5]

Living books would give me (and my children) eyes to see the wonder of nature, the beauty of humanity, and the transformative power of empathy, kindness, and integrity. The plethora of books that would inform my life and the lives of my children from that moment on are so numerous it is impossible to recall them all. But in many ways, I can trace the woman I became, the children I raised, and the work I have done to the visceral impact of those works of literature, history, biography, and poetry. The books that can transform your home will, like pebbles thrown in a pond, reverberate outside of your home into the culture at large.

When we were a family with four children under age six, we spent countless hours reading. We read the Little Bear books by Else Holmelund Minarik, the Dr. Seuss books, *Goodnight Moon* by Margaret Wise Brown, *The Snowy Day* by Ezra Jack Keats, *Corduroy* by Dan Freedman, *The Velveteen Rabbit* by Margery Williams, and all the books of Robert McCloskey: *Blueberries for Sal, One Morning in Maine, A Time of Wonder, Make Way for Ducklings, Homer Price, Lentil, Centerburg Tales,* and *Burt Dow.*

We had fun with poetry. *Mother Goose* illustrated by Tasha Tudor, Shel Silverstein's *A Light in the Attic* and *Where the Sidewalk Ends*, A. A. Milne's *When We Were Six*, and the crazy limericks of Edward Lear all brought goofy silliness, laughter, and comic relief from the daily pressures of life. The beauty of poetry is that even the youngest listener, though they may not understand the concepts, is soothed and comforted by the lyrical cadence of meter and rhyme.

In *The Velveteen Rabbit*, we learned that when we love enough, our fur gets worn off, our glass eyes get scratched and drop out, and sometimes we lose our stuffing because we've loved and been loved so well. Loving like that makes us real. But becoming real doesn't happen to "people who break easily, or have sharp edges, or who have to be carefully kept."[6]

In Natalie Savage Carlson's *The Family Under the Bridge*, we learned to love a Parisian family who'd fallen on hard times and to see them as folks just like us. We found out that Romas (the often despised wandering folks of Europe) were people with great hearts who would take in a homeless family without judgment, offering them the warmth of their van and sharing whatever meager nourishment they had. As Armand learns in the course of the story, "It isn't walls and furniture that make a home, it's the family."[7] Homelessness became something more than a social ill; it is a fact of life that requires people of goodwill to respond with empathy.

Some of our most beloved books were read so faithfully that the dust jackets became worn or went missing, and pages have been torn, dog-eared, and marred by the prints of little hands. Robert McCloskey's works make that list. Gary D. Schmidt notes in his biography of Robert McCloskey that these beloved books were not written during a time of idyllic peace and harmony in America—quite the contrary.

> *Lentil* was published as France had fallen, England seemed about to succumb, and Roosevelt was rushing supplies to shore up the allies. *Blueberries for Sal* was issued during the beginning of the Cold War, and *One Morning in Maine* during the height of the Korean War. *Time of Wonder* came during one of the most intense periods of nuclear arms testing in the country's history, and *Burt Dow* came after the assassination of a president and during the move into Vietnam.[8]

Against these backgrounds, McCloskey created stories that transcended the chaos. As Schmidt points out, McCloskey's tales provide "warmth and security, family relationships, innocent joys, the freedom for children to grow and relish the unalloyed splendors and mysteries of the world that lives close about them."⁹ McCloskey's stories breathe beauty into the ordinary and ignite wonder of the natural world. In *Time of Wonder*, Jane and Sal are given the freedom of unstructured and unsupervised play to explore the Maine island on which they summer. They take the rowboat out by themselves at night, where they "snap off the light and row toward the dock as the stars are gazing down, their reflections gazing up. In the quiet of the night, one hundred pairs of eyes are watching you, while one pair of eyes is watching over all."¹⁰ There is a sublime beauty to the works crafted by McCloskey, and though it might seem like an idyllic, improbable world, hurricanes still come, boat engines break down, and young Jane loses her first baby tooth in the sand. Yet the adults are there—to belt out boisterous hymns with the girls as the hurricane rages, to rebuild the engine that needs fixing, and to help look for the lost tooth.

As my children grew, we advanced in our reading to Marguerite Henry's horse books: *King of the Wind, Misty of Chincoteague, Justin Morgan Had a Horse*, and many more. These books, all based on true stories, taught deep lessons of love and respect for the animal world, most notably the noble horse. We learned how powerful the love between a horse and a child can be and were inspired by the examples of self-sacrifice, particularly for the greater good.

We read all the Marguerite de Angeli books, such as *Thee, Hannah!, Yonie Wondernose, The Door in the Wall, Bright April*, and so many others. De Angeli wrote multicultural books before that was even a term in literary criticism. Reading her books, we walked in the shoes of the young Quaker girl Hannah, who is determined to wear something fancy—something with colorful fabric and lace—anything other than the plain brown homespun frock of her faith. But Hannah's perspective changes when a fugitive slave woman desperately needs to find a "safe house" and sees Hannah on the street. Hannah's simple Quaker dress identifies her as a Friend.

In de Angeli's *The Door in the Wall*—the first children's book to deal with disability—we learned empathy as we felt the pain of young Robin, a medieval boy who permanently lost the use of his legs during the plague. His struggles to accept his disability and overcome self-pity taught us powerful lessons of courage and perseverance. As the kind monk who helps Robin reminds him,

> A fine and beautiful life lies before thee because thou hast a lively mind and a good wit. . . . Fret not, my son. None of us is perfect. It is better to have crooked legs than a crooked spirit. We can only do the best we can with what we have. That, after all, is the measure of success. What we do with what we have.[11]

In de Angeli's *Bright April*, published in 1946, we see young April's pain as she is first confronted by how one of her fellow Brownie Scouts views her because of her skin color. This beloved tale remains the favorite childhood book of Dr. Carla Hayden, current Librarian of Congress, who recalls the transformative moment when, at age seven in Jamaica, Queens, a local librarian gave her a copy of *Bright April*: "That was the first time I saw myself—a brown girl—in a book."[12]

The groundbreaking reality of de Angeli's work is that not only did she feature a loving Black family as central to her story but she also exposed the systemic racism they faced—not overtly, but seamlessly throughout the story. At a Brownie meeting, when April expresses her dream to become "a hat designer and be the boss of a big store on Chestnut Street," a fellow Brownie replies, "'Why, they never let'—But she got no further, for Mrs. Cole quickly slipped her hand over the child's mouth."[13] April's father, a beloved postman in their Germantown neighborhood where he has served faithfully and honorably for twenty years, is passed over for a promotion, and her older brother Ken, who is a trained architect serving in the military, is kept on laundry duty and forced with his fellow Black soldiers to eat in a separate canteen. In each instance, de Angeli intentionally paints a realistic picture of racism that grieves her personally and is systemic to the world that the Bright family occupies.

Miss Bell, a White schoolteacher at April's integrated school, is a voice of reason as she teaches her students of the

> men and women in our nation's history who had given their time, their fortunes, and sometimes their lives in order that we might have a more perfect union. . . . This country is for all, and . . . to be unfair or unkind to anyone because of race or religion is neither Christian nor American.[14]

Miss Bell makes sure her students know the stories of Crispus Attucks, the first Black patriot killed in the Boston Massacre, and Haym Salomon, the Jewish financier who, as an American patriot, donated his entire fortune to "support the cause of liberty" in the early days of the Revolution.[15]

Later, we were enthralled by Laura Ingalls Wilder's Little House on the Prairie series. The beloved Ingalls family depicted in this series modeled much of what is best in the American spirit. Their skills in carving out lives from scratch, whether in the Big Woods, on the prairie, by the banks of Plum Creek, or on the shores of Silver Lake, display a profound and inspiring resourcefulness, cheerfulness, and gratitude that hold lasting lessons for anyone seeking wisdom in what comprises a meaningful life. Here are Ma and Pa building sod or log houses, milking cows, digging wells, mending wagons, churning butter, sewing quilts, hunting panthers, fishing, sowing and reaping, having babies, telling stories, showing hospitality to strangers, singing, and praying—all while facing wolf packs, sickness, prairie fires, crop failures, grasshopper infestations, drought, and in *The Long Winter* seven months of deadly blizzards.

While there is justified criticism of elements of racial blindness and insensitivity in the series, these present modern readers with opportune moments for thoughtful discussion and lessons in humanity. The lessons the Ingalls have to teach each generation include their particular cultural blindnesses, but more importantly, they teach us kindness, courage, neighborliness, perseverance, cheerfulness in the face of failure, the power of music, community spirit, and gratitude—timeless, universal lessons of the heart.

These lessons were so powerful that when General Douglass MacArthur oversaw the democratization of Japan at the end of World War II, the first book he authorized for translation into Japanese was *The Long Winter*. Japan was emerging from the country's total ban on works of English during the war years. MacArthur's wife, Jean, suggested the book to him as a way to "buoy the morale of a defeated and starving people."[16] Japan was humiliated and devastated at the end of World War II. As millions of Japanese read *The Long Winter*, Wilder's words gave hope and transmitted meaning to their own sufferings. The book was so popular that within a few short years, both *The Little House in the Big Woods* and *The Little House on the Prairie* were also translated into Japanese.

When our children reached their teen years, our reading became more sophisticated and challenging. We read Dostoyevsky, Conrad, Dumas, Harper Lee, and Dickens. We read the works of Mildred Taylor: *Roll of Thunder, Hear My Cry*, and *Let the Circle Be Unbroken*. A teenage son, normally stoic, had just finished the latter title when he walked into the kitchen where I was preparing dinner. Tears were streaming down his cheeks. "Mom, how can people treat others this way?" This is where empathy begins.

In a recent opinion piece for the *New York Times*, "How to Save a Sad, Lonely, Angry and Mean Society," David Brooks argues for the power of literature to transform us.

> We know from studies by the psychologists Raymond Mar and Keith Oatley that reading literature is associated with heightened empathy skills. Deep reading, immersing yourself in novels with complex characters, engaging with stories that explore the complexity of this character's motivations or that character's wounds, is a training ground for understanding human variety. It empowers us to see the real people in our lives more accurately and more generously, to better understand their intentions, fears and needs, the hidden kingdom of their unconscious drives. The resulting knowledge is not factual knowledge but emotional knowledge.[17]

While endeavoring to cultivate emotional intelligence in my children, I little knew how empathy was growing in my own heart. Forty years from when I first read *For the Children's Sake*, I look back in awe at a life of experiences undergirded by literature. And I wonder about all those books we read—the books with orphan protagonists, the books about folks suffering the injustices of prejudice, the books of heroes rescuing Jewish families during the Holocaust, the simple but powerful tales of common people simply loving their neighbors as themselves. As Gregory Boyle affirms in *Tattoos on the Heart*, "The measure of our compassion lies not in the service of those on the margins . . . but in our willingness to see ourselves in kinship with them."[18] I now know that stories led me to the local men's prison. Moral imagination opened those barred gates for me, and stories *keep me* going to those men behind walls. Because their stories are as important as any I've read in the pages of books.

Rea Berg loves to see abandoned and broken things brought back to life, like antique houses, classic children's books, and especially lives—like those of the men she is privileged to work with at her local prison. Through the company she founded, Beautiful Feet Books, she has brought many beloved children's books back into print and has crafted numerous guides for teaching history through literature. Rea has a graduate degree in children's literature from Simmons College, Boston. Follow Rea on Instagram @reaberg or read her blog on children's literature at ReaBerg.com.

Nurturing Wonder, Formation, and Belonging in the Home
Alberta Stevens

The 1998 film *Sliding Doors*, starring Gwyneth Paltrow, delves into the intricate psychological dance we engage in when contemplating alternate paths our lives could have taken. Paltrow's character, upon missing a train, unfolds into two divergent stories based on that pivotal moment. Similarly, I often contemplate the alternate course my homeschooling journey could have taken without the transformative impact of our cherished Morning Time Medley.

Our homeschooling journey began out of necessity, driven by the challenges posed by the traditional school system. The decision was prompted by concerns about my son's well-being and the inadequate provision within the school environment. I dedicated six weeks to researching and preparing for homeschooling, navigating the uncertainties with a mix of relief and apprehension. As a single parent with a demanding full-time job, the decision was both daunting and necessary.

Armed with the grandiose certainty that my son would not be left behind by his school peers, I studied various books, including Susan Wise Bauer's *The Well-Trained Mind* and Sarah McKenzie's *Teaching from Rest*.[19] Aware of my need for patience and divine guidance, I absorbed ideas and wisdom from various home educators who had walked the path before, but in the back of my mind, I remained committed to mimicking what my child would have gotten in school.

Less than a week into our homeschooling routine, I knew something was amiss. While my structured learning approach gave me confidence that I was ticking the right boxes, our atmosphere was one of tension, hurry, and stress. My son reminded me that I'd sold the idea of homeschooling to him on false pretenses. I had promised idyllic mornings of lounging on the sofa, reading our favorite books with hot chocolate in hand, mixed with afternoon visits to the park and his favorite museums. I concluded that my child needed time to adjust after leaving school, and the traditional academic learning approach didn't align well with my desire to teach leisurely from a place of rest.

Grasping for straws, I recalled reading about Charlotte Mason, a Christian education philosopher mentioned in Bauer's book. I was curious then but did not allow myself the luxury of exploring beyond my immediate goals. However, after listening to a podcast where a lady gave a riveting talk about what mornings looked and felt like in her home, I set out to learn more about this philosophy of education as a life "sustained by ideas."[20] Though I can no longer recall the woman's name, it was a pivotal moment in my journey. I was transfixed, as if she had handed me the key to the holy grail.

Harmonizing Learning and Life

Inspired by Mason's guidance to expose children to a daily feast of living ideas, our Morning Time Medley emerged as a transformative and gentle hour-long ritual in our home.[21] I learned how curating a blend of sacred and secular elements fosters wonder and intellectual curiosity. Rituals, recitations, and readings create a sense of belonging.

Just as in *Sliding Doors*, where a single moment alters the course of a character's life, our homeschooling journey took a decisive turn with the unfolding of our morning rhythms. I was smitten by the idea of this carved-out time in our day for several reasons. As a time-poor mom working from home full-time, the idea that I could introduce a feast of short but broad life-giving ideas that aligned with my classical education aspirations while feeding our faith and cultural identity all within a single hour floored me.[22]

I was attracted by the daily opportunity to deepen my bond with my child through reading, singing, recitation, and reenactment as we cozied up on a sofa or rested on a park blanket. I was also compelled by the call to start our day slowly in a relaxed atmosphere that fostered connection. An atmosphere that was an extension of the warmth and intimacy of our homelife rather than the rigidity of an austere classroom, which was where I was originally headed.

Blending Spiritual, Intellectual, and Cultural Rituals for Growth

Once I recognized the power of mornings to help cultivate the family culture and atmosphere I'd always envisioned, I needed little persuasion to start our days with the much-cherished practice. Like a musical conductor, I took great delight in composing our unique medley of sacred and secular living ideas to harmonize with my aspirations for spiritual, intellectual, and cultural growth for my family. Each prayer, song, poem, fable, or story was intentionally curated to cultivate the habit of loving God and appreciating his creation while stimulating intellectual exploration, fostering a sense of belonging, or firing up our moral imagination for a story-formed life.

Drawing from a wide palette of diverse offerings, our Morning Time Medley often began with a quiet prayer, rising to the soulful crescendo of the doxology or the uplifting words of Heather Small's soul anthem, "Proud." Our prayers were often rooted in a liturgical text like a psalm or well-known prayer like St. Francis of Assisi's Serenity Prayer, followed by a traditional hymn like "How Great Thou Art" or a modern equivalent like Hillsong's awe-inspiring "So Will I." We then affirmed an adapted version of Charlotte Mason's PNEU motto: "I am, I can, I ought, I will."

A short Bible reading would precede a series of nature-inspired poems, alongside classical and heritage poems from Black poets like Maya Angelou, Wole Soyinka, and Langston Hughes. We would then delve into a round of fables from *Aesop's Fables* or African and Caribbean folklore. Sometimes, I would share a fable handed down orally by my grandmother. If time permitted, we would close with a chapter of reading from our book of the month.

My son took to our Morning Time Medley like a fish to water, often engrossed in creative activities like LEGO or clay modeling while I read aloud. He especially enjoyed animated readings and occasionally requested to take over, showcasing his talent for impressions and accents. As a participatory guide, I joined my son in every aspect as we happily swung from the elegance of BBC Proms' classical music to an upbeat tune from a musical set in a brawling medieval pub. Variety sprinkled with spontaneity kept our routine ever fresh throughout the years, and witnessing his meaningful connections filled my heart with joy.

Living a Liturgy of Love, Learning, and Wonder

The daily practice of Morning Time helped me transcend the boundaries of deskbound structured learning and became a symphony of worship, wonder, and beauty in my home. As liturgical creatures, our mornings were a liturgy of love, daily rituals shaping our habits and aligning our desires with our faith and values. As James K. A. Smith explains, "You are what you love, and your ultimate loves are formed and aimed by your immersion in practices and cultural rituals . . . such practices fundamentally shape who you are. . . . This contest of cultural practices is a competition for your heart."[23] With Smith's cultural liturgical lens in mind, the Morning Time Medley can be seen as a dance of affections, guiding children and parents to align their loves with their ultimate concern—God.

If our daily practices mold us into who we become, I wanted to ensure I included sacred texts that would form the breeding ground of good character in my child. I started by introducing short chunks of texts like the Lord's Prayer, the Apostles' Creed, Psalm 23, or a verse of a well-known hymn as part of our monthly rotation. This practice served as an effortless way to introduce beautiful ideas through the simple practice of daily repetition.

When my son was younger, we translated the cadence of poems into a memorable rhythm or song, making liturgical texts engaging and facilitating memorization. Given my son's predisposition to visual learning, I would introduce new pieces with a video or musical rendition, followed by a few read-alouds. The more exposure he got to the text, the more familiar it became, and the quicker he internalized the words. Soon, if I paused halfway through reading a sentence from a newly introduced piece, he would quickly finish the sentence. Relaxed repetition, especially when served alongside music, helps our brains absorb new things more easily.

When learning traditional hymns, I often encouraged my son to interact with the music beyond solely singing the lyrics. We would read about the composer's life and their inspiration for the song. He would also experiment with the music by playing along on the piano or guitar as we sang. It didn't matter if he played well or not; my focus was on giving him license to naturally participate in worship within his own home.

As he got older, he created his own modern beats using GarageBand, while creating unique rap recitations of some hymns. Like an adoring fan, I would take immense pleasure in these creative moments, not for their excellence or creative genius—neither of which we could honestly boast of at the time—but because of his courage to have a go, to engage in the historical drama of worship through hymn singing, making a joyful noise unto the Lord like King David.

Nurturing Wonder and Beauty

Each morning's embrace turned our home into a sanctuary where spoken words and sung melodies nurtured wonder, language, and beauty. Poetry, much like excellent stories, is a masterful weaver of mental images that intricately shape our thought life, silently becoming the architect of our entire life's atmosphere. Charlotte Mason emphasized the importance of recitation in education, contending that beautiful words merited beautiful articulation, delivered with a certain roundness of tone and precision of utterance through the regular practice of recitation.[24] (For these reasons, I pay particular attention to my Morning Time Medley's poetic elements.)

Reciting poetry creates space for children to practice beautiful words aloud and offers a lens for experiencing words visually. According to a quote commonly attributed to Leonardo da Vinci, "Painting is poetry that is seen rather than felt, and poetry is painting that is felt rather than seen." This insightful reflection underscores the dual visual and emotional dimensions of poetry in our everyday experiences.

One crisp autumn morning, my son and I delved into Longfellow's "The Arrow and the Song." This classic poem unfolded before us like a living painting, evoking imagery that stirred nostalgia and longing in our hearts, albeit for different things. For my son, it became a melodic journey of shared secrets, echoing unexpectedly in the heart of a friend. For me, it unfolded as an ode to creative vulnerability, daring greatly to share a piece of oneself and unexpectedly finding resonance.

> I shot an arrow into the air,
> It fell to earth, I knew not where;
> For, so swiftly it flew, the sight
> Could not follow it in its flight.[25]

The poem's symbolism, drawn from Mother Nature, weaves a poignant narrative that transcends individual interpretations, uniting us in its timeless beauty. The words moved my son so profoundly that he decided to set music to them, allowing him the creative license to infuse hip-hop rhythms with a classic poem.

Reliving the Past Through Story

In the rich tapestry of our homeschool journey, where each day unfolds with the enchanting rhythm of living books, Morning Time Medley is a vessel for carrying captivating, identity-shaping stories that ignite the imagination and cultivate a sense of belonging. As we delve into the significance of reading aloud or oral storytelling, we uncover its power to shape identities and guide us in understanding life's intricate dance.

Storytelling is the ancient art that binds the fabric of humanity and emerges as the elixir that excitedly transforms a homeschool day. As tales are shared, a profound realization dawns on the storyteller: this is not a new experience. The stories begin to echo the familial aspirations encountered once before in the storyteller's heart.

In my home, the stories of my griot African grandmother stand as a testament to the power of oral tradition. Her "Bra Spida" (Anansi) stories, woven with lessons of craftiness and consequence, find their place in the heart of our Morning Time. The call and response, the shared narratives all resemble the ancestral storytelling rituals that once echoed through African villages and slave plantations alike.

I vividly recall the day I shared my first Bra Anansi story with my son. I recounted the tale in Krio, my mother tongue, then retold it in English, infusing it with as deep a West African accent as I could muster. My son was utterly captivated, his eyes wide as he absorbed every detail and nuance. I watched joyfully as his head bobbed to the song's rhythm, "Mod n' law, tiday na shake ead day." Before I knew it, he was singing along in Krio and eagerly asked if he could narrate the story to me.

Later that evening, my son eagerly retold the story to his grandma, complete with costumes and props. I watched with pride as the young griot performed while my mother joined in on the song at the end, tears of joy in her eyes. It was evident that my son had unknowingly resurrected long-buried childhood memories, as she possibly recalled her mother telling her the same story.

At that moment, I realized the profound power of oral storytelling as a bridge between generations, particularly for immigrant families whose childhood stories may not be readily available in mainstream bookstores. Through storytelling, connections are forged and moral lessons are passed from generation to generation, resonating and delighting new audiences hundreds of years apart.

Crafting a Flexible, Meaningful Experience

Morning Time profoundly shaped our home educational experience, transforming what could have been dry lessons on Shakespeare, Plutarch, or Isaac Newton into joyful and meaningful moments. This dedicated time allowed us to weave a tapestry of truth, goodness, and beauty in a relaxed, relational atmosphere. As a new and anxious homeschooling mom, this practice empowered me to engage authentically in my son's education, bringing my whole self—culturally, spiritually, and experientially—into the process.

Much like a conductor harmonizing a new orchestra, I blended our medley out of educational materials from various sacred, cultural, and intellectual traditions that reflected our multicultural, Christian, and neurodivergent family. Our unique morning time became a shared canvas for meaningful discussions, enriching our family bonds, faith, and moral values. It offered a respite from the busyness of life, allowing us to slow down, connect, and savor the beauty of words, music, and shared experiences. The transformative impact of our Morning Time Medley continues to shape our homeschooling journey, nurturing a love for learning, fostering meaningful connections, and creating lasting memories, even as it has changed through the years.

At the beginning of our homeschool journey, we conducted our daily liturgy religiously every morning on the sofa or by the dining table. As our schedules got busier, we took our readings in bite-size chunks wherever we went. We relied on our monthly Morning Time Medley playlist and audiobooks to serve our needs as we ferried from one place to another.

Now that my firstborn is a teenager and I have a toddler in tow, the cadence of our mornings is a hodgepodge of nursery rhymes and Sunday school sing-alongs juxtaposed against heated discussions on the symbolism of dystopian novels. We still recite poetry, but now it accompanies our weekly read-aloud sessions alongside tea and delicious cake. We continue to read fables and parables, appreciate art, and listen to beautiful music, but they're mostly accompanied by a hearty evening meal rather than breakfast. There are no strict rules for Morning Time (or any time); adapt it to your family's needs. Embrace flexibility and follow your instincts.

These set-aside moments are not meant to be rigid or burdensome but should be a time of joy, connection, and growth. It's not about perfection but an intentional act of creating space for meaningful moments. We are the maestros of this symphony of learning as we guide our children into the spaces they are destined to inhabit. Embrace the journey, savor the process, and cherish Morning Time as a treasured part of your family's daily rhythm.

Alberta Stevens, a British Christian home educator of Sierra Leonean heritage, lives in the UK with her two sons. As a writer, speaker, podcast host, and home education coach at Homegrown Sonshine, she empowers fellow home educators with culturally diverse resources and guidance. Alberta helps parents create life-giving rituals that bring wonder, meaning, and connection to family life. She also has over twenty years of experience assisting businesses in achieving social impact goals through strategic partnerships with nonprofits. Alberta holds a BA in marketing and politics and an MA in Christian leadership/theology from St Mellitus College, London. | @homegrown.sonshine

The Scenic Route That Is Homeschooling Middle School
Trisha Vuong

What are the core memories of your middle school years? I distinctly remember being short (still am) with a perm and bangs that I tried desperately to spread like a paper fan with plenty of Sebastian Shaper hair spray. Yes, I had the quality stuff. I was in my second of five years in braces and sported slouchy socks with white Keds.

I attended a public middle school with quite a few childhood friends from my elementary school. "Small fish in a big pond" was a gross understatement, as I felt like a teeny tiny tadpole in an ocean of eighth-grade sharks and whales, half of whom had already grown peach-fuzz mustaches and adolescent muscles. I hardly remember any lessons taught in my classes, but I most definitely remember feeling distracted and self-conscious.

My seventh-grade English teacher did not have the strongest classroom management skills, which meant the kids were brutal—stealing things from her purse when she wasn't looking, writing rude comments on the chalkboard, and leaving the room without permission. I have a strong memory of self-talk: *Trisha, do not EVER become a middle school teacher. This is the worst age to try to teach. They have no respect for adults and are reckless.*

Little did I know that decades later, I would be teaching middle schoolers. My own middle schoolers, no less. To be fair, I started homeschooling from the beginning, when my oldest was in kindergarten. Back then, I prided myself on being an intentional, communicative, and forgiving mommy and teacher. While there were the normal challenges, I had no idea what was just around the river bend. Since I did not personally know many others who were homeschooling, I felt like I was pioneering new territory, which was both terrifying and thrilling. I forgot all about my seventh-grade warning to myself and just kept homeschooling one year at a time.

Homeschooling in the early years often included some form of magic-making. Adding enchantment and whimsy to math and science. Creating a game out of spelling and finding picture books that told fascinating stories while sneakily teaching sentence structure. Numerous homeschool curriculum brands are designed with exactly this in mind, and I found that planning for ways to inspire young, curious minds was so much fun for me as well. The goal was to foster a love of learning, and to my surprise and delight, that was precisely what was happening. Homeschool life rocks!

But as my two older kids neared fifth grade, I began to notice a subtle shift. It wasn't sudden but gradual and sporadic. Every now and then, I encountered a dramatic increase in the amount of pushback to my ideas and requests. Moments that I expected to dazzle them often resulted in the most unresponsive faces you could ever imagine—not even a blink.

What happened to my sweet girl and my joy boy? was my initial thought. I prayed hard that God would help me navigate this new season with supernatural wisdom and incredible grace. Our tweens and teens face a quickly changing world. Smartphones with apps that replace traditional tools like dictionaries and the organic discovery of trends are also altering how authentic relationships are formed. In these shifting times, it's convenient to blame the culture. I hold on to Isaiah 25:1 dearly: "O Lord, you are my God; I will exalt you; I will praise your name, for you have done wonderful things, plans formed of old, faithful and sure" (ESV). Technology, media, and our children's social circles aren't inherently evil or our enemies. Our true adversary is far craftier, but through it all, God remains sovereign. Every challenge passes through his protective and guiding hands. This truth gave me assurance as I brought my concerns about my tween and teen to him directly.

What followed happened quickly. God began inspiring me with ideas, such as regularly meeting one-on-one with each child. I began setting aside weekly time to meet with my daughter. However, it wasn't quite what you might envision. These meetings weren't always filled with special intimacy devoid of conflict or frustration—far from it. Some sessions tested my patience to the fullest, and she felt similarly frustrated at times too.

But slowly, our protective walls came down, and we connected in a new way, distinct from our usual family dynamics. I'm amazed at how these meetings have unlocked opportunities for deeper connection and improved communication. If I could recommend one thing for this stage, it would be consistently meeting one-on-one with your teen, approaching each session with an open mind and heart. Staying deeply connected to our children during these formative years alleviates some strain over big issues like trust and respect.

With much discipline and commitment, I kept these meetings scheduled in my homeschool planner, maintaining our weekly discussions throughout her middle school and into her high school years. We loosely followed a curriculum covering topics like maturity, reproduction, and other themes guided by our faith. This journey led us to read books together on using screens purposefully, understanding true feminine beauty, and managing finances from a biblical perspective. These discussions weren't quick fixes for any challenges we faced but rather a meaningful journey of discovery—together. What initially filled me with apprehension turned out to be the intimate conversations I had prayed for with my daughter.

One of the conversations that interested and affected my daughter the most was when I shared about my experiences as a teen. I often forget that our children have a hard time seeing us as anything but Mommy and Daddy. The fact that we had a life before they were born, made significant mistakes, and were (gasp!) irresponsible was extremely shocking to her. Putting aside my mommy persona to reveal a real person, a woman, and a sinner really helped break down the image she had of me. I can't help but think it is like knowing that Jesus felt all our feelings as a human. He becomes relatable and even a friend—someone who has compassion for us because he's been there and done that. When I shared stories that related to my daughter's circumstances or feelings, I'll never forget how her eyes lit up and her posture leaned in. As a parent, is there anything that feels like a bigger win than your teen leaning in to you in conversation?

And all the moms with teens say, "Amen."

• • •

The beautiful residual effect of these moments is the humility and love I feel while sitting with my children. There's no hierarchy or power plays—there's no room for any of that. Even better, the significant revelation for my daughter is this: Mom does not have it all together. She cannot fix every situation. She is laden with potholes that need healing and repair. Mom needs forgiveness, and Mom needs Jesus. Now, that's a scenic route, don't you think?

My son is completely different. We've affectionately nicknamed him our "joy boy" for as long as I can remember. He had the charm factor down early on, often wanting to cuddle just to be near and speaking pure words in a little high-pitched voice that melted my heart. It's surprising how far charm can take you, but sin puts a hard stop to any shortcuts charm attempts to take.

When my son entered the tween years, the change was rapid. He experienced a huge physical growth spurt in just a few months, and his struggle with pride grew just as quickly. My joy boy began making many less-than-joyful faces in response to my requests, accompanied by less joyful words and actions at times. It's funny because when my oldest daughter was going through her tween phase, I'd asked my joy boy to remember what he witnessed and promise me he'd never go through the same phase. He promised . . . joyfully.

With the experience of my oldest under my belt, you would think I'd have mastered at least a certain level of patience, right? So I thought. But my joy boy's path to maturing is much different from anything I've experienced before. I never had a brother, and to this day, I still don't fully understand the male species. My son has had more vocal and physical expressions of frustration, but he also offers the most genuine and humble reconciliations. The boy knows how to apologize well.

My husband has started meeting with our son one-on-one, just as I did with our daughter. They read a chapter of a relevant book together and often walk laps in a parking lot side by side while discussing the week's happenings. They act as accountability partners, taking intentional time to connect and sometimes working toward healing from an incident earlier that week. It's truly amazing to see the impact of these walking talks on their understanding of each other and their father-son bond.

● ● ●

Parenting and *Age of Opportunity*, both by Paul David Tripp, have profoundly impacted me, and I highly recommend them to friends. Just take this quote:

> Parenting is *ambassadorial* work from beginning to end. It is not to be shaped and directed by personal interest, personal need, or cultural perspectives. Every parent everywhere is called to

recognize that they have been put on earth at a particular time and in a particular location to do one thing in the lives of their children. What is that one thing? It is God's will. Here's what this means at street level: parenting is not first about what we want for our children or *from* our children.[26]

Is that not freeing? Changing the mindset to shepherding God's kids takes some pressure off. Tripp shares that as parents, we are God's ambassadors, and while that assumes a high calling, it reminds us that we are not alone in raising image bearers.

Think about how you are when overseeing other people's kids. Maybe you have a playdate for your daughter and her friends. You easily respect the personhood of those friends, attending to their needs and engaging as you get to know them well, but you don't take on the full load of who they are becoming because you know they belong to others.

When friends with kids of the same age ask for my opinion or guidance, my mind is much clearer. I can think through the whole picture without the personal attachment, pride, or self-image my own kids can trigger. While this is not an exact parallel, it's eye-opening to notice the difference in my tone of voice and anxiety level between the two situations.

The two most powerful influences in your middle schooler's life are their parents and peers. While both are big players, they sometimes seem to be fighting for the throne. In *Hold On to Your Kids*, Gordon Neufeld states, "Absolutely missing in peer relationships are unconditional love and acceptance, the desire to nurture, the ability to extend oneself for the sake of the other, the willingness to sacrifice for the growth and development of the other."[27] This is where parents are vital in this stage of development.

In the journey from adolescence to adulthood, tweens and teens need their parents more than ever. Your availability and willingness to remain in their corner are crucial, even though it won't always feel natural or easy. If you can make this commitment early on, it will greatly help you on the days when it feels impossible to like their behavior.

This period, when your child may start looking like an adult and craving independence, is a great time to ramp up the "family memory-maker" meter a notch. Here are some simple and effective ways our family maintains consistent connection opportunities:

- **Have a board or video game or movie night.** In place of spelling, we would play a game to let off some steam and engage in something they enjoy. In the summer, I might watch a series like *Master Chef Jr.* or *The Amazing Race* with my teen.
- **Enjoy a sweet treat.** My kids love Asian desserts, and we keep those shaved ice with mochi runs for special occasions.
- **Allow the haircut of their choice.** Gasp! My daughter and I searched for photos of hairstyles she liked, and we went to a real salon for a more mature cut.
- **Invest time in their interests.** A pastor at our church knew his tween daughter loved Justin Bieber back in the day, and I'll never forget how he invested himself in taking her to his concert and meet-and-greets.
- **Go out to a revolving sushi bar or dim sum.** The more out of the ordinary experience this is for your family, the better! It makes for easy conversation in the present and future.
- **Engage in random acts of kindness.** Try ironing her outfit for church or giving him unexpected hugs for no reason at all except to show love and affection.
- **Surprise them with small gifts.** Picking up a small object every so often is an easy way to show you notice and care about their smaller needs or wants.

Do a family escape room. We did this for the first time last year as a family, and it was a BLAST!

These types of fun family "adventures" or outings, paired with affirming words, have long-lasting effects. It's like when you're dating and want to create special memories to show someone how much you care. While these activities aren't necessary, they align with the message "I am for you." When someone frequently shows they consider you in their daily lives (in a language you can receive), it makes you feel more connected, safe, and secure.

Once your children hit those middle school years, it can feel like time speeds up. They may look, speak, and act older, yet they still desperately need your unconditional love and attention. Their roots need nurturing to grow deep and strong. Homeschooling offers us a VIP ticket for bonus time with our teens, allowing us to share the incredible sunrises and sunsets of this significant season with God and our growing young people.

This opportunity is the blessing of a lifetime, so choose to embrace the scenic route!

Trisha Vuong, with experience in talent representation, church administration, and teaching, transitioned to homeschooling after feeling unexpectedly called to it. Based in Southern California with her husband and three children, she brings a contagious passion for home education. Noticing a lack of discussion around the challenges and triumphs of homeschooling, especially in middle and high school, she started her blog, JuiceBoxHomeschool.com, to offer encouragement. With over a decade of experience, Trisha provides valuable insights and fosters a supportive community for moms. Her dedication to empowering fellow homeschooling parents highlights her belief in the transformative power of personalized education. | @juiceboxhomeschool

Preparing to Launch: Navigating the High School Years
Susan Seay

Homeschooling through high school is like embarking on a journey through uncharted territory. The winding roads and unpredictable twists can often leave even the most seasoned homeschooling parent disoriented and uncertain. The transition from middle school to high school is not just a change in scenery; it's a pivotal moment where you see a major fork in the road ahead, symbolizing your child's journey into adulthood. As Gretchen Rubin aptly puts it, "The days are long, but the years are short."[28]

When we started homeschooling in 2000, high school seemed a distant future. I felt unprepared for how quickly the elementary years passed, and in a blink the time to transition from middle school to high school was right in front of me. I vividly remember how much I longed for a seasoned traveler, a wise mentor, to shed some light on the path ahead. I knew I needed help to find my way.

Today, when planning a trip, most of us rely on GPS, a Global Positioning System. It's an invaluable tool when navigating unfamiliar roads. Instead of functioning like a travel GPS, offering precise routes with turn-by-turn instructions, think of me as providing your homeschool GPS—Game-changing Principles and Strategies. I'm here to guide you toward principles and strategies to set you on the right path.

I've spent the past twenty-four years on this homeschooling road. As a mom of seven, I've seen more than a few passengers embark on their unique path after finishing high school. So far, five of our seven children have graduated from high school and enrolled in college. The same principles and strategies that helped launch my older kids are guiding me as I prepare my last two, who are currently in high school. For each of our children, I strive to avoid a narrow focus on college readiness. I want them prepared to live a fulfilling life of purpose.

Join me as I take you on a journey through three pivotal decisions that have shaped our homeschooling experience and paved the way for successfully launching our children into adulthood. Along the way, I'll provide you with practical next steps so that you, too, can implement these ideas with confidence. Yes, you!

1. Interest-Led Internships

High school is the perfect time for exploring the world beyond the classroom. A blend of textbook knowledge with hands-on experience creates a powerful plan for a bright future. But how do you help your child figure out their interests?

Over the years, I've discovered that most high schoolers hate being asked, "What are your plans after high school?" This well-meaning question casts a cloud of uncertainty over an already mysterious road ahead. Even the most confident student will question their readiness to enter the next phase of life. Let's normalize the feelings of uncertainty in this season. After all, they are preparing to venture into a world that's constantly changing. But there is hope! This is where interest-led internships step onto the scene, offering a warm ray of sunshine to banish the fog of uncertainty.

Interest-led internships show what a career looks like in the real world, offering your child a personalized work opportunity. Imagine giving your child the chance to shadow someone who excels in a field they're interested in exploring. These internships go beyond just gaining skills for future employment; they're about absorbing invaluable insights from a mentor eager to share their expertise and hopefully help your child determine if this interest will one day become a career.

At age eleven, my daughter Aisha expressed an interest in becoming a photographer. Little did we know that this spark of interest would ignite her journey to becoming the youngest professional photographer in our city. This remarkable achievement was the direct result of her unwavering dedication and the invaluable mentorship she received from two seasoned photographers in our local community: a studio photographer and a lifestyle photographer.

Each mentor generously shared their daily work routines, favorite tools and resources, pricing strategies, and marketing techniques. They were thrilled by Aisha's eagerness to learn and offered her chances to shadow them and take on smaller tasks. Through these apprenticeships, she created a portfolio featuring photos from festivals, concerts, and premiere events at our performing arts center—long before she was even old enough to drive.

These experiences opened her eyes to the many possibilities in photography. However, they also made her realize that despite the widespread recognition she gained for her talent, photography was not the ultimate career she wanted to pursue.

Interest-led internships go beyond pursuit of a job. They're about having a mentor who allows you to see not only the process but also the possibilities within a particular field. As you all work together, the mentor can offer feedback on unique skills your child may possess and offer ideas on ways to leverage those skills, whether within the current field or in other areas down the road.

Practical next step: Take a minute to consider God's sovereignty over the details of life. When you do, it becomes clear that every connection in your life holds purpose. Now, reflect on the individuals in your high schooler's life. Who stands out to you? Perhaps it's their profession, their daily routine, or the path that led to their career choice. Make a list of each person that comes to mind. Then, reach out to them one by one. You never know—one of them may hold the key to unlocking your child's next step in the journey of life.

2. 360 Life Check-In

As children age, they don't need you less; they need you differently. Having mastered the foundational blocks of learning—reading, writing, and arithmetic—your high schooler is in a crucial time to learn how to use their foundational tools to build a life beyond textbooks.

At the heart of homeschooling through high school is our weekly 360 Life Check-In. I carve out a dedicated time slot each week to meet with each child individually. During these meetings, I take on several roles—teacher, guidance counselor, coach, accountability partner, and adviser, to name a few.

These weekly check-ins keep me informed about their academic progress and personal development. This dedicated time empowers them to take ownership of their learning journey while receiving personalized support. These meetings are a cornerstone of communication and connection, ensuring my children know they don't have to navigate life's challenges alone, even though they're getting older.

The atmosphere in each meeting is positive and full of encouragement. I do my best to maintain a warm smile and friendly tone throughout our conversation. I encourage each of my children to maintain a personal calendar to stay organized and proactive in managing their commitments. We begin by reviewing upcoming events and deadlines on their personal planner, emphasizing time management and personal responsibility.

Next, we review upcoming assignments to ensure they have given themselves plenty of time to study and complete them. My role here is to provide accountability and guidance. This is especially important when I notice what I like to call "bad life math." Life math involves applying basic math principles like adding, subtracting, multiplying, and dividing to everyday life. When I notice one of my children adding more and more to their calendar without removing anything, I step in to wave the warning flag and help them reevaluate their decisions.

Toward the end of the meeting, we focus on health and wellness. This is when I ask about their mental, emotional, and physical well-being. A 360 Life Check-In not only emphasizes their academic achievements but also ensures their overall well-being—body, mind, and spirit. These practices have been particularly impactful for our family, helping each child feel supported and understood during their formative years.

Practical next step: Choose a consistent day each week that works for both of you to meet. Cultivate a positive and supportive environment for your comprehensive check-in on all aspects of your child's life. These weekly sessions may range from thirty minutes to two hours or more, depending on the events in their lives and the level of support they require.

Stay organized by taking notes on your computer, using a single document for each week's meeting. Begin each session by reviewing your previous notes, addressing any outstanding details, and then updating the document with new information during your meeting each week. Remember, we are not just preparing them to launch out of homeschool; we are preparing them to launch into a full and flourishing life.

3. Community and Online Resources

One of the greatest benefits of homeschooling through high school is the ability to discover the many treasures of community and online resources available at your fingertips. Think of these as the roadside stops on your grand adventure—moments that will make your trip memorable and provide a breadcrumb trail for interests to cultivate in the days ahead.

From the public library to nature centers, museums, performing arts centers, and the many resources these organizations offer online, there's an all-you-can-eat buffet of opportunities to enrich your child's high school experience. Let's challenge the stereotype that libraries are only for story time. There's a treasure trove of resources waiting to be discovered by high schoolers too! Beyond the rows of books, many libraries now offer access to technology tools like laptops, cameras, and even 3D printers. Building a relationship with your local librarians can unlock a world of opportunities such as scholarships, exclusive events, and insider knowledge that can fuel your child's passions.

Don't stop there—venture out to explore local attractions. Whether historical sites, art galleries, or science centers, there's something for everyone. Encourage your child to engage in this discovery process. These experiences aren't just about fun; they're a direct pathway to shaping future possibilities.

For example, my youngest daughter loves planes and wants to become a pilot. Her interest led to an internet search that quickly revealed several municipal airports within a short driving distance from our home. To our astonishment, many of these airports offer aspiring junior pilots the chance to experience free test flights. I surprised her on her fourteenth birthday with her first flight. Witnessing her excitement as she took to the skies reminded me of the endless possibilities within the homeschool journey—opportunities I never imagined possible when I was her age.

Another often overlooked opportunity is for high school students to enroll in courses at the local community college, often at no cost. This allows students to gauge their academic and time management skills in a collegiate setting while also earning college credits in the most cost-effective manner possible, outside of grants and scholarships. By the time they graduate from homeschooling, they can have a substantial number of college credits, which sometimes allows them to bypass standardized testing requirements for incoming college students.

Taking advantage of community resources unlocks a world of possibilities throughout the homeschool journey, providing high school students with the tools, experiences, and knowledge to flourish academically, professionally, and personally both now and in life beyond high school.

Practical next step: Make a list of community resources in your area. Circle the ones of interest and plan a date to visit them, either online or in person, to learn more about what they offer. Be sure to spread the word about your desire to give your high school student as many opportunities as possible to explore and learn. Follow up on your progress through this list at each 360 Life Check-In.

● ● ●

I hope this homeschool GPS helps smooth your journey through the high school years. Your journey will be unique, and that's what makes it special. Before I go, I offer you this anchoring truth: Time is not on your side in this homeschool journey; it's in God's hands. More than creating the perfect plan, your greatest gift to your child is to prepare them to live life pursuing God and his path of purpose for their life. You were made for this!

Susan Seay hosts the highly successful podcast *Mentor for Moms*, once ranked in the top 1.5 percent of all podcasts. As you listen, you get a sense of Susan's heart to provide practical tools and loads of encouragement to busy moms who struggle with burnout and boundaries. Her uncommon wisdom as a mentor allows exhausted high-achieving moms to be more intentional without any soul-sucking perfectionism in tow. She aims to help moms be better, not just do better. She's married to her college sweetheart Ron and is almost at the end of her twenty-three-plus years of homeschooling the seven Seays. Find Susan online at SusanSeay.com and @susanlseay.

4
The Relationships That Carry Us Through

Cultivating Relationships Through Mentoring
Sally Clarkson

Six of us were tucked here and there between blankets on couches, with mugs of hot chocolate and marshmallows in hand, enjoying the crackling fire in our den. On that freezing December day long ago, with snow falling heavily outside, we sat warm in body and soul in the fine company of each other. For the first time in several years, all of my adult children were home for the Christmas season. Gathering them home from far corners of the world over the holidays was just the gift I needed to fill my heart.

As I sat there, I found myself appreciating the closeness and connection we shared as a family. I thought of the many people I had encountered or knew my children had encountered who might not have experienced stability or connection in their lives. We've certainly faced our share of trying circumstances—no family is immune to life's difficulties—but in that moment, I felt grateful for the love and understanding that anchored us, even when things didn't go as planned. Being together within this culture of love reminded me of how reassuring it is to have a familiar, supportive place where we each feel safe and truly at home.

A culture of love. It was my first time thinking of it that way, but it spoke volumes to my mother heart. All of us create a family culture of some kind. The traditions we keep, the meals we make, the routines we practice, the values we hold, the movies that become our favorites, the church we attend, the generosity we practice, the ways we invest time, the company we keep—all of these come together to craft our particular family culture. While we can also, sometimes unintentionally, create a culture marked by tension, neglect, or discord, it's never too late to make changes that nurture the kind of environment we want. By choosing meaningful traditions or practicing small acts of kindness, we can create a warmer, more loving culture in our homes, no matter where we're starting from.

It has been several years since this family story took place. Still, in this season of life, I am amazed at how often my children call and how much they love to come home or be with Clay and me for meals. And we are still the ones our children seek for advice, encouragement, and friendship. I can now see that my children, in their thirties and early forties, still thrive in the family culture of love we shaped. Giving children teachable hearts for all the faith, values, and ideals we want to pass on to their generation is the most productive, foundational influence we can have on their lives.

As idealists committed to educating our children, we can be so caught up in education as a way of knowing facts or simply learning reading, writing, and arithmetic skills. We seek to provide every bit of instructive curriculum and wonderful mind-developing experiences we can fit into our children's young lives. And yet, as I interact with my adult children regularly, I understand even more that the foundation of unconditional love invested in time and space was a much more critical part of their education than I understood.

They looked to us with favor and listened to our instruction because, as mentors, we sought to win their hearts through affection, encouragement, and acceptance. We wanted them to see that the God we spoke of is also loving, encouraging, and affirming. Most of life revolves around relationships: marriage, family, friends, and work, as well as experiencing influence, feeling a sense of belonging, and finding hope and encouragement through life's trials. These relationships rely heavily on the strength and presence of solid, healthy connections and the modeling that helps shape a vision for healthy interactions and commitments. Having the highest test scores becomes meaningless without a flourishing foundation of love and acceptance, job success, faithfulness in marriage, the ability to work well with others, and a positive sense of self. Unconditional love and acceptance provide the foundation upon which all other areas of life are built, ensuring stability and productivity.

In 1 Corinthians 13, Paul tells us that faith, hope, and love are the most profoundly important aspects of life—but that the greatest of these attributes, in reference to the needs of all humans, is love. Over time, I have realized that "the greatest of these is love" is the most critical factor in living a virtuous, strong life.

The Role of a Mentor

What we store up in our hearts is the truth and message our children will draw from in their daily lives. Beyond the curriculum and teaching all the facts, I have come to believe that the most important aspect of education and imparting a sound view of life comes from the heart, mind, and soul of the teacher. Our children will face a chaotic and challenging world for many more years than they will spend being educated at home. Therefore, we must instill in them excellent truths and virtues that will guide them through all the seasons of their lives and provide leadership that will give them confidence throughout their journey.

We are called not just to pass on knowledge but to mentor, coach, encourage, and inspire our children from the wellspring of excellence and truth we have cultivated in our own lives. A mentor is defined as an experienced and trusted adviser. Having experience and wisdom is essential for all we will teach, but the integrity of our lives will lead our children to trust our perspectives.

My children's need for me to help shape and guide them has called me to become more excellent, more faithful, and more generous in serving them. What comes out of my heart and mind is indeed what teaches them and sparks their desire to live a good and excellent story. I have realized over many years that crafting a culture of love required that I, as a mom, become the conductor of a loving and generous heart that led my children to understand gracious, generous, sacrificial, validating, and forgiving love. Creating such a culture required planning, intention, mature responses, words of life and affirmation, patience, and just lots and lots of unconditional love. My goal was also to provide rigorous reading, discussing, writing, and living out virtuous ideals so that my children would learn to think, to own their convictions, and to live with wisdom in all their ways.

Often, we as parents get caught up in the immediate tasks—housework, homework, paying bills, and disciplining our children. However, it's the air our children breathe and the principles we live by that will truly connect our children's hearts to ours and, ultimately, to God. Genuine influence and discipleship are formed intentionally by modeling ourselves after the ultimate lover—Jesus. He knelt to wash 120 toes; embraced sweet, wiggly children clamoring for attention; and touched and blessed the prostitute, giving her grace. His acts of love and sacrifice provide an ultimate pattern for living generously for the good of others. He ultimately gave everything, out of love, for our redemption. He is our source and inspiration for creating a culture of love. This example didn't come from a textbook but from real life.

How can we ensure that, amid life's busyness and demands, we provide enough genuine love to fill and nurture our children's hearts?

Personal Quality Time

Love is like oxygen for our souls. It brings life, health, and a stable sense of belonging. Building deep understanding and acceptance and nurturing a sense of security and self-acceptance require prioritizing intentional time with our children. This includes time to talk, play, listen, and interact so their hearts receive the strength and grace of a loving relationship. As the Bible says, "Greater love has no one than this: to lay down one's life for one's friends."

Words of Love and Acceptance

"You mean so much to me. You are a gift. I love being with you. I love you just as you are." Words are the food upon which great relationships feed. Jesus was called the Word of God (see John 1:1), showing that God is a communicator. He created us to thrive on communication. Speaking loving words is essential in building a person's confidence. Words of love can be recalled and cherished for a lifetime, just as words of anger, criticism, and guilt can be remembered. Choose your words wisely.

Serving and Meeting Practical Needs

The workload of homelife can often be daunting. Yet, when one of my own washes dishes without being told or thoughtfully makes me a cup of hot, steaming tea and brings it to me unasked, I feel the value of my worth in their eyes. We are all grateful when someone helps us with the tasks of life. Jesus made meals, healed the sick, spoke of helping the downcast (the good Samaritan), and washed toes! These were very practical services that reached the hearts of his disciples and showed them that love is not just words but actions.

Making delicious meals, helping a child with chores or a difficult task, patiently playing a game, or teaching a skill is another way to express love. I'll never forget offering to pack a bag for my child who was going away on a trip. She looked at me and said, "That makes me feel so loved and seen that you would help me with a dreadful task." It surprised me because packing was not a big deal to me, but it was a mountain of challenges to her. So, giving ourselves to help our children with the tasks and pressures of life is another way to love them through serving.

The Gift of Touch

One of my teenagers became more closed-lipped as he navigated the emotions and pressures of adolescence. Sometimes, he would go out at night to church or an activity with his friends. When he came home, I would ask, "Did you have a good time tonight?"

"Oh, I don't know," he would reply.

"Where did you go?"

"Nowhere."

"What did you do?"

"Nothing."

Then I would say, "Want a nice back scratch before you go to sleep?"

He would lie on the couch, and I would gently start scratching and tickling his back. And, of course, in my heart, I was saying, "Tell me your secrets!" Before I knew it, he would start talking about everything on his heart. Touch can be a magical way of opening a relationship. I used to massage my daughter's hands with lotion to achieve the same effect.

Teaching Truth, Inspiring Great Thoughts

When my children began to venture into a very secular world where their values were constantly questioned, it became crucial for them to have a deep understanding of truth, righteousness, integrity, courage, and strength. These qualities have been instilled in them through endless conversations day and night throughout their years. Our dinner table became a place for discussing great ideas, articles, politics, Scripture, cultures, and differing worldviews. I believe these discussions are what truly shaped our children into the intellectuals they are today.

The foundations of a person's thoughts and beliefs are more profoundly nuanced through countless hours spent engaging with hundreds of books, great stories, science articles, and biblical discussions covering every subject imaginable. Developing convictions and a sense of self occurs through an intentional effort to mentor, shape, and inspire our children day by day in a thousand ways. Passing on a legacy of intellect, strength of mind, depth of soul, and a compassionate heart demands that we ourselves grow and exemplify the qualities we hope our children will take away from our home.

Taking on the responsibility of shaping my children with the finest ideals and philosophy I could embody has pushed me to become my best self. I am far more educated now, having grappled with the contradictory ideas found in the books we've read together. Learning to cultivate an open mind and a humble heart was a lengthy process, but it gave my children a comprehensive picture of what a robust and fulfilling life entails. While our primary aim in mentoring our children was to instill in them a love for learning and growing, we unexpectedly found that we also fell in love with education and leadership, gathering wisdom in ways we had never experienced during our own educations. In essence, the process of shaping our children also shaped us.

A full-bodied and excellent education begins with the heart and mind of the teacher. It's not about mastering all the facts found in textbooks but about approaching our children with a teachable heart, a spirit of generosity, a readiness to love and serve them, and a commitment to lifelong growth and learning. Regardless of your educational philosophy or your children's personalities, all students crave love and acceptance from someone who believes in them. Loving well is the primary and most profound commitment you can make to shape and nurture your children as they flourish through life.

To keep my primary goal of loving and serving my children at the forefront of my mind, I memorized verses that resonated with me while teaching my children. These words to ponder guided my daily attitudes and efforts toward achieving my goals:

> Jesus replied: "'Love the Lord your God with all your heart and with all your soul and with all your mind.' This is the first and greatest commandment. And the second is like it: 'Love your neighbor as yourself.'" (Matt. 22:37–39)

> God is love. (1 John 4:8)

> If someone says, "I love God," and yet he hates his brother or sister, he is a liar; for the one who does not love his brother and sister whom he has seen, cannot love God, whom he has not seen. (1 John 4:20 NASB)

> And now these three remain: faith, hope and love. But the greatest of these is love. (1 Cor. 13:13)

> In addition to all these things put on love, which is the perfect bond of unity. (Col. 3:14 NASB)

> By this everyone will know that you are my disciples, if you love one another. (John 13:35)

> Above all, keep fervent in your love for one another, because love covers a multitude of sins. (1 Pet. 4:8 NASB)

Sally Clarkson is a bestselling author of over thirty books, with millions of copies sold globally. She hosts the popular podcast *At Home with Sally*, offering wisdom on motherhood, home, and education, and has garnered tens of millions of downloads. Married to Clay for forty-plus years, Sally cofounded Whole Heart Ministries to support families in raising faithful, healthy children. She has four accomplished children and four beloved grandchildren. Sally splits her time between Colorado and England, often enjoying tea with her golden retriever, Darcy. | @sally.clarkson

The Gift of Allohomeschooling
Delina Pryce McPhaull

We have the sweetest home video of my son walking out the back door. My three-year-old twin girls and I are standing there in pajamas, while my son, almost four, is fully dressed—hair brushed, sneakers on, coat zipped—and dragging an oversized backpack.

"Have a good day at school!" I say as he walks the seventy-eight steps to my sister's house.

Fast-forward eleven years, and I have pictures of my mom sitting with my teens at my dining room table, novels in hand, working through a complicated plot and admiring how authors weave stories together. A lot of life, growth, and changes happened in the years between these two snapshots of our homeschooling days, but one thing remained constant: I never homeschooled alone.

My husband, three children, and I live on a family compound. That sounds cultish, but it's not, I promise. My parents live in one house, my sister's family lives in another, and my home sits in the middle. My brother's family has a house about two hundred steps to the left of mine.

We didn't plan this communal living; it's just how life worked out. And even though there are many places in the world where I'd rather live, I know that what we have here is special and has been much of the reason I didn't thoroughly burn out and quit homeschooling altogether.

My parents were teachers and school administrators all of our lives, and thankfully, they didn't bristle or protest when we chose not to enroll our kids in traditional school. Instead, they offered to help.

And help they did. My dad, a retired science teacher, taught science and helped with math when we got stuck. My mom took charge of language arts. Before they could read and write their names, the kids would go to Grandma's for school. She started with reading aloud and expanded to spelling, grammar, and composition. My sister volunteered to lead nature study or Spanish (her interest area) at various times and taught them to play the piano (her expertise). My sister-in-law offered to teach art and help with math.

These adults were more than extended family; they became *allohomeschoolers*.

The term *alloparenting* was coined in the '70s by Edward Wilson, who studied the genetic basis of social behavior. As is evident to anyone who has parented for more than twenty-four hours, humans were not designed to raise children alone.[1] Alloparents are those who assist in providing care for a child who is not biologically their own.

Cooperative childrearing feels so removed from our reality, where the help we receive is more transactional than relational and often comes with a price tag and a contract (think coaches and co-op teachers). But around the world and throughout history, alloparenting is the norm. Extended families live in community, family friends are considered uncles and aunties, and grandparents naturally take on caregiving roles. When children need comfort, food, or play, they know they can receive it from more than just Mom and Dad.

In my case, the extended family that shared in the caregiving was also willing to share in the teaching duties that are part of parenting in a homeschooling family. It's what I've started calling allohomeschoolers—the community that forms around you to support your homeschooling efforts by sharing their expertise to educate your children. These allohomeschoolers aren't like the co-op teachers and tutors we pay to help in certain subjects. Instead, the education poured out by allohomeschoolers is an extension of their love for your family.

Sharing the load is good for everyone. Researchers have documented how involved grandmothers live happier and healthier lives for longer.[2] Children also benefit from knowing another dimension of their grandparents. It's incredible when kids realize that Grandma's knowledge stretches beyond cookie baking and reading picture books. Yes, she loves *Judge Judy* and *Dr. Phil*, but she also has expertise and life experience waiting to be shared. My mom found much joy in seeing her grandkids develop their writing skills and create stories and characters from their imaginations. There's nothing like the motivation of having a teacher who beams and thinks you're a genius.

I remember overhearing my mom telling the kids stories about her childhood that I'd never heard before—memories triggered by something they'd read in their language arts curriculum. These stories not only enriched their education but also strengthened the bond between generations. The wisdom, family lore, and values passed down from grandparents are priceless.

Knowing that my kids have close bonds, years of memories, and connections to their grandparents, aunts, and uncles is something I'm deeply grateful for. I sometimes (okay, always) complain about the rural area where we live, the lack of homeschooling families of color to commune with, and the long drive to connect with like-minded homeschoolers, but it's in those moments that I remind myself that my kids' homeschooling experience had something unique and special.

"Have You Been to See Grandma Today?"

But let's be honest, friends. One of the top reasons I loved allohomeschooling was because your girl needed a break! My sister will tell you that giving me some time alone motivated her to include my kids in their homeschool days, even though they were much younger than her son. The videos she sent of those moments were appropriately chaotic. I loved knowing they were having fun learning and interacting with their cousin while I started dinner or responded to emails.

We can't always easily absorb or redirect our kids' energy. It was helpful to have a place for them to go a couple of times a week that didn't interrupt but instead advanced our homeschool day. I could schedule a doctor's appointment, sit and have a moment with a cup of tea in hand, or gather my thoughts for the woke homeschool history lessons that would start after lunch.

Right around the dreary and cold days of February each year, I would start questioning my life choices, including homeschooling. But my allohomeschoolers helped me to stay the course. Sometimes, I just didn't feel like doing our regular school routine. But when my mom was done, I knew at least *some* quality, intentional educational engagement had occurred that day. Researchers say,

> The much lower prevalence of parental burnout in collectivistic countries—even when socioeconomic inequalities and other factors are controlled—suggests that strengthening the social network of mutual aid and solidarity around families might well help to decrease the prevalence of parental burnout in individualistic countries.[3]

Did you catch that? Strengthening our social networks of mutual aid and solidarity is critical.

Our Western individualistic culture expects us to parent alone. That expectation sometimes shows up as comments from friends and acquaintances who wonder out loud, "Are you even homeschooling? What do *you* teach them?" Don't spend your energy trying to justify your choices based on their ideas of what homeschooling means. What are *your* values? What are *your* practical needs? What arrangement would *your* kids benefit from?

There's a particular sort of shame of not being able to "do it all" like our mothers appeared to—or the mothers on Instagram seem to. For example, there's always going to be that person who thinks hiring a housekeeper is a shameful admission that you're not organized or disciplined or haven't acquired the proper habits to keep your own house. Don't listen to those voices because they're wrong. If your budget allows, get the help you need to lighten your load and live in peace.

To graciously and happily accept homeschooling help from those in our network, we've got to get over our determination to do it all. There are no prizes for wearing ourselves to the bone and burning out. Again, get the help you need to make homeschooling sustainable and life-giving for your family.

Allohomeschooling doesn't come without challenges. Navigating life in community requires honest and up-front communication, especially if one of your allohomeschoolers doesn't share your approach to education. One year, my dad made himself available to do another year of science curriculum with my kids. But the kids begged me to do science with them instead. "Grandpa is too serious about science," they said. My dad was strict about protocols and precise documentation. It was up to me to advocate for my kids but also for myself, so we compromised. I did the science lesson with the help of Mystery Science, and Grandpa did the experiments once a week.

Deciding how to handle the curriculum is an essential aspect of communal teaching. Have detailed conversations with your allohomeschoolers before you begin so the experience is enjoyable for everyone involved. Will your allohomeschoolers create their own lesson plans, or will you provide the scope, sequence, and instructions for each lesson? Remember that this arrangement is primarily about helping you and your kids. Maintain open communication with everyone about how things are going, and don't be afraid to pivot if something is not working.

You Can Do This Too

What happens if you don't live on a family compound? What if your family members are not supportive of your choice to homeschool? Where will you find like-minded people to be your partners in homeschooling? Maybe it's someone from church or your retired math teacher neighbor. Perhaps an old coworker would be delighted to share their expertise. Even if you don't live near your siblings and parents, you can find ways to incorporate your network into your homeschooling.

One year, my homeschooling friend Mariangela, who had been a talented art student, and my sister-in-law alternated teaching art lessons. "I'll make the snacks," I announced, happy to have my kids experience something that wasn't in my wheelhouse. Ms. Maria, as my children call her, is also my son's godparent. The chance to see and know her, not just on birthdays or when she drops off donuts but through her talent, was a gift.

Look around. I'm confident that the people you are in community with have knowledge and talent to share. Tap them on the shoulder and add them to the school schedule. More often than not, you'll find that friends will feel honored to be invited into your family's life in this meaningful way. Homeschooling allows you to expand and deepen your network if you're willing to interlock your lives with others as everyone flourishes.

We tend to spend time looking for the "perfect" curriculum and crafting the "perfect" schedule without giving nearly enough thought to who will implement those ambitious lesson plans and daily schedules. If this sounds all too familiar and the idea of allohomeschooling resonates with you, start slowly. You don't have to hand over an entire subject or make a long-term commitment. For example, a semester of once-a-week auntie time to work on math facts is plenty. If things go well for your kids and your allohomeschooler, discuss how to grow their level of engagement over time.

Your community will be proud to see your children reach milestones—graduations, careers, academic accomplishments. Friends applaud and send their congratulations when you post accolades in your Facebook feed, but those who partnered with you to homeschool will feel pride on a different level. When my daughter was accepted into a fine arts high school after auditioning and submitting a portfolio of her artwork, my friend Mariangela jokingly took the credit.

"Wow! Those art lessons I gave her sure paid off!" she joked. But in all seriousness, this was her win too.

It belonged to all of us.

It took a village.

Delina Pryce McPhaull is an editorial consultant and owner of Woke Homeschooling, a platform for sharing resources for conscious and inclusive families. Throughout her career, Delina has repurposed her journalism degree to create books, podcasts, websites, blogs, newsletters, and homeschool curricula. She has collaborated with small business owners, nonprofit organizations, and authors in various fields. Her commitment to lifelong learning has helped her to evolve and grow as a professional and a human. But work isn't everything. Her happiest days are spent with her loved ones enjoying good food, stimulating conversations, and basking in the beauty of the sunset and sea. She lives in Texas with her husband and teenagers. | @wokehomeschooling

Aristotle Smiles:
The Gift of Together Schooling
Erin Loechner

It was my husband's idea.

"What are your thoughts on Chinese?" he asked as he put away a stack of freshly folded T-shirts. The moon outside was full, swollen even, much like my eight-months-pregnant belly. I thought of dinner.

"Sounds great," I said. "Want me to order in?"

He laughed. "No, I'm talking foreign language. For the baby?"

My mind raced to the tower of parenting books on my nightstand. There was the one about tiger moms and helicopter dads urging their toddlers to become trilingual cellists and pint-size soccer stars. Another about biohacking education, including a family who was encouraging (coercing?) their daughter to graduate with a PhD in actuarial science before she hit puberty. Still another how-to guide on raising geniuses, pages filled with EQs, IQs, all manner of Qs. Stacks and stacks of bestselling bellwethers that told the tale of a coming generation of children predicted to experience academic and athletic pressure none other had seen.

I was wary. And hungry.

"No way," I argued, hormones raging as I spouted off the dozens of titles I'd read predicting infinite damage caused by offspring being dragged down paths paved with their parents' overreaching hopes and dreams. In an instant, I assumed my husband's simple question would catapult us into a tangled labyrinth where nothing short of raising a preschool chess savant or third-grade composer prodigy would suffice.

My husband smiled. He knew this outburst was likely more rooted in estrogen than logic, so wisely, he said, "Okay, then. Just a thought. Fried rice?"

But less than three years later, we'd find ourselves driving our daughter and her favorite stuffed panda to a friend's house for tea. Only we don't say tea. We say *chá*. And we don't say panda.

We say *xióngmāo*.

This is how our daughter began immersive Chinese lessons, although I can hardly call them that. The truth is much simpler: we met a friend from Taiwan, Shu-Hui, and we asked her if she'd be willing to share her language and culture with our family. She was delighted, and we began visiting Shu-Hui's home twice a week for an afternoon of cooking ban pao, writing characters, and crafting zhezhi.

My pregnancy outburst, as it turns out, was entirely unwarranted. My fear of coercing a toddler to learn a foreign language was rooted in my misconception that to learn a rigorous skill, one must be forced into a rigorous academic environment. *More flash cards! More memorization! Pencils chewed down to the quick!* I had failed to imagine that a small child could become fluent in a foreign language—or anything, for that matter—naturally, gently, and with great ease.

Now, over a decade later, I realize just how wrong I was. On every visit with Shu-Hui, our children pick up something new—a word or phrase, a long-standing tradition, a deeply held cultural belief. They are joyfully soaking up dialects and intonations, a whole new alphabet. But mostly, and I think most importantly, our children are discovering something far more foundational than the ABCs. They are realizing—as are we—that the best education rarely comes from a box, a book, or a building.

It comes from a friend.

The Many Teachers All Around Us

In our home, I like to think of our core learning method as "together schooling," an admittedly self-made pedagogy rooted in the idea that people are among the best curricula available to us. Whether at the butcher or the ballet, the playground or the pew, every encounter with someone else is an opportunity to give something lovely and to receive something even lovelier in return. From small kindnesses to specialized knowledge, learning begins the moment we acknowledge and invite the experience of another.

This very practice of together schooling is how our family has created a motley education where our kids speak Mandarin to each other while spinning nunchucks and toeside on skateboards as they rehearse an upcoming scene for their local theater troupe. This is how they've learned to bake lemon bars, master "Für Elise," recite Robert Frost, and nail the Charleston. Together schooling is why our kids can catch a bass or a wave and pull a quarter from behind your ear.

It's a philosophy that has expanded far past our children's learning experiences, revolutionizing my idea of education. Recognizing people as magnanimous guides to a worldwide classroom transforms my daily drudgery and tiring tasks into opportunities for everyday enrichment. After all, it takes only the slightest acknowledgment that the person behind the cheese counter is a human being with a mind full of experiences I'll never see, know, or understand to humble myself for the rest of the day—or at least until dinner.

Together schooling—noticing the many teachers all around us—is the simplest, most beautiful educational method I know. The method requires no tools except one available to us all: the boldness to live curiously. To ask your friend's daughter how to find the perfect lipstick shade. To ask your son's best friend's father how to paint a mural. To ask your barista for the best vegan scotcheroo recipe she's got.

There is no formula, no booklist, no schedule, no scope or sequence. Want to become a better gardener? Those delphiniums next door didn't grow themselves. Knock. Ask. Learn.

With every conversation, our family is building a village, a support system, a team. The gift of together schooling means never having to go at it alone. We mere parents are no longer the sole dispensers of information, life experience, and perspective. Instead, we're giving our children infinite possibilities for skills gained and endless opportunities for micro-apprenticeships offered by passionate, everyday experts. Our kids are learning to interact with different ages, cultures, and perspectives. They are learning to ask good questions and to notice and unearth passions hidden in other people.

But also . . . to notice and unearth passions in *themselves*.

When I trace back the highlights and experiences from my own passionate career—writing books, hosting a multi-season HGTV.com show, and keynoting stages at Walt Disney World—I see the seeds of together schooling sprouting wild. I recognize the many simple moments and conversations rooted in curiosity, slowly inching me toward a path not yet paved.

In college, knocking on the dorm room door of another girl on my floor. *You said you were majoring in interior design? This might be a dumb question, but can you tell me more about what that means? It sounds like a dream job!*

In Los Angeles, on the phone with a producer. *Wait, you don't have any shows streaming online for your network? I'm writing about interior design here in the city. Tell me everything you need. I have an idea.*

In Singapore, at a creative studio. *You're an editorial intern at Hachette? Can I take you out for dinner? I'd like to learn more about the publishing process from your perspective.*

Knock.
Ask.
Learn.

Have You Asked?

Much ink has been spilled on the many different pedagogies available to homeschooling families, and many more dollars have been funneled convincing us all that we're one book, one kit, one boxed curriculum, or one method away from achieving blissful success in the minds and hearts of our children. So we scour thrift stores for hardback volumes and watch influencers live stream their timetables and home libraries. We attend nature groups and co-ops and hybrids; we listen to audiobooks the whole way home, we pull into the garage to start dinner, and we settle in with a classic read-aloud before bed. We turn off the porch light, hunker down, and prep for the day ahead, where we'll march to our proven rhythms again.

We tell ourselves that learning is a fire to be kindled, a feast to be enjoyed, a treasure trove of ideas to be explored, discovered, and beautifully invited into.

But who else are we inviting into the beauty?

What might change if you knew your next-door neighbor owned every Landmark book and had read them twice? Or your best friend's brother won a nationwide banjo competition? Or your mother-in-law's friend's son was an Olympian? Or your dentist's cousin helped restore Notre Dame? Or your other neighbor is a retired rocket scientist?

Have you asked?

Together schooling begins by teaching our children that learning is free and available to all. That resources abound, unearthed by curiosity and connection. That everyone—our own children certainly included—has wisdom to give and to receive. That learning lies within our own reach, yes, but can also be reached for in someone else's story.

While the gift of living books is infinitely valuable, worthwhile, and good, we mustn't overlook the gift of living beings. If we surmise that stories matter and that living books offering authentic experiences of lives lived are one of the purest and most beautiful forms of education, we must also include the stories still unfolding around us.

And when I begin to doubt that together schooling will be "enough" for our children, I remember this: Aristotle was once someone's neighbor.

I am convinced we are walking among the greats. Daily, we pass people learning new ways to live, work, and be, and many are persevering against insurmountable odds. Our crossing guard is learning to live with a new diagnosis. Our hairdresser is teaching herself carpentry. Our best friend is working toward a PhD, our sister is learning embroidery, and our mother is finding her footing after retirement.

We are learning to lead, teach, and live well. To move through an ever-changing world as we develop the capacity to persevere, encourage, believe, dream, and begin anew.

Might that also be the hope for our children?

A few days ago, we welcomed a new friend into our home. "My son has been ill," she told me, explaining that after months of tests and lab work, doctors were still baffled by his symptoms. "I'm thinking it might be a food allergy. I just have a hunch."

So we sorted through piles of cookbooks, and I shared my own journey of a rare diagnosis. We talked of how difficult the adjustment can be, of finding a new normal, and of the gift of other people sharing stories, recipes, and hope. I ground some einkorn flour to give her and passed along my sourdough recipe and some starter. Moments later, the kids burst through the door, my eleven-year-old daughter proudly toting fresh dumplings she'd made at Shu-Hui's house.

"You take Chinese lessons?" my friend asked. "I've always wanted to learn that language!"

"Oh, really?" my daughter said, grabbing soy sauce from the fridge. "I'll teach you what I know!"

And somewhere, somehow, Aristotle smiles.

Author of *Chasing Slow* and *The Opt-Out Family*, **Erin Loechner** is the founder of the global early years homeschooling hybrid Other Goose. Her seminal work has been praised in *The New York Times*, *The Washington Post*, *The Wall Street Journal*, and *The TODAY Show*. When she's not scrawling on her trusty steno pad, Erin, her husband, and their three homeschooled kids spend their days chasing alpenglow, reading Kipling, and biking to town for more tortillas. Find more from Erin at ErinLoechner.com.

I Wasn't Supposed to Homeschool: A Father's Journey
Richard M. Smith, PhD

I wasn't supposed to homeschool.

Camille, my wife, and I never even considered it. What did it even mean to homeschool? How in the world would I do it? And what would happen to our children as a result of it? Homeschooling, or the idea of homeschooling, was a different world. I never thought about it, didn't see it, and didn't think it was feasible.

Additionally, I did not know how to do it as a dad. I knew very well that my wife, who had a master's degree in education and was a schoolteacher, had the ability, talent, and capability to do it. But what about me? What was my role? How would I contribute? How would I be a homeschool dad? These questions have been with me in some way since the beginning and throughout my journey. Some questions have been answered, while others have shifted or changed. Allow me to share a bit of my homeschool journey with you.

• • •

It was the latter part of 2005, and I was working on completing my degree at Temple University. Camille was a teacher in the Philadelphia school system. As we prepared to have our first child, we discussed and decided she would take maternity leave, and then we would find someone to watch our son while she went back to work and I completed my degree. There wasn't even a conversation about homeschooling.

However, all that changed once our son was born and even more when we were blessed with our daughter two years later. We started considering where we lived at the time and the state of our local school district. Additionally, we recognized that no one was more equipped than we were to raise our children and prepare them educationally and with the life lessons necessary. This was not a moment of arrogance or dismissal of our district's excellent teachers; it was about the fact that these were *our* children. We struggled with the idea that someone else would have most of their time during the day and that strangers would design and mold their experiences. We learned there was power in taking more control of our children's education.

Another factor in our decision to homeschool was something else we didn't see coming. When my firstborn son was two months old, we noticed he could not stop scratching. He was highly itchy, it seemed, all the time. We took him to his pediatrician, and they noted he had severe eczema and recommended visiting a dermatologist. Additionally, they recommended we see an allergist due to his heightened irritation. The dermatologist confirmed the severe eczema. They told us to "keep him greasy" and prescribed various ointments and creams.

We then went to the allergist, where he underwent allergy testing. He did not have just one but multiple food allergies, which included wheat, soy, dairy, eggs, nuts, shellfish, flaxseed, sunflower seeds, and coconut. This was the first time I remembered wanting to protect my son as a dad. I even prayed that all his ailments would become mine and that he would be free of them so he could have a normal life. I was frustrated and saddened that I could not protect my son from having these problems, but maybe I could shield him from being around foods that were dangerous to him. The idea of homeschooling later appealed to me as a way for me to protect my son.

While working on my doctorate in sociology, focusing on race, I delved into the racial inequities within the US educational system and how it has failed Black children. My studies revealed biased curricula, discriminatory disciplinary practices, and a lack of resources, perpetuating disadvantages for some students. Additionally, I explored broader struggles within US schools, including underfunding, overcrowded classrooms, and a one-size-fits-all approach to education that stifles creativity and critical thinking. In contrast, educational systems in some countries excelled by challenging their students academically and fostering discussion-based learning rather than merely instilling knowledge. These educational methods emphasized critical thinking, creativity, and student engagement, leading to better outcomes and more well-rounded individuals. Witnessing these stark differences made me reconsider the traditional schooling system and explore alternatives for my children, aiming to provide them with a more enriching and equitable educational experience.

At the same time, I became aware of the origins of the US homeschool movement. I read about how it gained momentum in response to the Civil Rights legislation of the 1960s and school integration. Many White parents, many of whom claimed to be Christian, chose to homeschool their children to avoid having them attend schools with Black students. Given this history, I was initially hesitant about homeschooling. However, I realized that while I might not be able to alleviate my son's medical issues, I could ensure he received a more personalized and focused education. This understanding led me to embrace homeschooling to protect and nurture his learning experience.

The Power of Community

Before my son turned five, I began noticing several African American families, in particular the fathers, who were homeschooling their children. I saw how deeply involved they were in their children's lives, educating them on standard curricula, cultural studies, and heritage. Observing these families and witnessing how they made learning a part of everyday experiences, not just something from a book, was inspiring. This exposure ignited a passion in me for the opportunity and privilege of educating my own children despite my appreciation for schoolteachers' hard work and dedication.

I was moved by how invested these fathers were in their children's lives, as I did not have that growing up. Their engagement made me reflect on my role as a parent. I observed men like Jason, Derek, and Marion, who provided great insights on being an involved father. Jason, in particular, stood out. As a scholar in English and literature, he regularly designed and taught classes for his children. He guided them through critical reading, thoughtful writing, and effective storytelling. He also taught debate and shared his knowledge with other children.

Marion was a strong father, guiding and directing his family while providing his children with experiences and opportunities in STEM, entrepreneurship, and marketing. With a military background, he set detailed goals for his family and empowered his children to set their own goals and pursue their interests. Despite a demanding schedule, Derek was a supportive father who made every effort to attend major family events and ensure his children had what they needed. Whenever he could attend an event, he actively supported the class or contributed to the homeschooling group's activities. The dedication of these men inspired me to reflect on how I wanted to impact my children's education and showed me the profound difference an involved parent can make.

Meeting these men was instrumental in growing my understanding of how fathers can participate in homeschooling. Initially, I hadn't realized there could be such a variety of approaches. I learned that homeschool fathers are diverse and unique in how they approach educating their children, each contributing their strengths and talents to their children's education. I also recognized that, as a homeschool dad, I could teach my children in various ways, including using unstructured approaches. I've learned to practice a form of mentorship, allowing my children to see what I do and where I work and involving them in critical areas of ministry. This hands-on approach has enriched our homeschooling experience, demonstrating that education extends beyond traditional methods and into everyday life.

When I cannot be present, it's usually because I'm working to support my wife's great ideas for our children's learning and growth. She helped me realize that my sacrifices of work and time make it possible for our children to have opportunities they might not otherwise have. This includes attending camps, taking various trips, and having beneficial experiences that allow them to see different parts of the country and, eventually, the world.

My wife and I are partners in educating our children, working together to support their growth and development. We collaborate to ensure our children receive the best education possible. Recognizing our children's unique qualities and leveraging our strengths, we create a supportive environment that equips them with everything they need to succeed.

Lessons Learned in Fatherhood

Looking back on my homeschooling journey, I've learned many lessons to share with other fathers considering homeschooling for the first time or those becoming more involved in homeschooling, especially those who are married or coparenting.

The first lesson: it is essential to recognize that a partnership between parents is crucial for leading the homeschool journey for your children. You have the power to craft and determine the path you want to take your children on. You are the leaders of your own academy. For example, when we talk about our children graduating or advancing to the next grade, they know they are continuing in "Smith Academy," which we view as one of the most elite educational spaces in the country. We have the power to ensure they receive a top-notch education because we are their teachers.

The second lesson is to recognize how you function best. I have been inspired and significantly grown in the company of other homeschooling dads. However, seeing some who are more involved than I could be has sometimes been discouraging. It seems like they are at every event for their children. I have felt discouraged not because of their dedication but because I couldn't spend as much time with my children in those places. However, I've learned that doing what I can is enough. There's no prototype or standard for homeschool fathering besides love.

Some dads can attend every event, class, field trip, and activity, which is fantastic! But others make it to what they can, and that's fine as long as it works for their family. It's a team effort. What's most important is that fathers thoroughly love their children and work to provide possibilities they may never have had. Some dads invest in their children's lives through their work and the opportunities they can give, and that's okay too.

The third lesson I learned was that any time spent with my children is valuable to both them and me. For example, I remember taking my youngest to the park, where I usually run, and we jogged together. He was about ten or eleven at the time. I didn't think much of it—I do it regularly, and I decided to ask if he wanted to join me. We went at his pace, jogging and walking. It soon became apparent through our interactions that it was special for him. He was happy to be with his dad, enjoying our father and son time. I also enjoyed every moment, especially after realizing how important it was to him. We don't have all the time in the world, but when we make time to be present and engaged, share space with our children, and show up whenever we can, it makes a real difference in their lives.

The final piece of advice I will share is that education can happen everywhere and anywhere. Traveling with our children without the constraints of a school schedule has been a wonderful experience. When I went to Birmingham, Alabama, for a conference, I brought my family along. We had been discussing the Civil Rights Movement, and having my children there by my side was beyond powerful. They walked the streets they had seen in documentaries of children protesting for equal rights and stood beside the Gaston Motel, where civil rights leaders had organized at the only Black-owned hotel in the area.

Visiting the various monuments and locations we had discussed or seen in books brought history to life for them. Beyond that, finding different ways to learn throughout the day—discussing events, focusing on current issues, or even talking about science around the dinner table—was remarkable. Such moments are priceless and demonstrate that education can truly happen everywhere and anywhere.

● ● ●

My homeschooling journey has been a true partnership with my wife. While I've learned much from other men, she has been my greatest teacher. Camille has shown me what it means to educate our children and maintain a passion for teaching, even when it seems our children aren't grasping or interested in what we share. She has taught me to be creative and to genuinely study our children to understand what excites them. From her, I have learned about the patience, care, time, and effort it takes to homeschool effectively.

Participating in this journey and witnessing how my wife teaches our children has been a pleasure. Although I can't do everything she does, I make sure our children know I am there and that I care. I walk this journey with them, and I love every moment. I am immensely proud to be a homeschooling father. This educational path was the right choice for us, and I hope more dads will consider making this choice too. Together, we're shaping a rich and fulfilling educational experience for our children that honors their individuality and inspires a deep passion for learning.

Richard M. Smith, PhD, is the associate provost for equity and belonging and a professor of sociology at McDaniel College. He is also the lead pastor of The Movement Church in Maryland. For nearly two decades, Dr. Smith has taught courses on race and racism, African American culture, social psychology, religion, and criminal justice. He cofounded the Racial Healing Clinic and cocreated the podcasts *Black Men Homeschool* and *Race and Faith Cyphers*. He holds a PhD in sociology from Temple University and has published research on race, African American culture, and religious organizations. Richard and his wife, Camille, have homeschooled their three children for fourteen years. | @blackmenhomeschool

Heartstrings and Hugs: Cultivating Connection with Our Children
Jennifer Pepito

We walked along the mossy trail as the waterfall roared over slippery rocks to the creek below. I, my husband, and our three children who still lived at home had been going in different directions for weeks. For the first time in my life as a mom, I wasn't full-time homeschooling. My teens were in charter school classes during the day while my husband and I took Bible and ministry classes at a local church.

I missed the beautiful moments of connection that we had curated over twenty-six years of homeschooling and was anxious to continue building those bridges even as we moved into a different season of life. This walk in the woods was a needed reset, bringing a sense of peace and calm as we enjoyed the beauty of nature together. I was fortunate to have the privilege of homeschooling for so long, but even as a homeschooling family, we had to fight for connection.

There can be a tendency to let our children take more authority over their time as they enter their teen years. However, with the invasive nature of electronics, we still made it a point to emphasize times of togetherness and shared values. As I evaluated our time and navigated new seasons, I found several ways to forge strong bonds as my children grew.

But why even bother with connection? Many families are content to let the tide of culture roll them along, each member encased in their own private world via their personal electronic devices. But is this the best thing for our families? Is it healthy for humanity to let go of connection and simply fade into virtual community? According to an article in *Psychology Today*, it isn't:

> Evidence has been growing that when our need for social relationships is not met, we fall apart mentally and even physically. There are effects on the brain and on the body. Some effects work subtly, through the exposure of multiple body systems to excess amounts of stress hormones. Yet the effects are distinct enough to be measured over time, so that unmet social needs take a serious toll on health, eroding our arteries, creating high blood pressure, even undermining learning and memory.[4]

And it isn't just the connection between humans that is destroyed by a lack of intentionality and an overreliance on electronic entertainment. An article in the *Journal of the Association for Consumer Research* found that cognitive capacity is significantly reduced whenever a smartphone is within reach, even when the phone is off. Researchers dubbed this effect the "brain drain hypothesis."[5] Essentially, we are less likely to rely on our own cognitive resources if we know an information source is readily available. So, overuse of electronics and lack of connection can damage our children's cognitive abilities, making it harder for them to think clearly and plan for the future.

However, when children are securely attached to their parents, and you've taken the time to build connection with your children, you equip them to be more resilient for their entire lives. In an article about attachment by Daniel Siegel, author of *The Whole-Brain Child*, researchers concluded:

> It's been shown repeatedly that children with histories of secure attachment are less vulnerable to stress and better able to take

advantage of growth opportunities. Moreover, when these same children go through a troubled period, their prior experience of feeling nurtured isn't erased, so it still influences their response to the new situation.[6]

We all want to raise children who are hopeful and resilient. We want to raise children who know how to form relationships and care about the world, and that goal isn't out of reach. The first step is often healing our own attachment issues; for me, that looked like getting curious about my story of origin and inviting Jesus to comfort me in times of childhood pain and stress. But while we are healing ourselves and becoming more regulated, we still need to connect with our children and help them develop healthy attachments.

● ● ●

We can help our children live lives of hope and purpose instead of merely following the stream of culture into lives of disconnection and mental degradation. We can cultivate sacred, connected homes by paying attention to a few simple practices. We've been highlighting these simple practices in the Restoration Home Community and have seen families experience more peace and joy due to their efforts.

1. **Make Eye Contact.** When you look your loved ones in the eyes for at least ten seconds daily, it builds close bonds and raises oxytocin levels, releasing joy. This simple practice can deepen connections and create a sense of closeness that both you and your children may come to crave. You can start this practice by having a staring contest with your children, looking at them when they speak to you, and taking time each day to ask how they are doing while you gaze at them with eyes of love.

2. **Give Hugs.** Hugging your loved ones increases feelings of warmth and love. Just as with eye contact, hugs release oxytocin, a bonding hormone. So, if you want to nurture a close and connected family, it might be as simple as creating a hugging habit. In our family, we hug often! Even my teens will ask for hugs, and while small children don't always know how to ask for hugs, they will show their need for affection in sibling fights or fussy behavior.

   By prioritizing daily hugs, you can alleviate some of these behavior issues. Take time every day to hug each child for at least thirty seconds. You can make it into a game where you chase them, call out "I got you," and give them a good squeeze, or pretend you are the mama or papa bear and give them a bear hug. Find ways to playfully incorporate more hugs, and you will strengthen the bonds in your family.

3. **Read Aloud.** Reading aloud has been one of the ways our family created strong bonds. The books we read became a shared vocabulary, and we often refer to them during family times. We still play "Pooh sticks" while walking by a mountain stream in honor of our years of reading Winnie the Pooh. We remember the hardships faced by Laura Ingalls Wilder and her family, and it gives us courage when we are struggling, and when we are feeling spiritually dry or weary, we remember the faith of Darlene Deibler Rose or Corrie ten Boom, whom we were witnesses to as we read their biographies. The books we read are bonding agents, and in the Peaceful Press Connection Challenge, we encourage families to read for at least fifteen minutes per day to strengthen their own family culture.

4. **Spend Time in Nature.** When we get outside, it soothes our nervous system and creates opportunities for us to

connect. In some of our most delightful family times, we've walked in snowy woods, canoed on the lake at sunset, or sat together on our front porch looking at the bees swirling around the lavender plants. Being outside is especially comforting because we are off our phones and enjoying each other. It makes conversation flow naturally and gives us the joy of shared experiences in a beautiful atmosphere.

As I thought about all of the research I've read about connection and its important role in nurturing mature and responsible adults, I was reminded of the gospel narrative. The entirety of the Bible is the story of God trying to restore his people to connection with him. Time began in a garden, with the first people living in intimate communion with God, but sin and shame broke the connection, and we've been trying to restore it ever since.

When connection to God is restored through faith in the finished work of Jesus, our faith provides a sure foundation that protects us in the storms of life. Even so, we must continually make choices that prioritize connection if we want to experience that peace. We must choose to spend time with Jesus, know his voice through reading his Word, and turn away from things that steal that connection.

It might seem like more work in the short term, but when we pursue knowing God and being in a relationship with him, our faith grows, and with it, joy and peace. John 14:27 says, "Peace I leave with you; my peace I give you. I do not give to you as the world gives. Do not let your hearts be troubled and do not be afraid." While there will always be trouble and opposition in this world, we can experience the peace of God even in the midst of it.

It's the same with our family life. If we want our children to be calmer and more loving and better able to accomplish their responsibilities, we have to make choices to look them in the eye, give them physical contact, listen and empathize with them, and spend time together, building a shared vocabulary and a love of nature. If, instead, we ignore them, rush them, and continually find fault, we will experience the result of those choices.

• • •

Connection and a more peaceful life are possible. It just takes a few simple steps done consistently over time. In their book *The 4 Habits of Joy-Filled People*, authors Marcus Warner and Chris M. Coursey explain:

> As infants, we are not born with joy pathways in our brains. Because of this, we have no ability to act like ourselves when we get upset. One of the primary tasks of a parent when it comes to their child's emotional development is to recognize when they are experiencing an upsetting emotion and help them quiet from that emotion and return to joy. The more this happens, the more emotionally stable children become.[7]

There is an imperative for connecting with our children; it's part of what helps them become calm and happy adults, but some of us didn't get this connection ourselves, and we may even feel like it's too late to create a more connected family. Perhaps your children are already in their teen years, and you don't feel like anything you do matters anymore. I've experienced the distance when older children begin living their own lives, and it feels like the ability to speak into their lives is diminished. However, the same steps we use to connect with younger children can also work with older children, except that instead of reading them stories, we start listening to theirs or telling them ours.

As we tell our stories as a family, it helps our children understand their lives. This is one of the first steps to repair broken connection with ourselves, God, and our children. So don't be discouraged if the theme of connection is new for you or if you feel like you've missed this with your children. A calm and connected family is within reach. Start by acknowledging to your children that your actions have caused them pain and expressing your sorrow for the pain they've experienced. Then start the four practices outlined above, replacing reading aloud with listening and telling your own stories if children are already teens or adults, and begin to enjoy the beauty of a more connected family.

One of my children especially missed out on connection as a small child. We went through a hard season as missionaries in Mexico, and my husband and I experienced a lot of conflict, which created stress and a lack of presence. I wrote about this season in *Mothering by the Book*, but in that book I didn't share about some of the disconnection this child and I experienced due to that season. I've since been applying these practices of listening, offering eye contact, and offering hugs, along with my regular Christian practice of praying for my children. I was delighted recently when this young adult came to me to say, "You know, Mom, I used to have some resentment toward you, but now I'm really enjoying our relationship. I love you."

I was thrilled! I adore my children, and I've diligently pursued excellence as a mom, but my own lack of connection as a small child caused trauma to my children. Thankfully, as I welcome Jesus into these broken parts of myself, I can be calmer and more present for my children. I'm overcoming fear and creating a joy-filled home, and the more our connection is repaired, the more my children can live lives of purpose, presence, and temperance.

It's a worthy journey as a family to love our children well and to confront our own broken, traumatic pasts so we can heal and offer healing to them. As we give ourselves to loving and healing, we'll reap the reward of close and connected families.

While family life will be bumpy, and the road to repair and connection will be rough at times, the joy of calm and loving relationships will be a bulwark against the storms of life.

To get started with these habits of connection, download the Peaceful Press Connection Challenge here: http://bit.ly/4e0b4WJ.

Jennifer Pepito is the host of the *Restoration Home* podcast, author of *Habits for a Sacred Home*, and the founder of the Peaceful Press (ThePeacefulPress.com). Jennifer is on a mission to help families overcome fear and live with wonder and purpose, and her homeschool curriculum empowers this through heroic stories, heartwarming poetry, and engaging life skills development. Her resources help create joyful memories among families, which leads to deeper connections and lasting relationships. Jennifer lives in the mountains with her beloved family, where she enjoys reading aloud, working in her garden, and watching the sunset. | @jenniferpepito

5

The Belonging We Crave

The Story of What Matters
Rachel Devenish Ford

How do you study the story of a family's homeschool life to find out what matters? Is it a timeline or a graph? Is it a spreadsheet or a painting? I am over halfway through our homeschool journey. My oldest son is twenty-one, and my youngest is eleven. I've been doing this for so many years, but still, I can't seem to find a simple way to describe the road we're on. I do think I can find other complex and layered ways to look back on this time. It takes study itself. It takes going in less like an executive and more like a scholar or anthropologist, putting together the story of our learning and what matters.

Here is something. For a time, if you searched the phrase "cute kids with dreadlocks" and then scrolled down the page for a while, you would find one of my photographs from about fifteen years ago. It went viral on Pinterest a while back and has lingered in the internet's memory of the most clicked photographs for this particular word combination.

The photo shows a biracial little girl lying on her stomach on a wide marble porch railing. There is a coral-colored house just out of focus in the background. She is frowning intently at a rock and using a paintbrush to dust it off. This is my daughter, Kenya, and she is tiny in the photo, probably just over four years old. At the time, we had been reading about archaeological anthropology and how scientists learn about whole villages based on the bits and pieces of pottery and buildings they find in the earth. So Kenya and her older brother, Kai, began their search immediately, collecting rocks and chunks of broken bricks and brushing away the dirt with paintbrushes and soft cloths for days and weeks.

In the photo, little Kenya is looking for the layers. She's looking for story. She doesn't know it yet, but her life is defined by layers, by a story that is too complex to tell without brushing away at the surface for a while. Her life is multilayered.

Looking closer at the photograph, you may notice the bars on the window behind her, a custom in Goa, India, where she lives. The marble slab under her is heavy and thick, cheaper and more plentiful than wood in India. Everything is different in this new place where Kenya's family lives. They are all still finding their way.

You might see only hints of these layers when you look at the photograph. But I know the story, and I can tell you. I can tell you that Kenya was (at the time) the second of four children, the only girl born to her Black American father and White Canadian mother. Her baby brother, Solo, was recently born during the wildest, rainiest, soggiest days of the Indian monsoon. The family is living in a little Christian community near the beach in Goa, far from Kenya's birthplace in California.

I am looking at this photograph like you, from the future, where this child of mine is now nearly twenty, and I find myself between worlds. I am looking back on our homeschool journey. I am still teaching three kids and looking toward the future of my college-age children. Kenya has just applied for an illustration degree course at a university in Canada. In Canada, I think she will find that simple description again eludes her. Where was she born? Where did she grow up? Who inspired her? Every question has layers in its answers. In the photo, I can also see layers about myself—the invisible young photographer—that eluded me back then. I can see my bravery and my fumbling, my overwhelming love for my children, and the things, good and bad, that I and their father will pass on to them.

∗ ∗ ∗

I can make similar inquiries with our family and our homeschool. Looking back, I can dig into the word itself, taking it apart, brushing at the layers. What is *home*? What is *school*? What do these words mean to you? Or me? What does it mean to have homes in many places? What does it mean to be lightly touching worlds, to be in between? And in examining the layers, we may also ask, What mattered? What stuck? What endured in all the words, books, equations, and days upon days? This last may be the most essential question.

I think about the cow, the bear, and the fragrance of eucalyptus. In this anthropological inquiry, we may learn about fermented turtle feet and the connections between jazz and rap. You should know about the rocket. I hope you hear the squeaky horn of the bread man, the prayer call of the mosque, the chants of the monks, and the many cups of tea in our community circles, the many languages and the many prayers.

You will need to look at the layers of us, the places we are separate, the places we touch, our maps of connection. You may begin to form a picture of our anthropology, and you may take some reassurance from the map of our own wilderness and how it wove together to create something we can truly call home and school. You may find our wilderness and what mattered encouraging because truly, really, honestly . . . I was winging it most of the time.

I had my children when I was a baby, by which I mean to say that when I look at old photographs of myself holding two toddlers and a newborn, I can see why I was often mistaken for the babysitter. I was so young. By the time I was twenty-eight, I was living in India with four young children. We were well on our way to what became a lifetime in the in between, a wandering life of homeschooling.

I still clearly remember the early days, sitting in the homes of mothers ahead of me in age, watching them do their thing, trying to absorb it by osmosis. How do we do this thing? What do we do when one child collapses in grief because they did not get the red cereal bowl? Do we collapse as well? No? What then? Remain calm? But *how*? One friend of mine was a homeschooler, and I remember sitting in her Northern California home with all the eucalyptus-fragrant breezes drifting through the windows, holding my new baby on my lap and watching as she listened to her young son reading aloud to her in between doing handstands on the couch.

"Homeschooling can feel very slow," she told me. "You might feel like you accomplish nothing, but it adds up. One new spelling word. One math problem. One reading sentence. That might be it for a day!" I'm not sure what I thought when I first heard these words. Back then, I was a delightful combination of terrified and overly confident. I needed help in every area but was also quite sure that nothing could really be as hard as everyone made it out to be. My friend's words stuck with me, though. They returned to me over the years to comfort me again and again on this long road of homeschooling. *You might feel like you are accomplishing nothing, but it adds up.*

And if I were talking to someone dear to me, some shining creature who wants to start their own homeschooling journey, I would add that it turns out that a lot of it doesn't matter. And some surprising things will. You'll never guess what they are, so you kind of *have* to wing it and just do your best.

For instance, the man with the holy cow. This man marched through the neighborhood often, looking for offerings for him and his decorated cow. Did the cow have something special about it, such as a fifth hoof? I can't remember that part. I remember the cow was small, painted, and covered in bright blankets and decorations. I remember the man standing at our gate, calling us to come and see, "Madam, come!" while alternately playing a squeaky wind instrument. I remember that every time he came, I had just gotten the baby to bed and everyone else seated for read-alouds or math. *Every time.* And then the man and the cow came, and off the kids went, inexorably drawn out to the dusty yard to see this intoxicating distraction, dancing away from me on their cute, maddening little legs.

I used to get so frustrated. It was hard to get the obstructions out of the way and start working. Their attention was like light on water, like birds landing briefly on a rooftop and then flying away again. We were schooling in the heat, without air-conditioning. We didn't have reliable internet or even libraries. Instead, we had the man with the cow. To me, it wasn't a good trade-off.

But now I brush at the layers of this memory, and it seems so different to me. I remember their attention on the cow, how wide their eyes were, and how some of Kenya's first life drawings were of cows. I remember their high, excited voices. And I can see that I was focusing on one part of the picture (understandably), but meanwhile, other, brilliant things were forming in their cells. Wonder. Learning. Questions.

Here are some other things we did besides getting our bookwork done: we swam, running through the coconut grove on our way to the beach, attempting to get to the water before a child collapsed of grumpiness. One day, when they forgot their shoes in the heat of the day, I rounded a corner to find the kids and their dad fashioning shoes out of cardboard and coconut fronds (problem-solving).

In Nepal, my kids and the village children watched a tractor digger outside our house for hours. In Northern India, we rode with boatmen on the ghats, and in the mountains, we talked gently to a sloth bear in a park. At one point, many workers came to help us put in a garden in Goa, bringing in rich earth and grass to replace our dust. I would look outside, maybe because I heard the horn of the bread man arriving, to find the worker women braiding Kenya's locs into thick braids while she sorted through tiny shells, singing.

How do you put these things into the words for where you are from? How do you put the evening sounds of the pressure cookers going off in our kitchen and all around the village? How do you tell people that you are from a place where the sun looks like a giant orange ball as it falls into the ocean?

People stared at us, and we stared at them. I still remember how it dawned on me that staring could go both ways. In countries where staring is the custom, you are welcome to stop and watch anything at all with your curious children, whether baby piglets or men fixing a car in the midday sun, yogurt making, fabric dyeing, or men trying to wrangle a large bull into submission. I am not trying to romanticize this life. Anyone who has tried to homeschool in the April heat in Goa or the monsoon rain in the Himalayas knows it sometimes feels impossible.

Not one part of my homeschool would be considered Pinterest-worthy except for my children's beautiful, wild freedom. I forgot deadlines, I couldn't keep up with the systems I started, and I set homework and then forgot to collect it. But I read to them, I did. I read, and I read, and we walked, and we walked, on beaches and hillsides and mountains and riversides. Kai and Kenya went searching for monkeys in the jungle with their dad, and though they didn't find any, we did learn a lot about civet cats when one fell into our well and we had to rescue it.

Later, we moved to Thailand, and here, also, were layers. Another son was born in another country, and people on the street still slowed to take photos of us. We made our way through the checklists. We got math and science done in schoolbooks as well as in life. Facts were shouted out in our family, daily, nightly, around the dinner table. We were musicians, artists, writers, and science nerds. Then and now, people listen to us and ask, "Do you always talk like this?" *Yes, yes, we do*, meaning that we get absorbed and go for it, and there are competing ideas, and it's hard to get a word in, and maybe we are making connections between jazz and rap, or we are talking about Star Wars or black holes.

I think back to the time the kids made a rocket for Isaac (our Thailand baby) out of a blanket and a little chair. He was so confident in the skills of his older siblings that he started crying, not sure that he really wanted to travel so far away from us, all the way to outer space. The time Leafy made a boat out of empty plastic milk containers. The time I came home from a trip away to find that Kenya had made a restaurant and a menu that included fermented frog feet (buy at your own risk). Conveniently, the restaurant was out of them. And then there was the Leafy boy, brimming with emotion and joy, coming into my studio to see what I was making and bouncing on his toes or running around to express how happy it made him. He loved to learn. He loved that I made things.

As I look back now, this seems to be the heart of what matters. We learned to learn, and we learned to make things. Home has been in so many different places, done so many different ways. Flexibility has been essential. It looks like, "It's too hot, let's go to the river," or "We're locked in, and there is a pandemic, and let's just lie on the floor." Flexibility is giving up on a book when it is too terrible to continue and seems to be written by someone who never had a conversation with an actual human. Flexibility is letting the kids write their frustration about a book that seemed to champion a "good slave" narrative into essays. Flexibility is tossing curriculum and looking for the books you *really* want your high schoolers to read.

● ● ●

Home has been the sounds of the mosque and the sounds of the temples and the sounds of our own singing, the sounds of our prayers. Home has been my husband, Chinua, playing piano, trumpet, saxophone, mandolin, and guitar. The basketball hoop in our yard or the monks coming out to play at the village hoop. It has been listening as my youngest son recites basketball stats to me, and my second youngest tells me about cars. It is making space for their interests as they learn to learn and learn to make things. It has been driving my son Leafy's piano out to the night market so he could busk. It has been watching Chinua teach Solo to weld so he could make a go-kart.

And maybe the most important of all in the anthropology of us are the maps and the bridges. All the wrestling we have done with our differences and with the events of the world in tumultuous times. The moment we talk it over, and the moment we let it rest. Learning to reach for one another. To give space or draw near. Talking about God. Asking questions.

I have learned that I can't actually plan the most significant times. We have to wing it. All we can do is make space. Out of the blue, it seems, you are sitting for hours with your teenagers, talking about the most profound things. You learn to let go of everything else when that happens. Just stay there for a while. Let this grow and breathe. Be quiet and listen as your sons talk with your husband about race. Talk softly about fears. Listen to new ideas. You learn to treat learning, to treat reaching and the parts of our maps that are distant from one another, reverently, softly. To cross bridges so, so carefully.

Kenya and I went for a long walk with our two little dogs yesterday. It is the hot season here in Thailand, and the weather gets dry in our village, making everything around us a little muted, crunchy, and pale. I learned that Kenya doesn't remember her season of archaeological obsession. She had seen the photograph and assumed she was painting layers, not removing them. All her life, she was learning to learn. Learning to make things. Learning what matters.

"I have so many things to be thankful for," she said out of the blue, simply because we were walking together in the quiet. "Thank you for letting me draw. For giving me time to draw." My daughter, the anthropologist, the artist. Out of everything that mattered, it was the support, the time to draw. And I would say, because I was there, that the love of drawing also came from the cow, from the women who braided her hair, from the light in India, and from all the layers, all the beautiful layers that we didn't even realize were school, were home.

Rachel Devenish Ford is a poet, novelist, and homeschooling mother of five incredible kids. She and her husband, Chinua, are founding members of a Jesus Devotional community called Shekina Garden, in the mountains of Northern Thailand. Rachel wakes early to write and dream up stories. She loves music, camping, and making her teenagers and young adults laugh. In her homeschooling journey, she hopes to help each one of her kids learn to do what they do best in the world with empathy, faith, and joy. You can find her work (including sixteen books of memoir, YA fantasy, literary fiction, and poetry) at JourneyMama.com.

Finding Home
Mandy Davis

In the vibrant world of social media, my story as the school principal who bravely transitioned into homeschooling has resonated with many. But this significant shift in my life wasn't an impulsive leap by any means. It wasn't just a simple solution to a single problem, and it wasn't the easy way out. No, this life-changing choice was a profound decision born from extensive introspection and a steadfast dedication to reimagining education. This path, chosen after much deliberation, symbolized more than a career change—it was a heartfelt commitment to create a nurturing and inclusive learning environment, not just for my children but for myself. In this new chapter of my life, I found more than an educational haven; I discovered a place where I truly belonged, hand in hand with my children, forging a path that resonated deeply with our values and aspirations.

Welcome to my story and my search for a place to belong.

Early Years: Searching for Belonging

My early years in school were marked by a pervasive feeling of being an outsider. Coming from Seoul, South Korea, and being adopted into a community that looked very different from me (hello, Nebraska), I frequently experienced feelings of isolation.

The halls and classrooms of the school, while brimming with activity, were paradoxically lonely spaces for me.

During my formative years, the question of identity cast a large shadow over me. As a child, wrestling with this profound concept was intimidating, especially in a school environment that highlighted my differences. And while I have many stories of feeling bullied or misunderstood, one particular memory stands out vividly, a moment that brought a stark realization to light.

What started like any other day shifted quickly when we were instructed to share a dish from our cultural heritage for a class project. While this should have been a proud celebration of roots, as my classmates joyously chattered as to which of their family's cherished recipes they would share, I was engulfed in a deep sense of loss. *What could I make that represented my heritage when I was a stranger to my origins?* I feared bringing in an English/German-rooted dish from my parents for fear of ridicule and confusion, but I also had an even bigger fear of bringing in a Korean dish to which I had no connection. The experience emphasized how disconnected I felt, not only because of my cultural differences but also through the realization of my longing to understand my heritage.

That day, as I entered the classroom where I constantly grappled with the sense of not belonging, I was suddenly hit with a harsh truth: I was a complete stranger even within my own body. This profound moment extended far beyond the boundaries of a simple school project. In this transformative moment, I realized the importance of embracing my identity and finding my purpose in a world where I frequently felt lost.

I silently shouldered the weight of these insecurities, carrying them as a solitary burden in my heart. And as I quietly tried to live a school life under the radar, I was far from *unseen*. Daily confrontations with bullying and an educational system that felt alien to my identity chipped away at my confidence. Yet, these very struggles became instrumental in carving my path. Through their teachings, I learned the importance of resilience. I developed a deep passion for creating an educational realm that was both empathetic and inclusive, where every child could confidently find their voice and place, just as I once strove to find mine.

Motivated by my own journey of feeling alone and out of place, I became deeply dedicated to creating a space of belonging for every child. Professional aspirations did not solely drive my commitment; instead, it was a personal mission that originated from the depths of these tough, early experiences. I wanted to make sure no child ever felt the same way I did. I wanted to create a place for them to belong.

Finding My Path: A Principal's Journey

As a young adult, I was tenacious with my burning mission in education. I was going to be everything my younger self had needed. I aspired to become that exceptional educator who possessed the ability to foster a genuine sense of belonging for each and every student. And while the dream was ambitious, I had no doubt that the work I needed to put in would change lives. As I began my career as a teacher, I embraced this path with a strong sense of purpose . . . and idealism.

As a twenty-two-year-old teacher in a classroom of fifth graders, I quickly realized my human limitations. Working against a clock, a set curriculum, an administration, and what felt like endless rules without reason (nor understanding their exact source), I would spend ten hours a day working in my classroom and even more at home. But hours and dedication aside, the facade of everything I had learned in college began to shatter. Each day, walking in to see twenty-six faces looking up to me, needing me, and in a place where they would spend the better half of their awake hours—they were many, and I was just . . . one.

I pushed hard, and at times my mission was blurred by the needs of my administration. A lingering thought troubled me as I was awarded in my first year for my dedication and performance. While I had successfully taught so my students could pass tests and managed to organize a classroom on a tight budget, I lacked a true understanding of my students' individual needs. Here I was, seeing my students each day without the time or ability to truly *see* them. It seemed the system believed that this part of the job and meeting my students' needs was irrelevant; they were expected to conform to a predetermined mold. This wasn't my mission. I needed to do better.

When confronted with the hard reality that my influence in the classroom had its boundaries, I questioned my ability to enact broader change. *If I cannot reach my students in my own classroom, I must get to a higher vantage point to shift this structure.* Oh, I wasn't even close to giving up, but I was incorrectly convinced I needed a platform that extended beyond the confines of a single classroom. My mission transcended overcoming day-to-day challenges: I sought to fundamentally transform how we nurture and educate our children. I was certain: as an administrator, I would have impact.

Many of you already know how this story goes for me. As I ascended the educational hierarchy to become a school principal, it became clear that this system didn't want reparations. I was soon stuck in a bureaucratic nightmare. I couldn't create an inclusive and caring environment, and surprisingly, my direct impact in the classroom had diminished significantly from my days teaching. I was fighting new uphill battles, but now I had to witness all the pain points.

The students I got to know best were the ones who found their way to my office, often for reasons that underscored the system's failings. And there I was, ironically still feeling like an outsider in the very system I had hoped to reshape. Many years had elapsed since that young girl from Korea had first wrestled with her sense of belonging, and yet here I was, still continuing the search. However, just as it seemed this journey might persist indefinitely, a life-changing role presented a new direction: motherhood.

Becoming a mother led to a profound shift in my perspective. I realized that the future of my children rested in my hands. The responsibility of guiding their educational journey and providing a nurturing environment where they genuinely belonged became a powerful motivator. This new role illuminated the importance of an education tailored to each individual, one that honors and nurtures their unique qualities.

This newfound maternal perspective marked a transformative moment in my educational journey. It brought a moment of clarity, revealing that while I might not be able to single-handedly overhaul the entire educational system, I did possess the power to influence my children's learning experiences. This wasn't a retreat from the broader battle for educational reform; rather, it signified a strategic redirection of my mission. My focus shifted toward creating a legacy where my children could genuinely express themselves, follow their passions, and develop with confidence and resilience.

A New Perspective: Embracing Homeschooling

Embarking on the journey of homeschooling my children has been a pivotal and transformative moment in my life. This choice necessitated a bold step away from the traditional educational frameworks to which I had long been accustomed and, significantly, a departure from a professional path I had passionately pursued. As a school principal, I was deeply invested in the mission of transforming education—but this mission has beautifully evolved. It's no longer about changing an entire system but about intimately nurturing and guiding my own children's education in a way that genuinely celebrates their individuality and supports their thriving.

While rich in rewards, this transition presented its own set of challenges. I had to adapt, grow, and reimagine the concept of a stimulating, nurturing educational space within the comfort of our home. It became a journey of exploration and experimentation as I navigated various teaching methodologies and curricula, each carefully chosen to align with my children's distinct strengths and interests.

One of the most remarkable aspects of my homeschooling journey has been witnessing my children flourish in an environment that wholeheartedly honors their individuality. As both their mother and their primary educator, I'm granted the precious opportunity to tailor their learning experiences to fit their unique abilities, interests, and learning paces. This approach distinguishes itself from the standardized, one-size-fits-all model prevalent in traditional schooling systems.

Observing my children's eyes sparkle with curiosity and zeal as they engage with topics that truly capture their interest is an unparalleled joy. Their educational path has been filled with imaginative exploration, engaging hands-on projects that make learning come alive, and a balanced integration of the arts, nature, and physical activities as core elements of our daily curriculum. But beyond the academic achievements and creative explorations, the most thoughtful insight from our homeschooling experience has been the intense sense of belonging we have found within the walls of our home.

It is an enlightening recognition that our sincerest place of belonging, where each unique identity is welcomed and celebrated, is right here in our personal sanctuary of learning. Our home has transformed into more than just a physical space; it is a haven of safety, nurturing, and understanding, where every member of our family feels deeply valued, respected, and an integral part of a loving educational family.

The Lasting Impact

The impact of homeschooling on my children's education and the overall dynamics of our family has been deep and lasting. See, as we embarked on this shared educational journey, something unusual unfolded: our bonds developed, solidifying unbreakable connections. This transformation exceeded the traditional realms of teachers and teaching, weaving its way into every aspect of our family life, enriching it with new dimensions of understanding and empathy. Each of my children—they are not one of twenty-six. My children are known.

This journey, however, is not just about my children's development; it's been a path of personal evolution for me as well. In rediscovering my roots, understanding my identity, and shaping my children's learning experiences, I've realized that the true purpose of education transcends mere knowledge transfer. It's about nurturing the spirit and potential of each unique individual. This realization has brought warmth to my heart in ways words can scarcely describe, echoing back to that young girl from Korea who longed to understand her place in the world. In this journey of homeschooling and motherhood, I've not only guided my children but also found the missing pieces of my own identity, completing a circle that began many years ago.

For the first time in my life, I know where I belong: right here, with my family, in the home we've created together. It's a journey filled with wonder, growth, and the most genuine form of love. Here's to giving our children back their childhood, creating lives they don't need to recover from, and embracing a journey where we no longer wonder about our place in the world. Here's to finding and cherishing our belonging, right here, in the *heart* of our home.

Mandy Davis, a former school principal and respected author of *A Matter of Principal*, stands as a powerful voice in the education arena. Her mission is straightforward: empower families to take control of their children's education. With deep insights into educational challenges and innovative ideas, she has emerged as a notable advocate. Garnering recognition from Fox News and the *New York Post*, and earning a place in *LA Weekly*'s "Top Ten Innovative Educators in the US," Mandy's impact is clear. More than a thought leader, she is a catalyst, actively driving the transformation of education's future. | @homebuilteducation

Revolutionary and Restorative: Getting Back to the Village
Jason B. Esters

"Man, I love to see that!"

I had just jumped out of the driver's seat of my minivan, walked over to the other side, slid open the passenger's side door, and was fumbling with a kid's shoe before I detached him from his car seat when I heard the words. I had to pause for a second because I had been in mid-conversation, talking to my kids while I hustled to get them out of the van. All of us had been talking, in fact—a six-year-old, a four-year-old, a two-year-old, and I were having an incessant conversation about airplanes, talking to each other, around each other, over each other. Speaking into each other. Joking about how ridiculous it seemed that something so heavy can stay in the air. Playing with ideas about how such a thing could be.

So when I got out of my van, I'd literally jumped out. The conversation had made me hyped, and I was animated. I remember I had just started what was shaping up to be an epic rant about the physics principle of lift, which I had recently become an expert on (thanks to the video I had watched online). The other man's voice cut across the parking lot, through the kids' chatter and my wannabe YouTube-inspired science lesson, with a clear, full voice:

"Man, I love to see that!"

With my hands busy with little shoes, I couldn't even turn around much to see who was speaking to us, but I could hear the smile in his voice. The way that brother spoke to us mirrored what he heard in us with our easy banter and intellectual curiosity. What he echoed back, in the middle of the mundane activity of getting out of our van at the edges of a parking lot, could only be described as . . . joy. Pure, unadulterated Black joy. Joy at seeing a father interacting with his children, building knowledge. I know it was joy because my clearest memory of that moment was his smile. His words and his smile. That brother affirmed me.

If it had not been for him reaching out to me—unsolicited, unpretentious—I would never have received this insight, this snapshot of living memory I'm sharing right now. It would have been one of a thousand forgotten moments. But because the moment was shared between me and my kids and shared between me and this used-to-be stranger, it became that much more valuable.

Our recognition of one another became more valuable, still, because we also recognized we had kinship. I don't mean this in the sense that we were family. We weren't related in that way. What I mean is that within his recognition and affirmation, I could see that this man I had never met and I were part of the same village, the same tribe, the same community, and it was a wonderful thing to behold.

● ● ●

We have probably all uttered the African maxim that "it takes a village to raise a child," so much so that the saying has become cliché, losing much of the wisdom and power gained through the lived experiences of the ancestors who gave voice to that proverb so many years ago. The truth is, this proverb we all quote and think we know isn't really about raising a child.

It's about the importance of raising a *village*.

The proverb is more than a reminder not to isolate our children. Or to plan get-togethers. Or even to attend homeschool co-ops. It's a call to action. We have to build and maintain the village. It's the village—the intentional community we create to love, nurture, and encourage our children—that needs to be restored. I believe that homeschooling is one step in reimagining how our children experience the world and can work to restore the village, the lost community. But if the goal is restoring the village, the men must be there.

Don't get me wrong: many men are already there. We show up for our families daily. We are providers. Protectors. Prayer warriors. Even more than that, when the Centers for Disease Control and Prevention studied fathers' involvement with their children in 2013, they found that compared to other racial and ethnic groups, Black fathers who lived with their children were more involved in the daily lives of their children than any other group.[1]

However, if we see homeschooling as an act that helps us to reclaim what it means to center the education of children within a holistically nurturing and generative environment, and if we believe this is also an opportunity to seize the time and reimagine what a healthy, liberating practice of education can be for our children, then we have to have a vision for more. For the restored village to be sustained, men need to take an active role in homeschooling their children and the children of their communities, not just as providers and protectors but also as elders, teachers, collaborators, and friends.

Fathers play a vital role in educating their own children and contributing to the educational growth of their communities.

The presence of Black men in homeschool spaces is both restorative and revolutionary. It is restorative because it empowers Black men and women to be actively involved in teaching their children, fostering a sense of unity and collective responsibility. It is revolutionary because, historically, Black people educating themselves in America—and many other parts of the world—has always been an act of defiance and self-empowerment. Black men teaching their children represents a daily act of revolution, radical imagination, and reconciliation. Being revolutionary means reimagining the educational experience not only for our own children but also for our entire community, creating a future where education is a powerful tool for empowerment and change.

Being in community with other Black men who homeschool their children has taught me valuable lessons about the importance of men taking an active role in our children's learning environments. The first is this: as men, we need a philosophy of "home" and "school" that centers on us being there. An unspoken and often uncomfortable truth is that while trying to do all the things good men aspire to do—be the breadwinner, be the first line of defense, be the broad shoulders that carry the weight of the world—it becomes easy not to be involved in homeschool.

This was true for me. A lot of times, I would feel like an interloper in homeschool gatherings when I first started my homeschool journey. Today, my wife is our homeschool's principal instructor and organizer, but in those early years, beginning in 2010, I was my kids' only homeschool teacher. I worked nights and would be with them during the day while my wife taught at a middle school. My wife and I often joked about the awkward times when I was the dad who broke up the harmony of the homeschool momspace.

Anytime I went to a park for a new homeschool meetup, as soon as I started walking toward the group, I would become very aware that the moms were very aware of my incoming presence. What's funny is that I would think about my approach constantly. I would use my kids as a buffer—not a fence but more like a safe place for people to rest their eyes. I would use all kinds of tactics to make sure the moms saw them first—before they saw me. Still, regardless of how uncomfortable it can be, men have to resist the temptation of believing that financially underwriting the education experience in the home is enough.

When I first started attending my current co-op almost ten years ago, I didn't know anyone there. I had no idea what a homeschool co-op was supposed to look like or what I was supposed to be doing there, so I was cool just sitting by the front door (I figured I'd be co-op "security"), content to answer some emails or complete some other kind of "real work" while I waited for the day to be over.

Then I started to notice the other men in the co-op. Their mere presence changed my thinking. There were Black fathers there who were already present and deeply invested in the co-op's daily routine—teaching classes, leading discussions, and playing games with children. Watching how they carried themselves made me realize I had fallen into two traps.

The first trap was that I was preoccupied with thinking about how the co-op would benefit my own children. I had not given any thought to how I could help other people's children. The second trap was thinking I had something more important to do than be part of the world of learning my children were engaged in. My attitude was more about using the co-op as an opportunity to take a break from teaching than a chance to build or be part of a community. Watching those brothers engrained a new expectation in me. I realized I had to step it up a notch.

Hanging out with those more seasoned men—hearing their stories, sharing my struggles, getting advice, being in their presence, celebrating each other—was the lifeline of fellowship I didn't know I needed. Iron sharpens iron; every opportunity

I had to walk and talk with those brothers when I first began homeschooling was a step toward wholeness. Men and boys learn lessons from other men that are vitally important. Sometimes, that lesson is simply that you're not alone.

Today, I'm actively part of the rhythms of our homeschool journey. I have a full-time job, but I carve out time to teach my children at home and in community with other children. And I still attend that same co-op for weekly meetups. I help set up, teach classes, watch the door in the morning, and help clean up when we're done. There's no doubt that my children benefit from learning from me. But they also benefit from seeing me interact with other kids, men, and women in this reimagined educational space. I didn't anticipate the influence I would have on the lives of other children in our community. The kids in our community *expect* to learn from me. I'm not just a father educator for my own kids; I'm also a "BaBa," a father educator for all children in our homeschool co-op.

This co-op and the others we belong to are culturally diverse and predominantly Black and Brown, especially in the older grades. Unlike most children in the United States, none of the kids in our homeschool community will have the narrative that they never had a Black man as a teacher. It is neither strange nor out of the ordinary for them to be taught by or learn from a Black man or woman. Because my presence and the presence of other men in the co-op over the years have normalized the pursuit of education as a collective endeavor (not exclusively manly or womanly), we've affirmed the sharing of knowledge and intellectual inquiry as a communal function.

Consistently demonstrating a connection between manhood, Blackness, and a commitment to intellectual activity not only destigmatizes being good at learning but also dismantles many of the often-accepted stereotypes about Black people, Black boys, and education. At the same time, when Black men are active in educational spaces, whether at home, at a co-op, or in a brick-and-mortar school, it builds a sense of community around a vision of education that everyone has access to.

According to a study shared by the Center for Black Educator Development, most Black students in US schools will go through their first thirteen years of public schooling without having a single Black teacher.[2] They also point out that "Black students who have just one Black teacher in K–3 are 13% more likely to graduate from high school and 19% more likely to go to college."[3] Those figures almost double if they have two Black teachers. Yet, most students of color will never have a teacher who looks like them.

Data from the National Center for Education Statistics reports that over half of students attending school in the United States are not White, while people of color make up less than 25 percent of teachers.[4] The likelihood that they will have a Black male teacher is even more disheartening. For the 2020–2021 school year, "Black, non-Hispanic men accounted for 1.3% of the nation's 3.8 million public school teachers."[5] Even though there are documented improvements in outcomes among students when Black men are in the classroom, there's clearly a dearth of Black male teachers in public school classrooms.

If this is the case, the question for homeschooling parents should be, Why duplicate that deficit in our homeschool practice? If we are conceiving of classrooms without traditional walls or borders, then we need to dream of a learning environment where we expect men, particularly Black men, to be active participants in all facets of learning. To do this, we have to let certain preconceptions go.

Part of our journey toward deschooling must eradicate the idea that teaching is women's work. The young people we teach are entering a world full of exploitative influences and dangerous conflict. Their liberation and well-being demand a new paradigm. This is true for all of our children, but it's especially true for Black children. I have three sons. I have a daughter.

They have all gained from having me as a consistent teacher in their homeschool experience. It has helped them see knowledge as their birthright. More than that, they have seen that my love and curation of their development is not an aberration. They have had other men who have taught, corrected, loved, and sown into them. They've seen their mother and me work together to shape their learning, and other men and women collaborate to make deposits into their lives as well.

I've said it before, but it bears repeating here: there is something powerful about Black men and women sharing the collective work of teaching our children by working together, nurturing together, playing together, and learning together. In that work, we get to model healthy relationships while we teach. The more children see that kind of modeling, the more confidence it builds in them. That confidence allows them to unlock their own creative intentionality.

• • •

At the co-op, I have a weekly high school survey of literature class called "Readings from Africa to America" with about twenty or so brilliant and rambunctious homeschooled teenagers. Our central theme this year is visions of the future. We've been reading dystopian literature, protest literature, Afrofuturism, you name it. One day recently, while discussing H. G. Wells's novel *The Time Machine*, we began to explore what it must have meant to envision a new future at the horizon of a new century when it was published in 1895.

Then, we started to think about who else was imagining a new future in 1895. We talked about Booker T. Washington, the founder of the Tuskegee Institute, and his "Atlanta Compromise" speech of 1895. We looked at journalist and activist Ida B. Wells (no relation) and read her detailed analysis and damning condemnation of lynching in her 1895 report *The Red Record*. We read one of abolitionist and orator Frederick Douglass's last letters before his death in 1895, wistful for a better, more just tomorrow as he lauded Wells, encouraging her to be brave and continue the work. I love finding connections like this, so I was hyped. I was animated.

And so were they.

I love to see that.

Jason B. Ester's love for reading began in childhood, as he devoured books from his parents' shelves with permission to read anything, even challenging material. He earned a PhD in English from Temple University and is currently an assistant professor of English at the Community College of Philadelphia. For nearly fifteen years, he has homeschooled his children and supported other families in subjects like US history, Africana studies, world literature, writing, and college prep. He is working on a book about substitute teaching and cohosts *The Black Men Homeschool Podcast*. Jason lives in the Philadelphia area with his beautiful wife, Dionne, and their four brilliant and rambunctious children. | @blackmenhomeschool

Honoring Our Home Field Advantage
Elsie Iudicello

"We recommend that you do not homeschool." Those were the final words at our intake evaluation for continued intervention services many years ago. I left that appointment with tears in my eyes. As heavy storm clouds gathered over the parking lot, I carried my two-year-old little boy to the car and strapped him into his car seat. His little grunts and chirps were the only functional language he possessed to tell me how much he'd hated that appointment. I got into my seat, placed a thick packet of paperwork on the seat beside me, dropped my forehead onto the steering wheel, and prayed, "Help me, help me, help me," over and over again. He chirped and I prayed, and the rain came down.

It's been nearly a decade since I sat in my car and wondered how on earth I would give my youngest little boy the same beautiful education I was aspiring to give my older boys. My heart was burdened by this tension: the desire to protect his childhood and nourish his soul and the desire to provide him access to avenues of aid located within a system we'd divorced from at the start of our homeschool life. He needed his childhood, but he also needed aid.

He was only two, and conflict was rising to meet us at nearly every appointment we attended. It was clear to me that common purpose, clear definitions, and wise company were of critical importance. Depending on the approach taken, those desires would either be in conflict or feed into one another and make room for flourishing.

The words "Help me, help me" were the first steps I took in finding a way to make the system serve us without being mastered by it. It was not easy or quick. We had to find the right map, choose our company with discretion, and protect what naturally belonged to our son.

Finding the Right Map

At first, there was the danger of getting lost in the shuffle of therapy appointments, doctors' offices, and a hundred rubrics. The flood of information was overwhelming. We quickly learned that new worlds come with new words whose meanings are subject to change depending on their context. For example, whenever someone said "intervention," we had to wait to see which version of the word they meant. Depending on who spoke it, *intervention* often meant disruption and upheaval: "Stop homeschooling so we can all be on the same map."

Many of the aides and therapists we spoke with based all their recommendations on a single statistical roadmap detailing at which point in time children should reach various milestones within a predetermined journey, regardless of their mode of transportation. Another problem with this map was its inherent inability to acknowledge who was on the trip in the first place, leaving it hopelessly misaligned with where we were going and how we wanted to get there. This map often kept my boy's navigation team—his parents and therapists—at odds with one another.

We met many therapists who could not rely on personal knowledge of our boy to guide them, so they relied on numbers. They were trained to read intake reports and find deficits so they could fill them and achieve that coveted standardized percentage. They had a map for solving problems.

We had another map.

Whenever we made decisions, we took personhood over percentages into account. We looked at our son's soul, his capacity and capability for wonder and imagination, and then looked for ways to make room for his flourishing. We didn't set our entire focus on percentages because we didn't see our boy as a problem. We saw him as a person. We had to stop and ask ourselves, Do we really want to embark on a trip using their map as our guide?

We had already tossed the equivalent map for neurotypical children when our other children began homeschooling. Reading by age four or five? No, thanks! But the map for the neurodivergent was not so easily tossed. After all, this new map was hard won. It came by way of hundreds of hours' worth of phone calls to insurance companies and several monthslong waitlists to get into the offices of various specialists who told us our boy needed this particular map. We bled to get our hands on their map. Was it right to toss it out the window too?

Our therapists needed their own map to function in their world, and we, as parents of our particular child, needed ours. We never did find an easy solution. We wanted a full map, ready-made and ready to use, that aligned with what we were doing. The truth was that we had to use a map that was still unveiling itself—a difficult thing to reconcile in an age of quick searches for fast answers.

There was a level of mystery to this map we had to accept if we wanted our boy to live like a person and not exist by percentages. The only real certainty we had was in knowing what maps we would not be using. Now we had to get comfortable with a mysterious one. No one wants to read uncertainty, so we learned to read possibilities. If we were going to follow this evolving map alongside a team, we had to agree on some basic definitions so we could live in the fullness of those possibilities.

Handing Out Invitations

It didn't take long to realize that the adults in the room weren't all using the same language. We had to stop and define our terms well if we had any hope of continuing on together. This led me to stop living at the mercy of what different people meant by the word *intervention* and start living by *fellowship* instead. Children are not standardized, and neither are therapists. My task as my son's teacher and captain of his health team was to find like-minded therapists and aides and flesh out our fellowship with those who were interested in his personhood so we could collectively protect his childhood.

Words are powerful. When I started asking questions of definition, I realized that I had approached the system with a posture of "Please say you'll accept us even though we homeschool," as if the system still had all the power. Steamrolled by statistics, I was moving through these appointments as though in a stupor. I would sit and listen to professionals tell me how my son measured up without asking, "Who are you? What do you believe? How would you define what *man* is?"

When I armed myself with a notebook and a pen and started holding interviews instead of just attending intake sessions, things changed. In this day and age, rights to educational freedom are protected. Before long, I began new meetings by saying, "I'm not here for permission; I am interviewing you for a possible partnership as we homeschool our son and build his team." I never apologized for asking questions and setting limits. The best therapists answered my questions and respected my limits.

The habit of exerting our right to discern who won a seat at the table with our boy for his educational feast was formed. I held the invitations. If anyone wanted to be a part of the fellowship, they needed to come by way of the truth that every child is born a person, as Charlotte Mason says. Their professional knowledge needed to be practically exercised by seeing my son as a person and not a problem to be solved.

They needed to come knowing, or at least willing to see, the value of our educational cornerstones. A feast of ideas told through good books, beautiful music, and art was nonnegotiable. They needed to respect the time limits on how much formal therapy we would engage in. I wanted aides who recognized the value of hours outdoors in the sun and wind instead of hours at a desk looking at pictures of nature. I needed people who could explain tools and then brainstorm creative applications.

Yes, there were therapists who tried to bully their way in and others who tried to angle for invitations by way of fear, pressure, or shame. More importantly, there were other therapists who brought their expertise and said, "Now, we need your expertise as his parents to figure out where we go from here." You can guess who received an invitation. I looked for kindred spirits, and I found them.

Years later, my boy and I attended another appointment on another rainy day with our favorite speech therapist, who was a beautiful woman born and raised in Jamaica. They bonded over their common love of raising goats, all things chocolate, Caribbean food, and listening to jazz music. She built a beautiful bridge of connection with him; with her support, he learned to put words to his ideas.

Having forgotten our umbrella, we ran from the car and dashed into the office under a tropical deluge. She was waiting by the door with a big smile. "Rain or shine, he is always running!" I laughed as we walked into her room. "Well, he loves you to pieces. Of course, he is running!"

She paused and looked at me. "I love him too, but it's not just me he is running after. He still loves learning. That's the difference. We see so many children his age who come in feeling defeated by testing, special groups, and extensive tutoring. Learning means school, and school is something they want to escape. Your boy still loves learning. It's something he runs toward. He loves learning, and it makes all the difference. You made the right choice. Homeschooling saved his love for learning."

When we returned to the car, I slid into my seat, let my forehead fall to the steering wheel, and uttered a simple prayer of praise. "Thank you, thank you, thank you," fell from my lips while the rain came down. If I were to dilute the ocean of rain between "Help me, help me, help me" and "Thank you, thank you, thank you" into a mere glass of water, this is what it would hold: the knowledge that we parents of children with special needs should not walk as if we need permission to advocate for our children. We are the cartographers, navigators, interpreters, adventurers, and guides.

We hold the map. We have a home field advantage. We hold the invitations. We see our children. We set the limits and break the barriers. We reach for truth, goodness, and beauty, and we offer it to our children. We find the possibilities that open the door to a love of learning.

Remembering What Belongs to Us

The first question was always the covertly whispered, "Are you the homeschool family?" This was the start of many conversations held in waiting rooms where families with weekly appointments gathered in the days before COVID-19.

"Where can I buy this curriculum?" The inevitable follow-up question. Unsurprising when we've been conditioned to find solutions by clicking.

"Wait, so he studies actual art and music? How much are you reading? Your lessons are how short!? My brain is racing. I just assumed the beautiful stuff was out of reach until we could get the basic stuff."

The realization that beauty is for everyone hits some people hard when they realize how ugly and sterile things can become when all energies are focused on children being programmed as if they were machines. When remediation renders foundational things unlovely. Why shouldn't these children have a beautiful education too?

When I was a little girl, the vast majority of my community was composed of immigrants. I vividly remember hearing my abuelo tell the story of his struggle to pass his journeyman plumber's exam with only a third-grade education from rural Cuba under his belt. He had to take some of his exams repeatedly.

Every time he failed, he went back to studying. No one lowered the standard for him. He simply kept at it. Late into the night, he studied the universal truth of mathematical principles revealed to humanity. By repeating humility more often than failure, he passed his exams and eventually went on to become the chief plumbing inspector of a large city in South Florida.

He wasn't the only one struggling through those late-night study sessions. He began inviting other men who lacked formal education, all political exiles from Cuba, into his small apartment in the evenings after long days of hard manual labor. Abuelo set aside a little money and eventually purchased a large chalkboard. He made a one-room schoolhouse and welcomed others to learn what already belonged to them. They fought hard for it.

Whenever my son climbs a tree, I think of Abuelo. They have the same wildness about them. Always windblown and barefoot, always smelling of either sunshine or rain, always aware of what animals are about and which trees will flower soon. The same unbridled laughter and sense of mischief. The same right to inherit a rich education full of truth, goodness, and beauty, simply because they are human. Their culture is not merely Cuban or American, it is the culture of human thinking, creation, and flourishing too.

Cindy Rollins writes in her excellent book *Mere Motherhood*, "We stand in the gap between our children and all that came before. We are the keepers of the culture. If our culture commits suicide, we cannot wring our hands and point the finger. We are the ones responsible."[6]

I stand in the gap between my abuelo and my son as a keeper of culture. It is my deep joy to give my son beautiful words, art, and music. An honor to say, "This is called a gumbo limbo tree. This bird here is known as a painted bunting. This poem is by a woman named Phillis Wheatley. Look at this Monet. Listen to this symphony by Yamada. Monday follows Sunday. This is the recipe we use for mojo when making lechon." An honor to introduce him to the great beauty of the world and the things of this life that cannot be measured while helping bring order to his mind and soul. An honor to remember Abuelo's story as we live out our own.

It is no coincidence that these are the things that have unveiled more of our map and helped him connect with others we've invited in. My son's inability to distinguish the days of the week did not build bridges the way a shared love of Joplin did. One day, when I least expected it, out came the words, "Mama, we listened to 'Pineapple Rag,' and Thursday is before Friday!"

Years later, the same boy would say to me, "I'm going to go read this outside since I can focus more in an open space. I'm going to do twenty minutes, and then I need a break!" Nothing special in this statement at first glance, until I break it down and consider that he knows himself and how he learns.

He recognizes that he is not a machine with an endless capacity for output, so he sets limits for himself and determines when he needs to rest. He loves being outside, and the book he is referring to isn't assigned in his lessons. He picks it up because he wants to know what will happen next in a small Alaskan school now that Ms. Agnes has unfurled the map and placed an array of colored pencils on the table for her students to use as they behold the size of the world for the first time. He wants to know more about this world of possibilities he is living in as a person. He thinks about how he will contribute by remembering all that came before. He is living in the echo of every "Help me" and "Thank you" I prayed, and the sound of it resonates like "Hallelujah!"

Elsie Iudicello is a homemaker, homesteader, and homeschooler, living on a small farm in South Florida with her husband and four boys. She writes for various publications and speaks at homestead and homeschool conferences. You can find more of her work @farmhouse_schoolhouse.

6

The Encouragement That Spurs Us Ahead

Connecting Through the Unexpected
Alisha Roth

I began homeschooling a decade ago with whimsical dreams of children who loved art and music and family trips to historical sites. I envisioned a close-knit family that spent many years learning together and enjoying one another's company, with farm animals and musical talents to boot. So, the divorce came as a shock to me and my well-laid plans.

After five years of successful homeschooling and the addition of my three younger daughters to our school days, I experienced the disruption of our family unit as I signed papers that would end my twelve-year marriage. At that time, I didn't know anyone who was divorced *and* homeschooled their kids. I knew many homeschool families, but they all included two still-married parents.

I didn't have a vision of what homeschooling while divorced could look like, but I knew one thing: I was determined to continue this way of schooling. When the rest of life was uprooted and changing, I wanted to provide this area of stability for my kids.

Life isn't always neat and tidy, no matter how hard we try. Families encounter many unknowns and difficulties, and homeschoolers aren't exempt from these trials. Homeschooling allows increased control over our days and more involvement with our children, but the belief that we can fully determine the outcome of our children's experiences is a misconception. Life is mysterious in all its ways.

At some point or another, we'll all be hit with hardships and heartache. It comes in different packages for each of us—divorce, a child with a learning disability, a sickness or chronic disease. It could be the loss of someone dear, continued marital issues, or infertility.

Whatever your hardship, I hope you know that you're not alone. There are others on this homeschooling journey who carry a similar weight. But I also hope you know that you are a hero. You carry deep wounds and heavy burdens, but you continue on. You wake up each morning and bravely care for your children's minds and bodies with all the love you have.

The beauty of homeschooling is that it gives us connection amid the chaos. When divorce caused everything else in our lives to change, from the house we lived in to the family unit we were used to, homeschooling held us together and remained a steady rock to which we clung. It gave us time together—to learn, to grieve, and mostly to connect.

Academics is only one part of homeschooling. The days we spend together are not just about shaping young minds but also about nurturing our bodies and souls. We weave our lives together in such a way that we refine each other through intimate connection. We connect now, in these mundane days, so that we have each other in the future when hardship or loneliness or unknowns strike. The moments of teaching math concepts may result in a child who excels in numbers or studies mathematics at the collegiate level, but they also give us time to sit shoulder to shoulder while patiently and lovingly bonding until new concepts become familiar knowledge.

I imagine most of us begin our homeschooling journeys with the vision of smooth days, bright children, and happy families.

We believe that for homeschooling to be possible, our families, our lives, and our health must be in perfect order. But I've come to believe that homeschooling is for the hard times; it's the glue that holds us together as we face trials.

It's normal to consider the academic aspect of homeschooling and spend a lot of time researching and choosing the best curriculum or method. I did this when I began homeschooling ten years ago, and I'm glad I did. But as homeschool parents, we're not just teachers. We are mothers (and fathers). We're mentors, nurses, and counselors, guiding our children's days while also setting the tone for our homes.

I don't think this means we do it all alone. Community is essential to our homeschool lives, and we trust others to also be a part of our children's lives. But much of our work is done in the home. When we sit with our children through sibling squabbles, mentor them through tough decisions, train habits of cleanliness and healthy eating, and wipe bloody noses, we're forming an atmosphere while educating our children. We're creating an environment that has a lasting impact.

Since change is inevitable, whether planned or unexpected, the home environment is just as meaningful as the academic curricula we choose. We may need to change curriculum for a season or just focus on the essentials of reading, writing, and math. But an environment can remain stable through academic changes. An environment isn't a specific house or room but rather a feeling of comfort and security.

Charlotte Mason says, "Education is an atmosphere," and she elaborated on this idea several times throughout her years as an educational leader and mentor, emphasizing that everything in a child's home and life impacts their becoming.[1] Discussing this concept, Sonya Shafer of Simply Charlotte Mason writes,

> Interestingly, the atmosphere of your home does not depend on how many members you have in your family or where you

happen to live, whether you are rooted in one place the whole time or travel around a lot, if you live in one country or two or three, what kind of house you have, or any of the other circumstances that are just "packaging." No matter what your situation, the culture of your family—the atmosphere—is made up of one thing and one thing only: the ideas that rule your life as the parent.[2]

By establishing this atmosphere within our family, we can navigate all the waves life brings our way. Our foundation remains solid, even amid the storms. This atmosphere encompasses both abstract and concrete ideas to guide our days, as many concepts can rule a parent's life. Below are some examples from our own home culture. While your family may share similar guiding principles, each is unique. Some guiding ideas will last a lifetime, while others will evolve over the years.

Abstract Ideas
Love one another.
Maintain hearts of gratitude.
Be considerate of others.

Concrete Ideas
Clean up after yourself.
Put forth your best work.
Complete schoolwork before free play or technology usage.
Eat healthfully.
Use kind words.
Books are important.
Physical touch and showing affection are valued.

After my divorce, this atmosphere carried my daughters and me from our beloved farmhouse to a new-to-us home in town that we affectionately called "The Yellow House." Our location changed, and we no longer had chickens and goats, but the guiding principles of our home remained the same. We gathered in the mornings and read books together on the couch, snuggling close. We ate healthy meals, though I relied on simple dishes on my most exhausting days as a single mom. We kept journals to put into practice our hearts of gratitude.

I cherish these moments despite their challenges. We navigated physical changes and heavy emotions as I figured out how to function as a single parent. When we moved into our new home, I lit candles, and we ate ice cream on the floor while I said a blessing over our new space. It was a way of acknowledging the change in our lives while also setting the atmosphere in this new place. Above all, I let love guide us. This was the idea that I knew was most important to maintain within our atmosphere.

At the time, I didn't know any other single mothers who homeschooled. The small handful of homeschooling moms I knew who had gotten a divorce chose to send their kids to public school afterward. Everyone's situation with divorce is different, and I respect the difficult and challenging decision each woman has had to make. As for myself, though, I had a fierce fire in my soul that knew homeschooling was my highest priority. I realized this may not always be the case, but at least in those early days while my daughters were still young and the divorce was fresh, I had a deep desire to provide the consistency and comfort of the homeschooling atmosphere we had always known.

I think of Charlotte Mason's quote: "Mothers work wonders once they are convinced that wonders are demanded of them."[3] So many mothers have taken the difficult moments in their lives, including overwhelming change, and turned them into masterpieces. Not because they've done more or have maintained a superhuman level of functioning and caring for their children but because they've focused on matters of the heart above all and have trusted the wisdom of their soul to guide them.

However, navigating academics during challenging times can be daunting. While academics aren't everything, they still hold significant importance, which can be overwhelming for parents during difficult and devastating seasons. Establishing a sustaining atmosphere will support us through these changes, but we still have decisions to make about academics. Learning must continue, even through hardship, but there are many ways to achieve this. Approaches to handling academics during these times include unschooling, focusing on the basics, centering on activities that spark joy, or outsourcing educational responsibilities.

Unschooling

All of life provides opportunities to learn, and for some families, an unschooling approach during this time allows them to take care of their basic needs while learning along the way. Meals still must be prepared, and cooking and baking together can incorporate math skills, family life skills, and even science. Writing can be utilized to make lists or send letters. Reading can be done individually or at bedtime. If moving to a new place, geography can be done by learning new surroundings.

Back to the Basics

Many choose to focus on just the basics during difficult times. For most, this is the "three R's"—reading, writing, and math. These are recognized as essential subjects for functioning well in the world, and therefore, when life requires less academically to make it through each day, keeping it simple with these three subjects allows education to continue while not being overwhelming.

Igniting Joy

Times of crisis and change can be emotionally taxing on both parents and children, so some choose to focus on the subjects that bring joy. While experiencing sadness and loss, studying beautiful art and music can often be just what our souls need. Maybe this is a time to set aside the left-brain mathematics to indulge in drawing, painting, and creating. Maybe you just pursue your favorite subjects, listen to audiobooks, or write letters to friends. Whatever ignites joy and makes your soul sing, allow those to guide your days during times of trial and transition.

Outsourcing

The beauty of homeschooling in the twenty-first century is the abundance of available resources. You don't have to do everything all the time. Hardship and change present the perfect opportunity to outsource parts of your homeschool curriculum. This might mean asking a family member for help, using online programs, or enrolling your kids in local classes and groups. Find ways to lighten your load while still providing a beautiful home education. Maybe in this season of life, *you* need to get out of the house too. If you need a change of scenery, explore local places to learn from and let field trips guide your education.

Even if taking a few months off from homeschooling is the best option for you, trust that your children will be just fine. The fear of "Am I doing enough?" can creep in even in normal times. One of my greatest comforts on this homeschool journey is remembering that learning is a lifelong endeavor. My goal is to set my kids up to thrive on that path. I aim to teach them *how* to learn and trust that *what* they learn is secondary, as they have a lifetime to pursue useful and interesting information.

During both the toughest of seasons and the best of times, I prioritize maintaining our connection—as a family and with each child—because I know this is what the human heart longs for most. This connection is our anchor through life's storms and the essential foundation for all our studies. By nurturing these bonds, we create a supportive environment where learning and growth can flourish.

When we moved into town, our books were all in boxes. I apologized repeatedly to the kind souls who helped me move, given the sheer number and weight of the books. Books are such a foundation in our lives that I quickly unpacked the ones we needed. Despite the change of address, we continued our reading traditions. We read Ezra Jack Keats's *The Snowy Day* in the dead of winter just like we had at the farmhouse. We read *Goodnight Moon* before bed and *Little House on the Prairie* during our school day. In December, we eagerly opened our box of Christmas books, anticipating which familiar story we would read next.

We put on our snow gear when the snow fell, and even though our backyard was now measured in square feet rather than acreage, we made snow angels and caught flakes on our tongues. We sat around the table at dinnertime, and though the number of chairs was different, we ate food that nourished our bodies and engaged in conversation that nourished our souls. While so much had changed, so much also remained the same.

Life makes no promises, and homeschooling doesn't protect us from the pain or challenges of this world. We will all, at one time or another, find ourselves wondering if we can continue on. Change is inevitable, but connection is a candle that will guide us faithfully through our days at home as we love and learn together.

Alisha Roth has been writing and editing for Wild + Free for five years and has a book releasing next year. She loves to write about homeschooling, raising children, spirituality, and sharing an honest look into her life of divorce, coparenting, love, and evolving faith. As a woman and a mother to five daughters, she's passionate about encouraging women to empowerment and wholeness. | @littlewomenfarmhouse

Navigating Life's Wildfires
Torrie Oglesby

Our lives are gardens we cultivate with every choice, thought, and action. From the moment I got married, I profoundly understood this truth and decided to use the garden of love and family to grow an abundance of legacy, memories, and traditions. As a young bride and mother, I found myself unprepared for life's unpredictability and the occasional cruelty of its plot twists. These changes—whether a sickness in the family, loss of a job, spiritual introspection, divorce, or death of a loved one—come into our lives like wildfires: forceful, sudden, and all-consuming.

Divorce was the wildfire that led to the complete deconstruction of my life. It is an awful beast that takes nearly everything and leaves a deficit in the heart, mind, and sometimes even the soul. While I could write a book on separation and divorce, I want to emphasize our response and determination to hold tightly to what matters amid the apparent destruction of a garden and the life it once fostered.

When I first envisioned my life as a homeschooler, I pictured my three kids and me nestled together on our fluffy brown sectional, immersed in our latest read-aloud. I imagined us exploring unpaved nature trails and gathering around the kitchen table, our hands kneading bread dough as a symbol of liberation and education. I pictured days filled with teatime and poetry, with jazz music, vivid colors, and textures from art lessons accompanying us—a blend of culture, simplicity, and fullness as the banner over our lives. If I'm honest, education had little to do with my desire to homeschool. For me, it was about stealing time to be with family and creating a lifestyle that prioritized slow days, freedom, and togetherness. Perhaps it was a selfish attempt to freeze our family's "good old days." Nonetheless, it was a vision I clung to tightly.

When I became a mother, I knew I wanted to experience the days with my children, not apart from them. As a young mom and military spouse in Hawaii, raising just my oldest child, I filled our days with story time, beach days, afternoon hikes, and trips to the park. Watching my little one discover and play freely with the world around her was so heartwarming that the thought of her eventually going to preschool and kindergarten, missing out on these holistic and fulfilling experiences with me, made my heart ache.

I remember telling my family that I was considering homeschooling. This was on top of my choice to have a home birth, breastfeed, and follow a delayed vaccine schedule—decisions that already made my family think I was losing my mind. In 2012, homeschooling was less common and often seen as something for "weird families with weird kids." Despite this, my desire to live a more connected life only intensified as our family expanded with the birth of our two little boys.

Once I committed to homeschooling, the vision quickly began to manifest. Almost overnight, our home transformed into a homeschool haven. Every corner had a thrift basket full of novels and poetry collections. Every sitting area was adorned with fluffy pillows and cozy blankets. My children's father bought the perfect table and chairs for the center of the room, and together, we transformed the dull guest bedroom into a lively learning space. It was here that wonder abounded, with Duke Ellington and Miles Davis providing the soundtrack to our slow and free days. My dream was finally beginning to take form.

Despite starting our homeschool journey in the middle of a deployment, homeschooling brought us a sense of stability. In a military family, there's rarely a feeling of being rooted, yet homeschooling felt like the remedy to constantly feeling like a dandelion in the wind. After seven years of moves and changes, things felt firmly established. Because of the nature of homeschooling, we had something planted that would never get uprooted. Homeschooling became a pillar in our lives.

It's fascinating when our prayers become the reality in which we get the privilege of living. Every day felt intentional and unique. It was a time when the ordinary became extraordinary. Even on our challenging homeschool days, it was still exactly where I wanted to be. I never wanted to stop homeschooling or change the way we were living. I was delighted with the life we had beautifully made. But life had different plans. What happens when what we prayed for gets threatened? What happens when our most treasured gift is taken away? What happens when wildfires start to form outside the gates of our gardens?

● ● ●

I remember the day my garden caught fire when divorce became a reality in my life. I felt frozen; everything began to burn to the ground. I remember lying there for hours, staring at the ceiling or crying my heart out. I felt like I couldn't breathe, eat, or move. I felt so helpless and lost as the scenery of my life shifted, disappeared, and changed. With every panic attack, I felt defeated, and the abruptness of its devastating entry into my life left me vulnerable and afraid of what was to come. What was life going to look like now?

One day, as I lay on my closet floor in a fetal position, with nothing left to give, God wrapped himself around me. He held me as the wildfire consumed everything in its path. He preserved me as every detail of the garden I had built burned to the ground. This began my season of refinement—a time of sitting in the fire as God, like a master blacksmith, forged, sculpted, welded, and finished what needed to be done in me.

The beginning season of separation and divorce was daunting and involved plenty of therapy sessions with and without my ex-husband, but I wouldn't trade those days for anything. Nothing generates humility like losing everything you once held dear, and humility is the breeding ground for transformation. Transformation happens when we let go of Plans A, B, and even C to embrace God's plan for our lives. It isn't pretty, and it isn't easy, but what lies on the other side of transformation is always worth it.

I held on to homeschooling for as long as I could, but eventually, it became clear that homeschooling my children wasn't the best choice for that season of our lives. It's easy to feel like a failure when you're forced to surrender something significant. As if divorce hadn't already taken enough from me, it now seemed to have the final win by stripping me of my homeschool duties.

However, an interesting thing happened once I reluctantly did what I absolutely did not want to do and let go of homeschooling: a weight lifted off my chest. A weight I didn't even realize had been there for the past three years. Amid fighting for my marriage, being a military spouse, being a homemaker, working on my own growth and development, and monitoring my children's well-being as we all healed from divorce, holding on to homeschooling did more harm to me than good. This isn't because homeschooling is inherently bad or good but because seasons change, and we must transform with them. My unwillingness to transform had led to an overly tired, overly stressed, and excessively worried version of myself.

People often don't understand that wildfires are good for the earth. They are nature's way of preserving and renewing itself. Some plant species even depend on burned ground to grow.

Wildfires can create their own wind, leap across highways, and destroy things that threaten the forest. Dead leaves and logs that gather on the forest floor can prevent new plants from sprouting, so the forest naturally burns away what blocks its growth. Robin Wall Kimmerer, author of *Braiding Sweetgrass*, writes:

> I take my guidance from the forests, who teach us something about change. The forces of creation and destruction are so tightly linked that sometimes we can't tell where one begins and the other leaves off. A long-lived overstory can dominate the forest for generations, setting the ecological conditions for its own thriving while suppressing others by exploiting all the resources with a self-serving dominance. But, all the while it sets the stage for what happens next and something always happens that is more powerful than that overstory: a fire, a windstorm, a disease. Eventually, the old forest is disrupted and replaced by the understory, by the buried seedbank that has been readying itself for this moment of transformation and renewal. A whole new ecosystem rises to replace that which no longer works in a changed world.[4]

Sometimes, we make the wildfires of our lives worse by holding on to the old story. The new is so overwhelmingly unknown that we desperately want what was. It's easier to cling to what we know than to launch into something different. We fail to realize what many Indigenous cultures understand: what appears to be a threat to the forest is an attempt to preserve and renew it. There needs to be a breakdown or destruction for what was there all along to spring forth, but you have to be willing to let the old burn before you can see the promise of the new. We must trust the uncharted journeys of our lives, seeing beyond what was to imagine what can be.

Our legacy, memories, and traditions are not tied to homeschooling alone. A family culture of art, jazz, poetry, and tea can thrive outside the walls of homeschooling. Family Bible study can still happen every evening, with or without homeschooling. Nature walks have the same effect, whether they occur on a Tuesday morning or a Saturday afternoon. Togetherness, family meals, and conversations about culture and the world can continue whether we homeschool or not.

I had to learn to reimagine my vision of family. Would I let everything good die because homeschooling was no longer an option, or would I embrace a new way of living while integrating aspects and cornerstones in our lives that could still flourish? The wildfires that arise in our lives ask us to do just that—to embrace what has come while also holding space for what has been.

We must be brave enough to reenvision our lives again and again and again. We need to stay flexible while cultivating the things we love. The visions we are given are worth being stubborn about, but they will also require grit and endurance to see through to the end. We must be mindful not to worship our plan more than we desire the outcome. Often, God has a better plan than we can ever imagine, and that plan not only fulfills the vision but also builds the character that the easy route—or our Plan A and Plan B and Plan C—would never be able to produce.

When you see the flames of change, embrace them, want them, and trust them. Homeschooling was a dream come true that I never thought I would have to surrender. Yet surrendering it, though difficult, taught my children and me how to adjust course while valuing and pursuing what matters. Whether you have the privilege to homeschool for the entirety of your children's education, choose a different route, or find that homeschooling simply no longer fits into your life, as a parent, you possess the resilience, dedication, and adaptability needed to nurture your children's growth and achieve your own goals and desires amid any circumstance.

When faced with seasons of transition and the need to surrender beloved things and ways of being, remember that our lives are gardens cultivated not only by our choices, thoughts, and actions but also by the detours, the scrapped plans, and the beautiful wildfires that come disguised as destruction. Inside each one of them is the opportunity for new creation.

Torrie Oglesby is a free-spirited mom of three with a passion for coffee, connection, women's development, and community. She dislikes rigid schedules and practices that are too restricted or formal. Her goal is to remind every woman of their freedom in Christ. She is about deep conversation, belly laughs, truth-seeking, and growth. You can find her building community in The Womanhood, a platform she built for every woman, every season, every time, and on YouTube, where she talks about honest homeschooling and parenting. | @the_womanhood_co

---

Joy Comes in the Morning
Erika Alicea

It was an ordinary Tuesday morning, filled with regular tasks and routines. By 9:00 a.m., I had driven my mom to her job in NYC, spent quiet time with the Lord on the way back, and prepared school assignments for my thirteen-year-old. I needed her to work independently because I had a dentist appointment in the middle of the day.

My husband, Efrain, was the senior pastor of our church, Elements, in the Bronx and a coach at Tim Keller's Redeemer City to City. He was getting ready to meet virtually with a few young pastors he was coaching. When I entered his home office, Efrain sat at his desk under the canopy of his extensive comic book collection and superhero mini figures. I handed him his "light and sweet" coffee, as was his preference, despite being so unlike our Puerto Rican family's choice of pure Bustelo.

He thanked me and joked about his recent Amazon purchase for the fireplace of our new home. Building fires was fast becoming a fun pastime for the kid inside him, who grew up in Spanish Harlem and never dreamed of owning a house, let alone a fireplace. As usual, Efrain's sense of humor made me laugh, and I closed the door behind me to give him privacy.

Not long after, I was in a zone, listening to an audiobook while washing the dishes left over from breakfast. My daughter was completing her math lesson upstairs. I was almost ready to leave for the dentist when I passed by my husband's office and heard an unfamiliar voice calling from the computer, "Efrain, get up!" I immediately swung open the door—and there was my husband, lying face down on the wooden floor, motionless and unresponsive.

As I screamed out Efrain's name and dropped to his side, desperately trying to revive him, my daughter raced down the stairs to witness a scene no child should ever see of their parents. In the chaos, I managed to dial 911 as my brave daughter called her brother, godmother, and grandmother. The ambulance quickly arrived and took my husband. My stepson drove me to the hospital while my daughter stayed home waiting with her godmother.

Within a couple of hours, Efrain was officially pronounced dead, killed by undetected heart disease. Just like that, our church lost their shepherd, our children lost their father, and I lost my husband of twenty years. We were left in utter shock and completely broken.

How Much Can We Bear?

It wasn't the first time our family had faced adversity as homeschoolers. When we began homeschooling, my daughter was in second grade, and transitioning from traditional school was ridiculously challenging. My child, who excelled in formal school, resisted learning from me, her first teacher, leading to recurring challenges every year.

To make matters more complicated, for the first six years of our homeschool journey, I was also a part-time caregiver to my retired father, who was battling cancer, while my mother remained working outside of the home. As a result, much of our homeschooling was done on the road, in doctor's offices, or at my parents' house, lugging tons of books back and forth. Sadly, this season came to an end when my dad went to be with the Lord in 2021, leaving us to navigate that grief and care for my mom, who had to learn to live without her husband of more than half a century.

The following year brought *new* stress as we merged two households into one by purchasing a two-family house with my mother, ensuring she wouldn't live alone. The bulk of moving two homes simultaneously fell upon my shoulders and overwhelmed me to the point of excessive hair loss. It took months to get to a healthy place, set up two functional homes in our new house, and restore an atmosphere of peace and order.

But my husband's passing, less than two years after my dad's, was like nothing I'd experienced before or could have imagined occurring this early in life. *How could this even happen to us?* There was still so much work for my husband to do, for *us* to do together, and more memories to make. Why would the Lord take E, as we affectionately called him, so soon? A million questions bombarded my mind. Yet none were more paralyzing than this one: *How do I raise my daughter without her father?*

Lifelines to Keep Us from Drowning

What I'm about to share may sound like just a lot of "faith" talk, but homeschooling *is* an act of faith. In whichever unique fashion you're called to homeschool, you research, find resources, and finally set off on this journey of the unknown while hoping you won't do your child a disservice in any shape or form. Soon, this hope turns to faith that home education is precisely what your child needs to fulfill the purpose they were created for.

Still, what do you do when you've done the best you know how and have given 100 percent of yourself in the process, and BOOM, tragedy strikes, or adversity just keeps knocking at your door? Dear friend, I can only share the lifelines that have kept me from drowning in the sea of despair in hopes they may come to your rescue in your hour of need.

Faith

What has helped me persevere in trying times has been holding on to God's promises in his Word, such as these:

I will never leave you nor forsake you. (Heb. 13:5 ESV)

> When you pass through the waters,
>   I will be with you;
> and when you pass through the rivers,
>   they will not sweep over you.
> When you walk through the fire,
>   you will not be burned;
>   the flames will not set you ablaze. (Isa. 43:2)

Peace I leave with you; my peace I give you. I do not give to you as the world gives. Do not let your hearts be troubled and do not be afraid. (John 14:27)

These Scriptures, and countless others, spring up from within, where I have hidden them, and are a balm to my weary soul. God's Word revitalizes my spirit, taking me from *knowing* Psalm 23 to *living* it, where I fear no evil in the valley of the shadow of death, for I feel his rod's protection. His Holy Spirit embraces me, and his staff comforts me with the supernatural peace of the Savior. I am not alone.

No matter how broken or discouraged the heart is, the Word breathes life, strength, healing, and peace, surpassing anything we could ever fathom. It whispers to every piece of a shattered heart, *I love you with an everlasting love*, and commands the storm inside, *Peace. Be still.* God is faithful to all his promises. Therefore, he will fulfill the promises he's made to you.

Community

From the instant my husband passed, my homeschooling community swooped in like a legion of angels, providing daily meals for our family, collecting funds for us, and covering us in prayer. And what of my daughter? These parents and their children literally took my girl under their wings, caring for her from morning till night for days. They organized a DIY spa day with her friends, took her to youth group where they cried with her and prayed over her, and let their abounding love comfort her.

Their love for my daughter allowed me the space to tend to funeral arrangements and other daunting tasks. This outpouring was not the outcome of an overnight calamity. On the contrary, this love stemmed from relationships forged over years of community, creating friendships for both my daughter and me.

I find the term *homeschooling* to be a bit misleading. It initially causes many, like me, to believe home education can only be done in isolation. I cannot stress enough the vital importance of community, for extroverts and introverts alike. Every family has unique needs, and the focus is usually on providing opportunities for our kids to make friends outside of their siblings to foster personal growth. However, these friendships are equally as important for parents.

While I've always had non-homeschooling friends who have proven to be tried and true, I also needed to connect with other moms who could understand the hills and valleys of homeschooling. I needed "colleagues" with whom I could journey alongside, share ideas, and provide mutual encouragement—a tribe of my own. Thus, I prayed and intentionally joined homeschool groups, and often created our own gatherings.

Eventually, my girl and I were blessed with an overflow of new friends who have made our homeschool experience richer and fuller than would be possible on our own. In my moments of confusion and doubt, they've brought clarity, and in my low moments, they've been the hands and feet of God, lifting me and carrying me forward. We found our tribe, and I honestly have no idea where we would be without them.

Hence, my passionate emphasis is on building community. Some simple ways to do so are joining co-ops, extracurricular activities, informal groups, weekly meetups at the park, or group nature walks. Use social media as a platform to find or create events. Consider organizing trips to museums, theaters, or nature preserves. If there aren't existing groups that suit your interests, start your own interest-based meetup, like a nature club or book club. It may sound intimidating to start a group from scratch. Nevertheless, as you pray for wisdom and discernment, you can also pray for provision and creativity. Trust me. If you build it, they will come.

Another way to build community is through special homeschool celebrations. Group gatherings such as a Thanksgiving potluck, a night of recitation, an education fair, a multicultural day, a reading masquerade where children present as book characters, or a history fair where kids dress up as historical figures are fun and educational, and they create an occasion for all kids to interact.

Book celebrations were a favorite of ours. After we finished a book for school, we'd put together a themed "party" and invite friends to participate. Sometimes we dressed as the characters, created activities based on the book, and cooked foods from the story. We've done the Narnia series, *Anne of Green Gables*, and quite a few other titles.

The list of what can be done as a community is endless because the sky's the limit in homeschooling. Regardless of the activity, you can partner with any homeschool support group in your area or your local library, allowing fellowship for the parents afterward and tons of playtime for the kiddos.

Grace

Homeschooling demands an abundance of grace, both given and received. Even more grace is required when homeschooling through hardship. You may long to return to your previous routines during the worst of times. However, brokenness and loss have caused a devastating disruption in your world and that of your children. This reality cannot be ignored and swept to the side.

You must acknowledge that this is the season you're in, and seasons take time to change. Ecclesiastes 3 tells us there is a time for everything and a season for every purpose under heaven:

> a time to weep and a time to laugh,
> a time to mourn and a time to dance . . .
> a time to be silent and a time to speak. (vv. 4, 7)

A time to heal, a time to embrace, a time to love. Accept that this season is what it is . . . for now. And always hold on to this truth: God makes everything *beautiful* in his time.

Give yourself grace without feeling guilty about what you're unable to provide for your children during this season. They are *not* missing out; instead, they are gaining a profound education in persevering through affliction, finding joy in sorrow, loving in brokenness, experiencing peace in pain, showing compassion toward others, and being allowed to grieve without being consumed by that very same grief. These are priceless lessons in a season of crisis. Allow yourselves to experience them freely.

For those of us juggling homeschooling alongside ministry commitments, side jobs, or pursuing passion projects, there are times when unplugging is necessary. It's not about isolating yourself; it's a temporary pause from less urgent responsibilities to recharge and focus on what truly matters at home.

When it comes to schooling, do what you can and encourage your children to do the same. When our world as a family fell apart, my daughter was already enrolled in a couple of outsourced classes. Despite our challenges, she continued with those teachers, participated in our co-op, and joined virtual classes with friends. Audiobooks remained a lifesaver during this challenging process.

With all the new responsibilities I was now shouldering in my husband's absence, I had just enough bandwidth to teach a couple of classes in our co-op. There was nothing more I could give. I had to accept that our homeschooling didn't meet my ideal standards. However, it was a season where my daughter and I did our best, and I needed the grace to be okay with that.

Support

For many independent parents, the following may be a tough realization. Ready?

It's okay to ask for help.

Why carry your burden alone? That's not how God intended us to live. Your family and friends are there for you—they celebrate your joys and share your sorrows. They're more than willing to lend a hand of love for you and your family. But how can they help if they don't know your needs?

We "strong" mamas (and papas) must set aside our pride and fear of inconveniencing others and ask for help when needed. It's okay to admit that your child may benefit from a class taught by someone else, even if you could teach it yourself. Asking for assistance could also mean asking for advice, researching needed resources, or requesting help with pickups or drop-offs. Despite the need, taking the first step of asking is essential.

I know firsthand how humbling it is to ask for help. Eight months into our new reality, the start of the school year was a total flop. My daughter was dealing with various emotions and obstacles that affected her learning. It was her first year of high school, and the added pressure left me feeling overwhelmed and unsure about what to do next. When I spoke with our family counselor, she suggested finding a friend who could assist by teaching some classes. The Lord immediately brought the right person to mind.

I felt embarrassed to make this request to my friend because I knew I could teach the classes myself. The reality, though, was that our current circumstances left me unable to do so. As I mentioned, our loved ones want to support us but need to know how. My dear friend was a beautiful reflection of Christ's love when she graciously agreed to help. She encouraged me to prioritize my family's needs and confidently assured me that if the tables were turned, she knew I would do the same for her. I will forever be grateful for her generosity and kindness.

Honestly, my feelings of relief and gratitude were still clouded by lingering shame. Yet God, always faithful and infinitely loving, revealed to my heart that in this season I was meant to focus on my daughter's mental, physical, emotional, and spiritual well-being without distractions.

He showed me I should use this time to intercede on my daughter's behalf for healing and ensure I was fully present for whatever she needed. This was to be my sole purpose for this season. My dear friend stepping in to teach my daughter allowed me to do so, and none of it would have been possible if I hadn't reached out for support.

Looking Forward with Hope

Even as I pen these words, we're only coming to my husband's first birthday in paradise. The last year has been a roller coaster of emotions. Yet, God's peace enables us to grieve with hope. His grace is sufficient for us; without question, he is our ultimate healing.

I am deeply grateful that God continues to use our family, friends, church, homeschooling community, and my daughter's dance community to support us during this challenging time. He answered my dreaded question, *How do I raise my daughter without her father?* His response came through the African proverb: "It takes a village to raise a child." I can do all things, including single parenting, through Christ who gives me strength and through the village he's graciously blessed us with. I am not alone. And neither are you.

Whether you're grappling with grief, divorce, sickness, rebellion, or any other heart-wrenching situation, understand that these losses are valid, and it's okay to grieve. Take time to acknowledge the reality of your situation and extend yourself grace as you navigate through it. Seek support from family, friends, and counselors. Hold on to your faith. You are *not* alone, and this difficult season will not last forever. Joy *will* come in the morning. Of God's promises, I am certain.

> Weeping may last for the night,
> But a shout of joy comes in the morning. (Ps. 30:5 NASB)

Erika Alicea's journey has been unconventional, encompassing her love story with her husband, motherhood, starting a church plant in NYC, entering the "foreign" world of homeschooling, and leaving behind a decade-long teaching career. By God's grace, Erika has navigated a unique path filled with challenges, including widowhood and single parenting. An aspiring children's author, she enjoys discovering beautiful literature and photographing nature treasures in the bustling city. With an eye for beauty and a heart that chooses joy, Erika hopes to inspire and encourage others facing life's challenges with the comfort she has found in Christ Jesus. | @cmcityliving

When Homeschooling Heals
Brytni McNeil

As spring graciously gave way to summer one year, our family was found in its usual flurry of activities and celebrations. Eastertide, the closing and commemorating of yet another school year, three birthdays, Mother's Day, and our wedding anniversary happened upon us in rapid succession, and we were barely able to keep up. But keep up, we most certainly did. We are unapologetically mirthful and merry McNeils, ever determined to mark the moments and memories of our lives with the goodness and many graces afforded us.

And to add to our collective seasonal joy, I had just finished recording a podcast interview with the long-admired Dr. Jemar Tisby, *The New York Times* bestselling author and noted historian of race and religion. From a bevy of hopeful applicants, I had been blessedly chosen to share the work I do at the intersection of motherhood, homeschooling, and racial justice on his popular podcast, raising awareness of a recent course I had created for parents seeking to guide their children along the paths of racial peace from a holistic, Christian perspective.

After several years of offering up my words and voice to the ongoing conversation surrounding racial justice across various platforms (and subsequently enduring many a raised austere eyebrow and seething word of condemnation as a result), being invited to share my heart and work with the likes of Dr. Tisby was truly an honor of epic proportions and a welcome affirmation and validation of both my mission and my message. Along with the interview was a written piece featured on Religion News.com, where I had the honor of chronicling a bit more of my story and expounding upon the unique opportunity home educators have to further the work of racial reconciliation and justice from the home front.

To round out the whole ordeal, I had a gnawing sense of urgency rattling about my spirit to spend that coming summer sharing about home education on Instagram, creating space for people who found themselves in the clutches of decision-making and potentially overwhelmed by the prospect. Thus, the podcast interview and written article were undeniable confirmations, freeing me to participate with as much passion and enthusiasm as I could muster.

Both would lend greater depth (and exposure!) to the conversations I so wished to facilitate. Things were most certainly looking up. The horizons seemed broad and bright, the possibilities endless, and my imaginative, creative heart was set wondrously ablaze.

This will be a summer for the books, I told myself in moments of quiet satisfaction. *They're finally coming into a cohesive whole, these seemingly (though not actually) disjointed worlds of motherhood, social responsibility, home education, and vocational aspirations.* I would spend the summer exhorting women, resting with my husband and children, and diligently setting our course for the new year of learning just on the horizon.

A summer for the books, it was indeed, though not in a way I could have ever foreseen.

● ● ●

Somewhere in the delightfully hazy, euphoric glow of what seemed to be long-tended fruit ripening unto ideal sweetness, a darkness not yet known in my thirty-five years of living fell mercilessly into my lap, its cold and calloused hands enveloping every corner of my mind and heart, its menacing presence shadowing every door and window of my life. It's not that the darkness was a foreign foe, per se. I've long battled its brazen attacks, taken cover from its fiery darts, wrestled in the ring with its ruthless uppercuts and sneaky left jabs, and writhed under its monstrous weight as it sought to draw out and extinguish the very breath in my lungs.

Anxiety and intrusive thought obsessive-compulsive disorder (OCD) has been a dreaded, fairly constant companion of mine as far back as my memory serves me. But through trial and error over the years, I had learned to order and subdue my life in such a way as to make living well possible, ever engaging in that delicate dance of making allowances for my very real brokenness and limitations yet striving with all my might to gracefully give form to the most treasured ideals of my heart.

I've long learned to anticipate seasons that intensify its presence, noting the triggers and factors that exacerbate it. Pregnancy is such a season, followed fast on its heels by postpartum recovery. Prolonged sleeplessness, busyness, superfluous clatter and clammer, and schedule rigidity also aggravate it. Suffice it to say, I'm most often able to anticipate when a bout is beginning and can thus scramble to hunker down and batten the hatches of mind, body, soul, and spirit whenever needed.

But this particular wave came seemingly out of nowhere, with a raging and unrelenting ferociousness, cresting rather rapidly along the shore of my soul and leaving an ominous froth of varied, ghastly fears in its wake. No sooner did I strive with all my might to fling them once more into the tempestuous waves, skittishly hopeful of their watery grave, did the current gather up even greater force and plunge the hideous, creeping creatures farther up along the beach. It seemed the tide was hopelessly beyond my bidding, the unwanted visitors stranded on what felt like the God-forsaken island of my troubled heart for days that heaped into weeks, and weeks that stretched into months.

As those who suffer from intrusive thought OCD will attest, the obsessions and subsequent compulsions can vary drastically, in both the scope of their contents and the severity of their intensity. My crashes have found me obsessively fearful of things as ordinary as heat (stoves, fire, curling irons) and of unlikely phenomena that one would categorize as "freak accidents." I've fretted over the possibility of losing my children or a limb, concealed eyes helplessly swelling with scalding tears in the middle of Costco—fearful that items stored above would shift and plummet onto a passerby before my watching eyes—and spent portions of my pregnancies in agony of losing my little ones to any number of hellish or horrific accidents. I've lain awake all hours of the night, white-knuckling wads of sheets in my clammy palms, desperate to stop a flare-up in its tracks.

But what made this episode so hauntingly grievous, so particularly insidious and downright wail-worthy, was that I couldn't shake the obsession with my own impending death; my very constitution was called into question every moment of every day. For reasons unbeknownst to me, the obsessive arrows were ruthlessly aimed in my direction, with no apparent escape in sight.

I found myself convinced my body was riddled with lumps where none were found, afflicted by diseases that were not actual, imprisoned to a heart I believed would give out at any moment.

So panicked was I over these phantom ailments that I soon inadvertently bruised portions of my body with constant (compulsive) "checking." The soreness eroded into severe muscle tension, inducing painful headaches. So dire the pain and the sense of hopelessness that I murmured to my husband through pursed lips one morning, "Do you think I'm really dying?"

How would I carry on?
How would I survive the summer?
Would I be able to continue my dream of homeschooling my children?

The fears inevitably dissolved into feelings of failure and relentless frustration. There's an eerily strange, deep-seated "knowing" that such thoughts are not real, and yet . . . they seemed as sure as the cold tile beneath my feet when I'd pace my halls, attempting to reason with myself. I'll tell you what: there's nothing quite so soul-gutting as rehearsing the words to write to one's children in the event of one's death. It's all the more horrific and disillusioning to know there is no need to write such letters—yet the words and your children's hypothetical reactions to said words race with a fury across the landscape of your mind like a stampede.

Out of desperation to return to some semblance of normalcy and restored order, I began to do the only things I knew to do and had done for many a summer beforehand: pray, plan, and proceed in peace (elusive as it was), though I knew not what the future held for me. I scoured resources and organized booklists. I contemplated each of my children and considered the needs of their souls. I began to piece together all my wishes and hopes for their coming school year, jotted down themes and topics of discussion, their areas of interest, and weighed the wonder that so enraptured them.

Though nearly drowning in unbearable emotions, I found myself willing my head to bob just far enough above the waves to breathe deeply and restore my lungs. And little by little, one faithful act followed by still another, I felt my lungs expand and the oxygen rush through my muscles. For brief moments scattered over several days, I found myself treading water.

The light of day had steadily begun to dawn in my spirit. But could I trust this light casting its purifying rays across my soul's dusty, dank corners? I desperately wanted to reach for it, to gather it—but I feared it would only slip through my fingers once more. I worried it would haunt and taunt me like an unwanted presence in the night, only to evade me. I was not yet ready to trust the healing being offered to me.

But then a kind of eucatastrophe materialized around and within me without much warning or fanfare. I found myself sitting one early, honey-hued morning with radiant light dappling every surface in sight, a steaming cup of brew nearby, dancing candlelight meeting my gaze, and words both ancient and new spread like a feast before me.

Out of sheer habit, I had daily willed myself up and out of slumber to partake of what I believed would nourish my soul and enliven my imagination before my children crept out of bed. As I sat in the hallowed hush that morning, I realized it had been the first day in quite some time that I hadn't awakened to an immediate, violent onslaught of intrusive thoughts. I was caught entirely and utterly by surprise, stunned at the clarity of mind, quietness of spirit, and settledness of soul that marked me at that moment, realities that had been so fretfully beyond my grasp for what felt like an eternity. For a brief second, I began to doubt what I was experiencing, hesitant to celebrate what appeared to be a longing suddenly and startlingly fulfilled.

I began to thumb anxiously through the worn and dearly beloved pages of one of my favorite Elizabeth Goudge novels, *The Rosemary Tree*, and my eyes were arrested by words I had highlighted many a time (for once is never enough for good excerpts!). It was the moment where the fierce and fiery redhead, Mary O'Hara, a loving yet increasingly pessimistic teacher at a school for girls (whose foundations were rapidly crumbling under the heavy hand of a sinister headmistress), is taken aback by a pupil's ability to see and experience potent beauty amid a pitifully broken environment.

> It seemed to her strange that Winkle could find a blue window in this place that always felt to her so profoundly unclean. "I expect you go back more often at home, Winkle," she said. "No, I go back more often here," said Winkle. Mary smiled. Why, yes, of course. The frontiers would move closer in a place like this. One was apt to forget that an increase of power upon the one side meant an increase of power upon the other. What waves of light there must be washing against all the dirty walls of all dark strongholds, what power, gentle, inexorable and undefeatable, an ocean of power and patience. If it was hard to abide its time it should not be hard to trust its power, and Mary's heart sang within her.[5]

Though the atmosphere of my home and the scope of my life were not "a dark stronghold" (for it was my mission and, further still, my duty to make heartily sure of that), the landscape of my mind, heart, and soul certainly *was*. After all, there's a noted hiddenness to OCD, given that its playing field is the unseen realm of the mind. And yet, piercing through the chinks of my soul-prison was a light so radiant it sent the darkness into a panicked retreat.

Against the immovable iron bars that seemed to bind me was God's sparking and jarring power as he began to forge me a way out. The "frontiers" were moving ever closer, the power of beauty gathering strength upon strength even as brokenness sought to dig in its heels. The battle between good and evil, light and darkness, death and life, was most decidedly on, like two ruthless, unyielding opponents squaring up for a final round. And though it was hard to "abide its time," as Goudge so aptly penned, I realized then that I needed to "trust its power." And my heart, too, began to joyously sing within me.

Surely, when the music of life is the dullest, heaven's symphony is the loudest. When the clutches of defeat are the strongest, the shouts of God's deliverance are stronger still! What was gifted to me that morning was a new mercy, a cup of cold water, a moment of refreshment under the shade of a tree.

My visceral experience was one of mystifying grace, a gift not to be taken lightly nor held with trembling hands in doubt. The healing that had seeped into my heart over time could never be lost. Sure, other moments, particularly unwanted ones, might spring up and rattle me to my core. But they won't change the truth of that moment: the lover of my soul had drawn near to me, gentle and lowly as he is, and imparted me peace. A peace that surpassed the full scope of my reasoning faculties.

● ● ●

Upon further reflection of the weeks leading up to this sacred moment, I realized that it was in the pursuit of beauty on behalf of my children that my soul had awakened, little by little, and my eyes set ablaze with hope and the tantalizing, quiet joy of possibility. In the perusing of books, the planning of lessons, and the prayers uttered on my feeble, motherly knees, grace began to rush into my soul, a cascading flood of refreshment and revitalization sweeping me up and into this moment of sheer transcendence.

It was through the laminating of updated responsibility charts, the stapling of freshly printed papers, and the hanging of words of affirmation in plain sight to be whispered in their ears each night. It was in the prereading of mighty words of prose and poetry and the choosing of riveting history streams. That summer, homeschooling and its joy, wonder, possibility, and scope for imagination held me.

The beauty I so wished to place into my children's hands, to hold them fast in their own life stories and gird them for their voyages of faith, had flown mercifully back to me. And I knew afresh that this homeschooling life is far more life-giving and grace-filled than its day-to-day scrapes and bruises may suggest. In the giving of our hearts and the consecrating of our homes, a healing balm is poured out in abundance . . . enough to soothe the soul-aches, mental agony, emotional fragility, and relational turmoil that are part and parcel of existence on this side of eternity. Enough to soldier on and saddle up when the terrain of life becomes bumpy. Enough to keep choosing defiant joy again and again and again. This I know is true:

Mercy rushes to find us.
Grace unrelentingly attends to us.
Love gently envelops us.
Beauty mightily heals us.
And sometimes . . . homeschooling will too.

Brytni McNeil is a wife, mother of five daughters, home-educating enthusiast, and passionate writer residing in the warm Phoenix, Arizona, desert. Most days, she can be found waxing philosophical about the beauty and brokenness of life whilst changing an astonishing number of diapers, homeschooling her children, feverishly writing words as they come, cooking many a meal, sipping endless cups of tea, and snatching moments to read "just one more page" of any good book. She believes mightily in the power of words and currently writes at the intersection of motherhood, home education, racial justice, and theology. | @athomeasitisinheaven

7

The Vision Inspiring Our Days

Engaging Imagination and Creativity Through Vision
Nicole Cottrell

If someone had asked me ten years ago, I would have told them that the idea of having a vision for my family and homeschool sounded old-fashioned. I wasn't interested.

I've heard the familiar verse quoted from the pulpit plenty of times: "Without a vision, the people perish" (see Prov. 29:18). It evoked thoughts of pillars of cloud and columns of fire. *They* were the people who needed vision. *They* were the ones wandering the desert aimlessly. Me? I was content, blissfully homeschooling my three children, spending my days reading aloud, enjoying poetry teatime, listening to my children recite poetry . . . until I wasn't.

I'm not quite sure when it happened, as is the case so often when things fall apart, but I woke one day feeling a heaviness in my chest and a pit in my stomach. I knew I needed something to change, though I wasn't sure what. I had a child struggling to read—and I don't mean I had a six-year-old who was having a tough time digesting *Macbeth*. I had a ten-year-old who worked hard every day just to read a single page of a book. I also had an eight-year-old who was convinced he would never, ever be able to spell, plus a rambunctious two-year-old whose primary mission in life was to place as many items as possible into the toilet bowl at one time before trying to flush it. I was worn down.

My personal issues felt like heavy weights I carried each day too. I was suffering from a condition that caused chronic daily pain and deep exhaustion. Some days, I homeschooled from my bed while my kids climbed up to strew their papers and books about my sheets. Honestly, I felt like a failure, certain I was failing my kids too.

Platitudes like "This too shall pass" and "It's just a season" felt hollow and meaningless. When will it pass, and how long is this season exactly? Any information on its duration would have been greatly welcomed. I was desperate for a timeline—and not just the one in my kids' book of centuries.

What I was slow to realize as I waded in my own self-pity, though, was that my children needed something to change too. Our homeschool wasn't just mine. It was ours. It was a daily reflection of our home, together, and we were all floating about, untethered. I didn't know it then, but I would come to find out that we needed a compass. We needed the thing I had turned my nose up at so many times before. *Vision*.

Some people will say that vision is the ability to see what's ahead and plan accordingly. For whatever reason, this never interested me. Perhaps it's because I'm a more spontaneous, free-spirited person. Maybe it's because I'm not much interested in thinking about the things to come; I would rather spend my time focusing on today. Whatever the reason, creating a vision for my family and homeschool felt like an unnecessary and, honestly, boring task.

But then, one day, a friend described casting a vision as an opportunity to engage my imagination and creativity. What? How had I never heard this idea before? I was intrigued. Vision no longer sounded like an ancient biblical concept. Now it sounded, well, sexy. It sounded compelling. My curiosity was piqued.

Some people define *vision* as the act or power of imagination. Power? Yes. Imagination? Absolutely. Creativity? Count me in. I knew my homeschool needed a change. I knew I served a creative God who shaped creative, imaginative people. I started to feel the shift inside me that perhaps I had this whole idea of vision wrong. Perhaps I had more to learn, and, Lord knows, I needed a new way forward.

More than that, I also had to invite my children into this process. If I meant to honor the word *home* in homeschool and acknowledge my children as born persons, full of their own passions, desires, and imagination, then their voice was just as important as mine. It wasn't long after this reimagining of vision that my husband, Jonathan, said excitedly, "We should create a family mission statement!" A what? *Nope, no, thank you*, I thought to myself. *I'm not a mission statement kind of gal. I'm not a goal-setter.*

But I wasn't exactly a vision-casting gal, either. Yet here I was, trying to lean into the idea of what a vision could look like. I couldn't have it both ways. I begrudgingly agreed, and soon thereafter realized there was much more to this process than I had first assumed.

We set about discussing our family values, dreams, and desires, as well as what we wanted and envisioned for both the future and the present. We read articles on writing a mission statement and found that reading other people's statements helped inspire our own. Interestingly, I discovered that mission statements often speak to the things to come but not always to the people we are today—every day—while we go about the hard work of life. A mission statement should ideally embrace both the people we hope to become and the people we already are.

We also asked our children how they would describe our family, what they saw as our purpose, and who we were, in their own words. Their answers surprised and delighted us. Sure, we got some "We love dogs and pizza." But we also got some "We love to love," and "The Cottrells don't quit."

After serious discussion and continued reflection, our family mission statement was born: "To live and love freely." We want to live and love others unhindered, in a way that embraces freedom. It was simple, reflective of our values, and aspirational. Seeing it on the page inspired me. It illustrated who we already were and gave me a glimpse into where we were headed as a family.

● ● ●

It's easy to read this and think that within a few short months, I went from having a breakdown to discovering the need for a vision, writing a mission statement, and having my life all tied up with a pretty bow; nothing could be further from the truth.

The truth is that my hope for a vision was derailed. My chronic pain condition worsened, leading me to have two extensive surgeries within a year. Another child began to seriously struggle with reading, but all I could do for months was recover in bed. When we talk about mom guilt, mine was as vast as the ocean, and I was drowning in it.

I could feel myself slipping away into the unknowns. *What if my kids never catch up? What if I'm not enough? What if they need someone else to teach them? How will I ever redeem the time I've lost?*

A symphony of what-ifs became my daily soundtrack. The concept of a vision now felt like a cruel joke. How could I engage my imagination and creativity in crafting a vision when I could barely get out of bed? All I had was an idea and a mission statement, both of which felt useless on their own, just words on a page.

Years passed, and I continued on as best I could, healing and gaining energy. After much experimentation, I clung to the practices that had proved successful: short lessons, time outdoors, reading poetry together, and read-alouds. Some days I did very little, and some days I could do more. But doubt was a familiar presence, and the feeling I was failing my children was unshakable.

One day, while reading *The Brave Learner* by Julie Bogart, I was struck by something she wrote. She encouraged homeschool moms who could hire a person to help clean their home to do so. She admonished her readers to do the things that could make homeschooling easier and more sustainable. Why had I never heard this idea communicated before? How had I spent so many years homeschooling without feeling the permission to embrace things that would allow me to homeschool more freely? I needed to ask myself not *Am I messing up my kids?* but rather *What help do I need to feel empowered to homeschool?*

I contemplated this question deeply. It initially felt a bit nebulous. I'm not known for being very good at assessing my own needs. Sure, I can help address and meet everyone else's—deliver a meal, host a baby shower, even deliver a baby. Those things were relatively easy. Expressing my own needs, however, was another matter.

What do I need in order to continue homeschooling—and to homeschool well?

I thought back to a previous time I had accepted help, and the freedom it had brought. My daughter's difficulty in reading weighed heavily on me then, and I felt like a failure as her primary teacher. I visited the local elementary school, convinced that enrolling her would be her only saving grace. Yes, I'd threatened to "send them to school" before (please tell me I'm not the only one), but this was different. I wasn't making this decision because of a bad day. I felt like I was a lousy homeschooler. Like I had no business homeschooling in the first place.

That same day, after I'd visited the school, a friend called me and shared a story about a family she met whose daughter was struggling to read. My friend explained the steps they had taken to help their daughter succeed, including hiring a tutor. She explained that, as she listened to this family, she immediately knew it was a message just for me.

It felt like an answer to prayer. I sighed with relief.

If I wanted to keep homeschooling, I had to embrace practices that would allow me to do that, and those practices had to bring peace, hope, and sustainability to our home. The line of thinking was no longer how to stop homeschooling but instead how to *keep* homeschooling. So, I hired a reading tutor.

The familiar tides attempted to pull me back into the crashing waves of mom guilt. It took me time to be okay with asking for "outside" help. Why do we homeschoolers—or moms in general—believe the lie that we should be the ones to do it all? No other area of life works that way. In no other arena do we tend to be solely responsible for every single outcome.

To move forward, I had to acknowledge my own limitations and needs, as well as my daughter's. She didn't just need help; I also needed it. Hiring a tutor quickly became one of the best decisions I could have made, and I watched my daughter make huge strides. It turned out that the whole asking for help thing wasn't so bad. Once I had received help in one area, I found it much more comfortable to find and accept it in others. Go figure.

● ● ●

As I thought back on the freedom that had come from saying yes to help and the practices that allowed me to homeschool well, another question came forward: *Who do I want my kids to be when they leave my home?*

Years in, I still struggled in certain ways as a homeschooler. I had a shiny new mission statement but little vision to speak of. The question echoed in my mind.

Jonathan and I began to discuss and answer this question together. In a very real sense, we were working backward, making progress toward helping to create a future outcome. Without realizing it, we were crafting a vision for our family. We brainstormed and continued throwing out ideas about the character traits and skills we hoped our children would possess when they launched into the world. We once again included them in the process, asking them about their hopes and dreams for the future. What kinds of people did they want to become? What values would they carry with them long after leaving our home?

Eventually, we landed on strong communication, problem-solving, and godly character. I looked at our list and felt a swell of pride at the characteristics they already displayed but also a lump in my throat around the areas I knew they lacked. *Gulp.* It wasn't long before I sighed deeply and reminded myself that they weren't graduating tomorrow. We still had time to help foster and cultivate these characteristics. And at least now we had a direction, a horizon, a picture of the future.

But I'm practical, and the *How in the world am I supposed to educate and then graduate three seemingly perfect earth angels?* question was not lost on me. In my brood, I have one deep-feeling, creative artist; one highly social, self-motivated go-getter; and one justice-minded truth teller. How was I supposed to educate all three of them to achieve this lofty list laid out before us? As I considered the differences between my children's personalities and passions, I felt the familiar swirl of overwhelm.

I was reminded once again why I didn't like to set goals or write mission statements: once they are on paper, I have to do something about them. They become real and require accountability. But I could engage my imagination, access my creativity, and let these tools help provide the power to live out our family's vision.

A vision is a guide we can follow or a path we can walk. More than that, a vision can help pave the practical steps toward an ultimate goal. For me, the practical how-tos required more working backward. And they required more questions. I began to consider what I needed to ask to uncover the practical steps for helping my children live out what we envisioned.

> What will best serve each child?
> What will best serve me?
> What will best serve our family as a whole?
> What, if anything, am I holding on to? An expectation? A stereotype? A lie? Is it something I need to let go?
> Is there a solution, addition, or supplement I haven't considered?
> When I consider it, which option brings me a sense of peace or relief?
> Does the option or outcome align with our three goals in helping raise strong communicators, problem solvers, and people with godly character?

If I want to raise strong communicators, for example, I can ask these questions with that vision in mind and almost assuredly uncover roadblocks or hindrances to reaching that goal. I can also unearth truths and practical steps to help get us there.

Not long ago, I felt that having a vision for my family was a dusty, outdated practice reserved for the aimless among us. But I was wrong. A vision is a powerful opportunity to engage our imagination and creativity. Visions are living too. They can evolve and grow. They can swell to support our dreams and be reshaped in each season. A vision is a framework and tool. In other words, a vision operates as a compass, not a fixed point on a map. It provides a direction, not a destination. Visions are meant to guide and serve us, not pressure or bully us. I've realized just how thrilling and life-changing a vision can be.

There was a time when I felt besieged by inadequacy and fear as a homeschooler—when the ocean of doubt felt endless.

I desperately wanted to have the peaceful, lovely homeschools I saw reflected in other people's homes, but what I needed was a vision for my own home. Like so many good things, getting there was difficult and took time. I don't have a perfect, social media–worthy homeschool, but I have a vision, a mission, and a plan. And most importantly, I've learned to ask for help along the way.

Nicole Cottrell has accurately been described as a lover and a fighter. It is this passion she brings to her everyday life while homeschooling her three creative and kind teenagers alongside her entrepreneurial husband, Jonathan. She is the founder and curator of Stories of Color (StoriesOfColor.com), a diverse book catalog and resource for homeschooling families and teachers pursuing a more representative education. When not watching true crime shows, Nicole enjoys teaching Shakespeare—but not necessarily geometry. She and her family call the Phoenix desert home, where the sunsets never disappoint. | @storiesofcolor

We Are Uniquely Equipped
Brenaea Fairchild

"I don't know if I have what it takes," Charelle confided in me, worry stretched across her face. I had seen this look before. I knew it from my work coaching other homeschool moms and from being one myself. These worries—*Do I have what it takes? Can I do this?*—show up on our hardest days.

What does it really take? Mother Teresa levels of patience? An advanced degree in mathematics? A perfectly designed homeschool room? It's tempting to believe we're missing the "special something" needed to homeschool well.

Too many of us go through our homeschool lives thinking we aren't enough. While we don't allow our doubts to get in the way of us showing up for our children, we can move forward with much more confidence and joy when we have simple truths to turn to in our hardest moments. Yet I know this is easier said than done.

I've always bristled at the idea of affirmations—and while I still don't love the idea of looking in the mirror and saying to myself what I want to be true, I have grown to appreciate the simple practice of reminding myself of what is actually true. Because in the daily rhythms of life, it's easy to lose sight of the bigger picture, and having certainties to count on makes all the difference. I hope you keep these simple truths, grounded in experience and research, in your back pocket and that they will inspire and encourage you on the toughest days.

Truth #1: You Are Uniquely Equipped to Homeschool Your Children

You are uniquely equipped to homeschool your children. You have the ability to impact, inspire, nurture, and lead your children in a way that no one else can. I first began to understand this during my undergraduate studies in education. A professor posed the question, What most impacts student achievement?

Our cohort first offered typical ideas on what might affect how well a child does, like their motivation, how early they begin reading, their parents' level of education, and their support structure at home. Then we explored the research of Nel Noddings and her study of the ethic of care, which has meaningful implications for learning: "Educators' caring is just as important—and in some cases, even more so—than larger structural conditions that influence student learning."[1]

Several studies have corroborated Noddings's research, such as a nationwide study of teenagers in which 75 percent of thirteen-to-seventeen-year-olds said they worked harder for the teachers "who care most for them," or a Texas school study that found that "the problem of 'underachievement'" was attributable to "poor school-based relationships and organizational structures," not the children's ability to learn or even the teacher's ability to teach—it has to do with relationships.[2] With the understanding that the relationships children have with their educators significantly impact their academic outcomes, as a parent, then, you have an advantage that no one else in this world does: the relationship you have with your children.

I appreciate that research affirms what we already know to be true: children thrive when supported by their most loving caregivers. Tashe, a mom who started homeschooling her neurodivergent eighth grader this past school year, shared with me that she pulled her son, Jamel, out of school because he was struggling; he could barely read and hated to even try. Tears filled her eyes and pride glowed on her face as she reflected on their first few months of homeschooling. "Now he's always reading, and he moved from a second-grade to a fourth-grade level. To some, it's not much, but to me, it's the world."

Her story inspires me because this mama knew her baby could grow, even with autism. While a myriad of factors kept him from experiencing this type of growth in traditional school, research tells us that his mother's care contributed significantly to his current success.

When we hear stories like Tashe's, it's tempting to think that maybe she has something that we do not—some special qualifications, all the time in the world, or specific tools that help support her son's growth. While special training and tools are quite helpful and should be embraced when available, the type of thinking that focuses on what we do not have, known as deficit thinking, is not helpful.

Deficit thinking limits our ability to grow and foster growth in ourselves and others. Unaware of this mindset, Jamel's previous teachers may have thought, *He can't sit still; of course, he'll always be behind in reading.* In the home, a detractive mindset could have discouraged Tashe from ever trying to homeschool. Thoughts like, *I'm so disorganized, I'll never be able to make sure my child completes their work*, can prevent us from appreciating how we can use our strengths to achieve our goals.

Alternatively, when we embrace strengths-based thinking by focusing on how our strengths can work for us, we become more confident in our ability to do hard things. In Tashe's case, she might consider how her creativity could help her craft systems to stay organized or how Jamel could practice his reading while standing up or walking. A strengths-based approach helps us find ways to achieve our goals by appreciating *who* we are and *how* we are. It shifts us from asking, "Do I have what it takes?" to "What do I have that equips me to do what it takes?" In every case, as dedicated caregiver educators, we have the unique advantage of the relationship we have with our children.

Notice here that the privilege is not strictly based on biology. It's based on relationships. Adoptive parents, grandparents, stepparents, aunts and uncles—we each enjoy the fruits of this privilege by way of the relationship we have with the children in our lives. We know this because, even in classrooms, caring teachers who have no biological connection to their students experience this advantage. With the understanding that we have a relationship with our children that uniquely positions us to encourage, inspire, and develop them, we can explore practical ways to nurture our relationships.

Truth #2: Expect Much and Love Big

First-generation homeschoolers are often conscious of not repeating the ills they experienced in school while growing up. The high-pressure and jam-packed days are things they resist in order to provide their children with a life-giving academic experience. We must all be careful, however, not to overcorrect and remember that nurturing our children isn't just about hugs and kisses. It's also about setting high expectations and giving them the tools they need to succeed.

As our children's most loving caregiver, we're in a unique position to expect and inspire growth. This is a delicate balance. If we have high expectations of our children without giving them the proper support, they'll feel defeated and unfairly judged. If we give them too much support, they won't enjoy the growth and pride that come only from wrestling with something difficult. I experienced this firsthand when I was a high school senior.

"Just apply so I can put it on the refrigerator if you get in." This was my mom's response to my teenage resistance to applying to Princeton University. As an eighteen-year-old, I didn't care about the prestige of an Ivy League school, but I *did* care about it being only forty-five minutes away from home. I wanted to attend school in Washington, DC, and kickstart my career advocating for educational equality. I had dreams and plans—and the university around the corner was not a part of them.

Rather than argue, force, or coerce, my mom made what in my teenage brain felt like a compromise: "Just apply; I'm not forcing you to go." I could do at least that. My private school required us to apply to at least nine colleges—three safety schools, three target institutions, and three stretch targets. After I shared my list with my guidance counselor, he looked at me and said, "Why are you applying to Princeton?" When I told him my mom told me to, he sort of just shrugged with an eye roll, and said, "Well, okay." This explains why, when I received my acceptance letter and went to thank him, he looked at me frankly and said, "I didn't do anything." That was true. He didn't. My mom and I did.

In this situation, I was in my ideal growth zone or zone of proximal development, the place where my skills were sharp enough for the expectations being set, yet I still had room to grow. My mom expected me to apply and put forth my best efforts. I was set up for success by the academic environment she raised me in, and I had teachers reviewing my essays and guiding me through the process. At the same time, Princeton's application was challenging, my mom didn't review it before submission, and I finished everything only minutes before the deadline.

While the application process was hard, I was able to finish it because my mom believed I could rise to the challenge, provided the right tools, and then gave me space to grow. Even if I had not been admitted, confronting a challenge that felt out of reach was a significant personal development that I am grateful for still today. It reminds me that nurturing our children includes letting them work and grow through challenges with our encouragement and support.

I did end up attending Princeton. As college is for many young people, Princeton was a formative experience for me. I grew to know and accept myself and my gifts more deeply. When I decided to pursue entrepreneurship instead of becoming a high school teacher or politician, I was taking a path unfamiliar to most of my peers. While they received pressure from their parents on what to major in and conditions tied to their parents' financial support, my family supported me paving my own way. By the time I graduated four years later, I had started two successful businesses, married, and welcomed our first child.

After my college years, I had the opportunity to mentor young women at my alma mater. In our weekly one-on-one meetings, one of these ladies, Brooke, shared how overwhelmed she felt as she applied to law school; it was an intense experience as she both completed her culminating undergraduate thesis and studied for the LSAT. As we talked and prayed together, one theme kept emerging: her mother's love.

On one of her hardest days, she shared, "My mom said, 'You can stop this all right now and come home if you want to. I'm proud of you. I love you.'" While I was mentoring this young woman, her mother's wisdom poured over me. Brooke's mom was simply saying, "This work, this achievement, is not what's most important. *You* are what's most important."

When I reflect on Brooke's last semester in college, what stands out most isn't that she got into a top law school; it's that her mother's love sustained her. We can have ambitious goals and expectations of our children without allowing our love to depend on their success. Understanding this balance is a critical element of loving our kids well.

When the love, support, and celebration our children experience with us are conditional on their success, they're likely to either play it safe to feel secure in our love or work tirelessly to prove they're worthy of it, both of which are recipes for a deeply unsatisfying life. Gratefully, it doesn't have to be this way. We can see the amazing things our children are capable of and love them right where they are. We can expect much and love big.

Truth #3: You Can Do Hard Things

Of course, expecting much and loving big are easier said than done. In fact, most of this homeschool journey is easier said than done. Homeschooling is hard. Yes, it's full of joy, laughter, love, and brightness—and still, it is hard. Hard things feel uncomfortable and are often unfamiliar for adults.

We routinely put our children in new situations and encourage them to take risks. As adults, however, we tend to stick to what we know and navigate life in our comfort zone. This often means that when things are hard, we feel like we're failing instead of realizing that we're growing. The simple truth is that you can do hard things. I don't offer this as a feel-good platitude. I'm saying that you can do hard and new things because science proves it; a piece of research from our neighbors across the pond illustrates this.

London is known for having excellent taxi service because one must study for about four years and memorize twenty-five thousand streets and twenty thousand landmarks within a twenty-five-mile radius to become a certified hackney carriage driver. Psychologists did an experiment comparing the brains of hackney carriage drivers to those of London bus drivers.[3] They discovered that during hackney drivers' training, the hippocampus, the part of the brain that specializes in acquiring information, grew significantly. As these drivers in training memorized streets and landmarks, their brains literally grew and made new connections that enabled them to maintain that information. On the other hand, the bus drivers who followed a simple daily route didn't experience the same amount of brain growth. Even more interesting is that after the hackney drivers retired, the hippocampus shrank back down, showing that their bodies and brains adapted to what they needed. This is a beautiful insight for us as homeschooling parents.

We can learn new skills, take on challenges, and sign ourselves up to do hard things, knowing that our brains grow with and for us. You can learn how to teach reading, understand new math, and prepare your children for college, and your body is designed to work with you in these efforts. However, another element that makes a significant difference in your success with taking on new and hard things is your mindset.

There are two primary types of mindsets: a growth mindset and a fixed mindset. When you have a fixed mindset, you believe that your talents, abilities, and skills are fixed traits. Either you are good at something or you're not. For example, you might think things like, *I'm just not a math person*, or *I don't know how to cook*.

Oftentimes, if you have a fixed mindset, you avoid attempting new things because you already know what you are good (or not good) at. The alternative to this way of thinking is known as a growth mindset. With a growth mindset, you know and believe that your intelligence, talents, and abilities can be developed with practice and effective effort. In this case, you might think to yourself, *I'm not a great cook yet. I will ask Nana to teach me some recipes*. With a growth mindset, you know that you can grow and, as a result, are more likely to grow.

You might contend that growth can still happen even if you don't believe it will. However, research shows that's not likely. In the fall of a school year, researchers gave seventh graders with similar levels of mathematical achievement an assessment to determine whether they had a fixed or growth mindset. Then they followed the academic achievement of these students for two school years.[4]

At the end of eighth grade, they found that students with a fixed mindset experienced almost no growth in their mathematical achievement over the two years; the scores they received in the fall of their seventh-grade year were nearly identical to those they received in the spring of their eighth-grade year on the same exact test. On the other hand, growth-minded students showed significant academic gains by the end of their eighth-grade year. Students who began with the same scores had different outcomes because of their mindsets. The takeaways from this research extend to us as adults: what we believe about ourselves matters.

On hard days, I encourage you to remember that your body and brain are designed to work with you as you take on the challenges that arise as you homeschool. You can do hard things, and your belief that you can grow through the challenges will sustain you on this journey.

Hold On to and Affirm Truth

A sobering reality is that no one on this earth will be with me longer than I will be with myself. No one will know my journey, my desires, or my insecurities better than me. And while sometimes that feels lonely, it's also empowering. It means that by design, I have the power to encourage myself in a way that directly speaks to my innermost being. It means that *you* have the power to encourage yourself in a way that speaks to your innermost being.

I encourage you to let the truths outlined here be just the beginning of the truths you speak to yourself throughout your homeschool days. You know your fears, your joys, your hopes. Seek out the truth and affirm it as often as you can. My friend, you are uniquely equipped to do this. You can homeschool with love and expectation, and you will be able to rise to the challenges that come your way.

Brenaea Fairchild is a former public school teacher, an educational entrepreneur, and a passionate advocate for homeschooling, which she enjoys alongside her husband, Matthew. Her decision to homeschool was influenced by her research at Princeton University, which highlighted the inaccuracies in US history textbooks regarding slavery and the Civil War. A trilingual mother of two boys, Brenaea delights in teaching world languages, particularly Spanish and French. She founded The Melanin Village to address the unique challenges Black families face in homeschooling, offering a supportive community and access to quality curricula and teaching resources. | @themelaninvillage

Taking Your Thoughts Captive
Julie H. Ross

I pulled the covers over my head, hoping to magically transport myself back to dreamland. Alas, no transportation occurred. I could still hear the shouting that had woken me wafting its way upstairs. What was it this time? The wrong colored cup, or maybe a toy dispute? Each morning felt like a repeat, me dragging myself through the day until I could retreat to my bed. I could feel the shame punch in my stomach as the repetitive thoughts started playing their well-known tune. *You are a horrible mom; your kids would be better off in school; you don't know what you are doing.* I pulled the covers tighter, hoping to drown out the internal voices. Surely, this wasn't what life was meant to be.

This pattern had become a testament to my growing sense of defeat. Balancing homeschooling and motherhood, especially with five young souls, felt like a mountain too steep. I was constantly overwhelmed, anxious, and hopeless, a stark contrast to the mom I'd envisioned myself to be.

• • •

Charlotte Mason, an educational philosopher from the early 1900s whom I deeply admire, wrote something that struck a chord with me. She said, in so many words, that a mother's anxiety and worry could unwittingly be transferred to her children, making them restless and difficult to manage. This wasn't about my actions, my children, or my circumstances needing to change; it was about my state of mind.

> Let not the nervous, anxious, worried mother think this easy, happy relation with her children is for her. She may be the best mother in the world, but the thing that her children will get from her in these moods is a touch of her nervousness—most catching of complaints. She will find them fractious, rebellious, unmanageable, and will be slow to realize that it is her fault; not the fault of her act but of her *state*.[5]

A 2005 study by the National Science Foundation found that we have anywhere between twelve thousand and sixty thousand thoughts per day, 80 percent of which are negative and 95 percent of which are repetitive.[6] We think the same thoughts repeatedly, creating stronger neural pathways and making them a habit. They become automatic programming, running constantly in the background of our lives.

Mason put it this way:

> But what if from childhood they had been warned, "Take care of your thoughts, and the rest will take care of itself; let a thought in, and it will stay; will come again tomorrow and the next day, will make a place for itself in your brain, and will bring many other thoughts like itself. **Your business is to look at the thoughts as they come, to keep out the wrong thoughts, and let in the right.** See that ye *enter* not into temptation." This sort of teaching is not so hard to understand as the rules for the English nominative, and is of infinitely more profit in the conduct of life. **It is a great safeguard to know that your "reason" is capable of proving any theory you allow yourself to entertain.**[7]

When we think a thought repeatedly, it becomes habitual. These thoughts become our beliefs. Our brains' "reason" then finds evidence in our daily lives to support our beliefs. Our brains are amazing filters, specifically the reticular activating system in the brain stem. This part takes in important information, leaving out the other billions of pieces of sensory data bombarding us constantly. Since our brains are neuroplastic, we can actually train our brains what to focus on. When we start to believe new thoughts, our brains will find evidence to support these new beliefs.

Let's take my example from the beginning of this chapter. When I woke up to the sound of my kids bickering, my mind offered me thoughts like these:

You are a horrible mom. Other moms wouldn't have kids who fight.
Today is going to be rough.
Here we go again.
Why does this always have to be so hard?

All these thoughts made me feel horrible. The shame made me want to do one thing: pull the covers over my head in the hopes of escaping. On other days, I might think along these lines:

My kids are so difficult.
Why can't everyone just get along?
I was an only child; they should be grateful to have each other.
Why can't they respect that I'm trying to get some well-deserved rest?

This line of thinking would fill me with a slow, simmering anger, leading me to march downstairs and start barking orders like a boot camp drill sergeant.

Surprisingly, neither of these scenarios gave me the results I wanted. The calm, loving, serene mornings I pictured when

I started homeschooling were far from my reality. The gap between my expectations and my daily life only added fuel to my discouragement.

If you have ever found yourself stuck in a similar pattern, you know that our first inclination is often to try to change our circumstances.

> *Maybe I just need a better morning routine.*
> *Maybe I need a sticker chart to reinforce positive morning time behaviors.*
> *Maybe we need a new house (or new kids)—did I just actually write that?!*

While those are all possible solutions that may help for a time, they don't address the real root of the issue: our thinking. Eventually, our negative thought patterns will reemerge, perhaps in a different area.

It can be challenging to work on our thinking because, well, most of us are clueless about what we are thinking. We know we don't like the results we are getting. We know we don't like feeling these negative emotions, but we don't pause to ask ourselves, *What am I thinking that is leading to these results and feelings?* Metacognition—that big, fancy neuroscience term for thinking about our thinking—isn't something we naturally do, so most of us run our lives unaware of the default negative thoughts running in the background. Awareness of your thoughts is the first step to breaking free from these mental ruts.

Think back to a recent challenging situation in your homeschool.

1. What thoughts came to your mind during this event?
2. Did you make any assumptions about others' thoughts or feelings?

3. How did the situation make you feel?
4. Can you identify any patterns in your thoughts and feelings?
5. What do these thoughts reveal about your beliefs?
6. Are these thoughts helping you achieve the results you want?
7. How would you prefer to respond?
8. What thoughts would support that preferred response?

Once we are aware of what we are thinking, we can take the next step to create new thought patterns by intentionally telling ourselves what to think instead.

> In this way, we think *as we are accustomed to think*; ideas come and go and carry on a ceaseless traffic in the rut—let us call it—you have made for them in the very nerve substance of the brain. You do not deliberately intend to think these thoughts; you may, indeed, object strongly to the line they are taking (two "trains" of thought going on at one and the same time!), and objecting, you may be able to barricade the way, to put up **"No Road"** in big letters, and to compel the busy populace of the brain-world to take another route.[8]

To help my brain travel down a new road of thinking, I made a list ahead of time of the thoughts I could think the next time I woke up to the sound of bickering:

> *It's normal for siblings to argue. This isn't a reflection on my abilities as a mother.*
> *Children are immature and need help expressing negative emotions. I can help model this for them by regulating myself.*
> *I'm grateful to be home with my kids.*
> *I can do hard things.*

These thoughts make me feel confident and empathetic, and I was able to jump into the situation with a combination of Wonder Woman's determination and Mr. Rogers's understanding. (Okay, well, maybe I just pictured that in my head, but I did start to show up differently.)

Let me give you some more examples to see if you can relate. I often had thoughts like these:

We are so far behind.
My child should be reading better by now.
We are never going to get caught up with our plans.
I'm failing my kids.

These thoughts would fill me with so much worry and anxiety. I would then feel the need to micromanage and control my kids all day, trying to squeeze in as many lessons as possible. My kids would pick up on my stress and couldn't focus at their best. They would resist my nagging and prodding. And guess what this led to?

Ding, ding, ding! And the winner is—you guessed it—we got less done. This reinforced my belief that we were so far behind. Can someone cue the facepalm, please?!

What's sad is that this cycle repeated for years before I realized the issue wasn't my children's lack of motivation, our curriculum, our daily schedule, or how cluttered our house was. The problem was how my thoughts were making me show up in a way that was not beneficial. The good news was that I could work on changing them. So I started to think new thoughts:

We are progressing at the perfect pace.
Every day, we are making progress.
Mistakes are opportunities to learn and grow.
I'm the perfect person to be teaching my children.

As these thoughts became more natural, something miraculous occurred. I started to show up calmer and more patient. I was able to relax and have fun during our days. I could allow my children the space they needed to work through hard problems or a difficult book without jumping in to fix it. Our days became peaceful and enjoyable. And here's the real kicker: we got MORE done and had more FUN doing it! All I changed was my thinking. Yep—no new schoolroom decor, shiny new curriculum, or color-coded planner needed.

By changing my thinking, I started to feel different, which changed the way I showed up each day. This slowly transformed the atmosphere of our home. I was no longer constantly vacillating between fight and flight. I started to approach each day with calm confidence, excited for the adventures that awaited us.

Another skill that will help transform our thinking and train the reticular activating system in our brains to filter for the positive is spending time daily reflecting on our small wins. Gratitude is a practice that takes the focus off our problems to refocus on all the good that we often miss. We can so easily fall into the trap of all-or-nothing thinking.

Either the day was perfect, *or* it was a complete disaster.

Either my child gleefully approaches every lesson, *or* they have such an attitude.

Either my house is spotless, *or* I'm a failure at balancing home and school.

In this trap, we miss out on all the small blessings right before us. Daily journaling the small wins can help us appreciate all the joys and small steps forward. This helps build confidence and motivation to keep making consistent progress, and it can be as simple as writing down three "wins" from the day in a lesson planner or a journal at the end of the school day. This will probably seem challenging at first, but the more you do it, the easier it will be for your brain to seek the good. Charlotte Mason refers to this as the habit of appreciation.

> We all know that it is easy to appreciate or depreciate the same thing. An appreciative habit of feeling is a cause of tranquil joy to its possessor, and of ease and contentment to the people connected with him. A depreciative habit, on the contrary, though it affords a little pleasurable excitement because it ministers to the vanity of the *ego*, disturbs tranquility and puts the person out of harmony with himself and with his surroundings; no stable joy comes of depreciation.[9]

If I'm honest, I was at the gold medal level in what Miss Mason refers to as the habit of depreciation. In plain ole modern English, that's straight-up complaining. This habit can be sneaky because we don't often notice how it creeps into our daily behaviors. It can be as subtle as a sigh, eye roll, or folded arms. It can be as blatant as the words we utter that we think are "helpful" but are actually harmful: "Why aren't you finished with that assignment by now?" "How many times do I have to repeat myself?" "You should know this by now." As Mason writes, this habit puts us out of harmony. So, if you want a more peaceful home atmosphere, start to notice the ways you habitually fall into deprecation and purposefully choose to cultivate the habit of gratitude instead.

• • •

Now that you know the tools, you can escape the negative mental ruts that keep you from creating a life and homeschool you love. Here are the simple steps:

1. Become aware. Choose one challenging situation daily and use your journal as a prompt to start noticing your thinking. Eventually, you will notice belief patterns.

2. Write out a new, empowering thought for each recurring pattern.
3. Make it a daily practice to write out these new beliefs. Posting them somewhere you can see them throughout your day may be helpful.
4. Take your thoughts captive. When you start thinking an old thought, hold up your imaginary "NO ROAD" sign and tell your brain you aren't going down that path anymore. Tell your brain what thoughts to think instead.
5. Write down your small daily wins and cultivate the habit of appreciation.

Above all, be patient with yourself. Creating new neural pathways takes time. It's like making a new path in the forest: there will be lots of weeds and debris to clean through. It's tough work at first, but once that new path is cleared, it becomes easier to travel. I encourage you to reflect on your thoughts and how they shape your homeschooling experience. Remember, the key to change lies within your mindset. I'm cheering you on every step of the way.

Julie H. Ross believes that every child needs a feast of living ideas to grow intellectually, emotionally, and spiritually. A former public school teacher, curriculum coordinator, and assistant director of a homeschool academy, she has worked with hundreds of students and parents. She has also homeschooled her five children for the past twenty years. Julie developed the Charlotte Mason curriculum *A Gentle Feast* to equip parents with resources for a rich education filled with books, beauty, and biblical truth. She lives in South Carolina with her family and enjoys reading children's books, hiking, writing curriculum for AGentleFeast.com, and taking naps. | @julie.h.ross

The Holy Audacity of an Unhurried Mama

Min Hwang

[I pray] that according to the riches of his glory he may grant you to be strengthened with power through his Spirit in your inner being. (Eph. 3:16 ESV)

Discovering Courage: A Homeschool Origin Story

It was unheard of. A Korean-Canadian, first-time mom saying she'd be homeschooling her daughter? Furrowed brows, disapproving questions, and criticism were all that met me.

"How will you homeschool when, as a pastor's wife, you should be giving every waking hour to serving your church?"

"What is this thing called 'homeschooling,' anyway?"

I actually didn't know much myself. I just knew that even before our long-awaited (seven years, to be exact) child arrived, God was training me to follow the "mother's intuition" he was growing in me. This intuition told me that when God would grant me a child to steward for him, I was to hold her close. More than anyone else on earth, I'd be given the gift of knowing, loving, and wanting the very best for her.

Through the trials of being an immigrant child in Canada in the seventies, later multiplied through the challenging call to be a pastor's wife, God trained me to search things out for myself and to discern his voice above the din of others. An early prayer as a pastor's wife was for thick skin. Maybe he answered a little too well. Apparently, I'd become known as that odd pastor's wife who moved to the beat of a different drum.

As a Christ-following homeschool mom, I think you'll know what I mean when I say that "God's still small voice" grows louder each time you heed him. At each juncture, I listened to the Holy Spirit telling me to hold my baby girl closer, despite the norm of pushing children away from their parents as toddlers to church nurseries, day cares, and preschools. As I did, he filled me with the courage I needed to persevere through the clash with my culture, context, and times. Moreover, he was training me to understand my role as a mother and to whom I was answerable.

As the Lord graciously added more children to our family, this early season of motherhood was when I began to unfurl from the claustrophobic ideas I had about motherhood, children, and education. How small my paradigm had been! I didn't know it until God began to shatter it to reveal a new paradigm too exquisite for words.

As I grew in realization of the freedom I had to pave my own path of motherhood, I dreamed of what our home atmosphere would be. We'd fill our days with wonder, exploration of God's creation, and falling in love with God's Word together. I'd be intentional in ensuring my children's hearts remained soft toward me, and therefore toward God their Maker.

I also made intentional choices about the kind of mother I wanted to be. I wanted to be an unhurried mama—one who would linger during the childhood days that passed too quickly. I wanted to listen thoughtfully to my child's thoughts, to carefully observe ants with her, to include her in our homemaking, to tell make-believe stories under blanket tents, and to never be too rushed to climb large rocks and small trees. I wanted to ensure our home felt safe and warm, a place where her whole being could find rest and let go of all tensions from the outside world—a safe zone from dragons.

This was difficult for me due to the borderline OCD tendencies I've had since childhood. It took conscious, intentional, painstaking effort to choose against my nature. Moreover, I had started a nonprofit rescuing women from threatened forced abortion, including foreign nationals and aged-out orphans who were victims of sex trafficking. With my babies in tow, I was turning apartments into safe houses, taking the women to prenatal appointments, giving workshops at the local hospital, orchestrating rescues with churches, and, of course, fundraising. Always fundraising.

Do you feel exhausted just reading that? I do just writing it! All that was going on as I took my first steps into homeschooling. I researched late into the night beside my sleeping babies. That was the only time I had.

God always answers, my friend. It was during one of those nights that I came across the "code of education from the Gospels": the Charlotte Mason philosophy of education.[10] I won't go into it, but suffice it to say, I had finally found a philosophy not only of education but of living that aligned with our family's vision. My bones were on fire as I consumed her words, and I began implementing them, as best I could, in my home.

I share my homeschool origin story with you because I believe we're made of the same stuff. We're called to the same calling. I also know that we have faced, are facing, or will be facing similar challenges.

I quickly knew that my strength was not enough to get through the days. I didn't want to just "get through" them, either. I wanted to soar on eagle's wings (see Isa. 40:31). Motherhood is extremely hard. Add to it the call from God to homeschool, and the need for vigilance, inspiration, insight, discernment, knowledge, and a kindred-spirit community is multiplied a hundred times. We're in dire need of abundant grace and supernatural strength—strength that, when we experience it, we know without a doubt is God's arms uplifting us. It is his life coursing through our veins to accomplish what he has set before us.

So now, the question before us is, How do we do this? How do we know what to cultivate in our homes? Let's dive in.

Nurturing the "Kingdom of Mansoul" as a Priority

In John 5:19, Jesus said, "The Son can do nothing of his own accord, but only what he sees the Father doing" (ESV). It occurred to me: If Jesus did only what he saw the Father doing, shouldn't *we* make it our aim to live in dependence on the Father?

So here's the secret: prioritize the nurturing of *your* inner life. These intentional acts of nourishing are what I like to call "Mother Nurture." As we delve into what Mother Nurture is and what it means to prioritize the nourishment of your inner life, let's simultaneously explore what the inner life is. All human beings have one. But what is it, exactly?

Unlike other books, which can be simplistic and reductionistic, the Bible shows us that this inner life is immensely complex. We see this in the detailed records of David's inner life. One of my favorite images, which I think does some justice, was described by Charlotte Mason. She called this inner life "The Kingdom of Mansoul," which she further detailed as consisting of five Houses: Body, Mind, Heart, Will, and Soul (where King Jesus dwells).[11]

This inner life includes our physical body, our emotions, our thoughts, and our spirit. There is no "faculty" or idea of segregation here. The Bible describes us as whole beings, made in God's image and formed by his breath.

To better understand the inner life and how Mother Nurture nourishes it, let's take each House in turn. Then, we'll see how Mother Nurture empowers the will with wisdom and discernment, for the soul's sake.

1. The House of Body: The Temple for the Inner Life

Have you ever traversed the "Valley of Burnout"? I have. At least my body was burning out, but I didn't recognize the signs until alopecia finally struck. As I stared at the large bald spots on my head, I was intrigued. I didn't feel stressed. My heart had been at peace as I adventured with my little tribe while supporting my husband in pastoral ministry. Yet, along the way, I had not been caring for my body. During this time, my body birthed and nourished three babies. (After recovery, I'd experience the joy of a fourth.) I didn't remember the last time I'd slept for more than a couple of hours at a time. My body needed urgent care.

We were able to visit my parents in Vancouver. My heartbroken parents immediately took me to a doctor who practiced traditional Korean medicine. He treated me daily with needles attached to electricity and strong herbal medicine. Gradually, I felt my spirit reviving, and my hair started to grow back too.

What a wake-up call! I learned to stop pushing my body too far beyond its limits and to be more attentive to its rhythm, which changed with the seasons and even the time of day. I learned to read its cues for sleep, sunlight, exercise, and gut health nutrition. I also educated myself on environmental toxins and made my home safer while not growing anxious or forgetting God's priority of people and relationships over bodily health.

Taking her cue from the biblical tabernacle, Mason describes the House of Body as the outer courts.[12] In this house, there are servants such as hunger and thirst. They are good if we're careful to keep them in their rightful place. But when we allow them to become masters, problems can ensue. Within this house, chronic illnesses may arise, but also, because God made us whole, the servants of the House of Body can wreak havoc on the heart and mind. (I don't believe all ailments result from a lack of watchfulness. We would be attributing too much control and power to ourselves. However, we must cooperate with the

Holy Spirit in stewarding our bodies well, according to God's grace in each season.)

So, what does applying Mother Nurture to the body look like? Taking care of the body's needs. Just as we are instructed on flights to put our oxygen mask on first before assisting our child, we must heed our body's needs so that we can do the good works God prepared for us (see Eph. 2:10). Of course, not to the point of indulgence. But the essentials are worth our attention.

Mother Nurture, then, is seeking wisdom from our Father to meet our bodily needs—not as an end in itself, but so that we may have the ability to cooperate with him with a sound mind.

2. The House of Mind: Ideas That Fuel the Inner Life

Do you remember when the idea of homeschooling first entered your mind? I do. It was during my junior high science class. The teacher said we evolved from apes while showing a diagram of an ape transforming into an upright, walking man. That's when the thought, *If God were to call me to motherhood, I'd homeschool*, burst into my mind. I remember clearly thinking that was odd because I wanted to be a celibate missionary. Moreover, I didn't know a single homeschool family. Years later, God brought this memory to my mind when I became pregnant.

The mind is the digestive system of our inner life. This is where ideas, whether good or bad, enter and become the building blocks of our character. How important it is to discern which ideas we allow to feed the mind!

As homeschool parents, we get to prayerfully choose each resource we want to introduce to our children's Mansoul. As a bibliophile, I love this part. Mason says, "Children must have the best books."[13] We need them too!

This notion of ideas being living as they pass from mind to mind via books, music, art, conversation, nature, and certain environments is not a fairy tale. I've seen a great idea move from one person to another because the first person didn't act upon it. An idea is like a living organism. When it is time to be realized in the world, it will find someone with the courage to birth it.

Mother Nurture, then, is nourishing your mind with ideas by

> Reading the best books from the best minds. Nothing compares to God's Word, through which we have the mind of Christ. Begin there. Then add by asking your spiritual mentors what *they* are reading.
>
> Creating space to ruminate upon those living ideas. When do you get the best ideas? In the shower? Extend this time. Give your mind opportunity to digest.
>
> Exploring your locale to nurture your imagination.
>
> Acting upon the living ideas to multiply them. God will provide a continuous supply when you are faithful and obedient to act.

3. The House of Heart: Relationships for the Inner Life

It was the summer of fifth grade, three years after my brother's tragic death. I'm not sure if my parents were deeply concerned, but they sent me alone on a plane to a friend in Alberta. While I was there, my friend and I had the opportunity to attend a youth retreat. Little did I know that Jesus had planned to invade my withdrawn, hurting heart. I remember it like it was yesterday. Three ten-year-olds sat in a circle, holding hands to pray. Suddenly, something like a mighty waterfall drenched us. I can only describe it as God embracing me fiercely with his holy love. He shattered the hard shell around my heart with a piercing, white-hot flash of light. Hot tears of relief poured down my cheeks. All the weight of the sorrowful burden in my heart dissipated. God rescued me, not only from my sins but from myself. Thus began the most crucial relationship of my life.

All the virtues necessary to cultivate relationships live in the House of Heart. After all, the tabernacle itself was a physical manifestation of relationship: God dwelling with humankind; God reaching out to us, chasing after us, rescuing us, and making a way for us through Jesus.

The Bible speaks of the heart as the place our core commitments lie—i.e., the things we fundamentally love, trust, and live for. Therefore, our relationships belong here. They reflect our core commitments since they tell us to what and to whom we are committed. Here we find all the virtues we need for relating to and serving others, including love, compassion, benevolence, kindness, generosity, gratitude, courage, loyalty, humility, and justice.

Mother Nurture, then, involves intentional acts of nurturing our relationships, with our relationship with God taking primacy. From that relationship, all others flow. The condition of our relationships with people and things is determined by our foundational relationship with God.

Thus, for our heart's commitments to remain vitalizing, the most important act is to sit before the Lord every morning. Give God the firstfruits of your day by meditating on his Word and listening for instructions as you ask the Holy Spirit to fill you. We can do nothing good apart from him, so we must choose this lifestyle.

4. The House of Will: Wisdom and Discernment for the Inner Life

At our children's graduation, we envision them possessing integrity, wisdom, and discernment. But what would you say if, in order to do so, we needed to strengthen their will? According to Mason, a weak will gives in to every whim and emotion; it is a slave to chance desires. In contrast, a strong will can keep the "servants" of Mansoul in their proper places. A strong will filters ideas, discerning the ones that would bring health to the inner life.

Coming across this idea from Mason, I realized it was not only my children who needed their wills strengthened. I did too.

Mother Nurture, then, is a way we can strengthen our will to choose what is true and good. Ultimately, to choose to please God. Here are some ways we can do this:

1. Carve out space to contemplate with God, which leads to an examined life.
2. Engage in prayerful, God-led goal planning.
3. Choose habits carefully and create habit-action plans.
4. Assess regularly with an accountability community.

I encourage you to include what you can in your morning date with Jesus. As you do so, you'll actually have more joyful energy because of whom you broke your fast with.

Holy Audacity, Being Unhurried, and the Gospel

At last, we're in the Holy of Holies to be immersed in the gospel of Jesus—the soul, where the ark of the covenant rests. Christ dwells here and waits for us.

There is nothing more important than maintaining your inner being where God dwells. A strong spirit can sustain a broken body, but a crushed spirit cannot be sustained even by the strongest of bodies. The treatment for the malady of a hurried, faceless, persistent, zombielike state is not to go inward toward self but rather upward toward God.

As parents, we wish to give our best to our children. We want to be present. We want to listen to their hearts with our own—undivided and uncluttered. For that is what our Father does with us. Experience it first with him. Proactive, intentional Mother Nurture rhythms can make the space to do just that.

When I was eight, I was gifted the loveliest diary I'd ever seen. It had a pretty gold lock and a key to match. At first, I simply wrote my thoughts. But once Jesus became my one magnificent obsession, I couldn't stop writing to him. Journal after journal, my prayers poured out. I didn't know it, but I had naturally started a life-giving habit. I needed to meet with my Jesus each morning, in the Holy of Holies of my soul.

That's where we remember not just *what* we are—created, beloved, rescued, dependent beings—but *whose* we are. Linger there. Just as Joshua did after Moses left the tent of meeting. Dwell there. Just as King David sat before the Lord when his infant son died. It was then the Lord bestowed upon him the staggering, astonishing, gloriously gracious Davidic covenant. Hear him renewing his everlasting covenant with *you*.

Ultimately, Mother Nurture is cultivating intentional habits that propel you to the Holy of Holies of your soul to face Jesus with your authentic face—the one he is restoring to you, which you will fully grow into when the new creation comes. Therefore, Mother Nurture is not an act of striving but of *resting*—trusting that God will bring all things to completion in his unhurried, perfect time. And when you come to see that God is faithful to uphold you, *his* holy audacity will become your own.

Min Hwang could not have imagined God's plans for her as a pastor's wife with four creative children, getting to live out her passion for Christ through homeschooling, mentoring mothers, and capturing beauty through art for Truth and Beauty Studio. She is the founder of the nonprofit Life-Giving Motherhood and shares her homeschool and home culture resources on her ever-evolving website, MinJungHwang.com, while also serving on the board of the Charlotte Mason Institute. Min's desire is to help mothers curate the Christ-centered education their hearts ache to give their children—cooperating with God to build a legacy aligned with his everlasting kingdom. | @min.j.hwang

Conclusion

This collection of essays is more than just a resource; it is a testament to the multifaceted and deeply personal journey of homeschooling. The voices of these thirty diverse and dedicated parents provide an invitation into a world where education is not merely an academic pursuit but a holistic way of life. These moms and dads illuminate the myriad ways in which homeschooling shapes not only the minds of our children but also the hearts and spirits of those who guide them.

The beauty of homeschooling lies in its ability to mold itself to the unique needs and values of each family. Whether it's integrating cultural heritage into the curriculum, fostering a deep connection with nature, or navigating the complexities of modern life, each story in *Homegrown* reveals the adaptability and constancy required for this journey. The contributors share their triumphs and struggles, their moments of doubt, and their unwavering commitment to providing a nurturing and enriching educational environment for their children.

One of the most profound insights that emerges from this anthology is the dual education that occurs within homeschooling. As parents teach their children, they themselves become students once more. They embark on a second education, one that is rich with personal growth, self-discovery, and the cultivation of virtues such as patience, compassion, and courage.

In the process of teaching our children, we uncover new dimensions of ourselves. We learn to see the world through fresh eyes, embracing curiosity and wonder alongside our children. We face challenges that test our limits, only to emerge stronger and more resourceful. We forge bonds with our children that are deepened by shared learning and mutual discovery. This unpredictable by-product of homeschooling is a gift that enriches the lives of parents, adding depth and meaning to our own journeys.

The home educators in this collection acknowledge the difficult choices, the moments of doubt, and the relentless pursuit of balance in a world that often demands more than we feel we can give. Yet, through it all, we see a community bound by a shared vision of what education can be—a beautiful, life-encompassing endeavor that nurtures not only the intellect but also the heart and soul.

We recognize the profound impact that home education has on our lives. It is a journey that requires wholehearted dedication, boundless creativity, and an unshakable belief in the potential of our children. It is a path marked by steadfastness in the face of adversity, the courage to forge our own way, and the joy of witnessing our children grow and flourish in an environment tailored to their unique needs and strengths.

Here's to the continued adventure of learning and growing together, hand in hand, heart to heart. Let us embrace the unpredictability and beauty of the homeschooling journey, knowing that it is not just about imparting knowledge but about nurturing a love of learning, fostering strong family bonds, and cultivating a life of purpose and meaning. Let us celebrate the diversity of our community, recognizing that there is no one-size-fits-all approach to homeschooling and that each family's journey is unique and valuable.

May we go forth with renewed confidence and vision, inspired by those who share their wisdom with us, and may we continue to forge a path that is true to our values, our dreams, and our unwavering commitment to raising homegrown kids.

Notes

Chapter 1 The Beauty We Find at Home

1. *Hook*, directed by Steven Spielberg, produced by Kathleen Kennedy, Frank Marshall, and Gerald R. Molen (Amblin Entertainment and TriStar Pictures, 1991).

2. Betty Smith, *A Tree Grows in Brooklyn*, 2001 Perennial Classics edition (HarperCollins, 2001), 83.

3. John Taylor Gatto, *Dumbing Us Down: The Hidden Curriculum of Compulsory Schooling* (New Society Publishers, 1992), 20.

4. Elaine Cooper, ed., *When Children Love to Learn: A Practical Application of Charlotte Mason's Philosophy for Today* (Crossway, 2004), 164.

Chapter 2 The Elements We Rely on Most

1. "Jim Gaffigan: Mr. Universe—4 KIDS," YouTube video, 7:16, uploaded by jimgaffigan, October 9, 2012, https://www.youtube.com/watch?v=GEbZrY0G9PI.

2. Kim Martinez, "No Child Left Inside: Be Out There," *NWF Blog* (blog), January 8, 2016, https://blog.nwf.org/2011/03/no-child-left-inside-be-out-there/.

3. Carla Hannaford, *Smart Moves: Why Learning Is Not All in Your Head* (Great River Books, 2005), 143.

4. Kim John Payne and Lisa M. Ross, *Simplicity Parenting: Using the Extraordinary Power of Less to Raise Calmer, Happier, and More Secure Kids* (Ballantine Books, 2009), 83.

5. Peter Gray, *Free to Learn: Why Unleashing the Instinct to Play Will Make Our Children Happier, More Self-Reliant, and Better Students for Life* (Basic Books, 2013).

6. The Cornell Lab of Ornithology, "The Basics: Feather Molt," All About Birds, April 20, 2008, https://www.allaboutbirds.org/news/the-basics-feather-molt/.

7. Leslie Martino, *The Joy of Slow: Restoring Balance and Wonder to Homeschool Learning* (TarcherPerigee, 2024), 219.

8. Deborah Meier, *The Power of Their Ideas: Lessons for America from a Small School in Harlem* (Beacon Press, 1995), 170, emphasis in original.

9. Brooke Nielson, "Writing as a Second Language: Psycholinguistic Processes in Composing," PhD dissertation (University of California at San Diego, 1979).

10. Mike Rose, *Lives on the Boundary: A Moving Account of the Struggles and Achievements of America's Educationally Underprepared* (Penguin Books, 1989), 188–89.

11. Tania Luna and LeeAnn Renninger, *Surprise: Embrace the Unpredictable and Engineer the Unexpected* (TarcherPerigee, 2015), 46–60.

12. Hannah Anderson, *Humble Roots: How Humility Grounds and Nourishes Your Soul* (Moody, 2016), 12.

13. The Cornell Lab of Ornithology, "How Birds Make Colorful Feathers," All About Birds, accessed November 19, 2024, https://academy.allaboutbirds.org/how-birds-make-colorful-feathers/.

14. James Clear, *Atomic Habits: An Easy & Proven Way to Build Good Habits & Break Bad Ones* (Avery, 2018).

15. Benjamin Hardy, *Willpower Doesn't Work: Discover the Hidden Keys to Success* (Hachette, 2018), 77.

16. Charlotte Mason, *Home Education* (Simply Charlotte Mason, 2009), 136.

17. Charlotte Mason, *Parents and Children* (Simply Charlotte Mason, 2009), 159.

Chapter 3 The Roadmap for Forging Our Way

1. Charlotte M. Mason, *Home Education: Training and Educating Children Under Nine*, Homeschooler Series, vol. 1 (Tyndale, 1989), 153.

2. Charlotte M. Mason, *Towards a Philosophy of Education* (Tyndale, 1998), 99.

3. Mason, *Home Education* (1989), 231.

4. Charlotte M. Mason, *Home Education: Training and Educating Children Under Nine Years of Age* (Tyndale, 1998), 174.

5. Susan Schaeffer Macaulay, *For the Children's Sake: Foundations of Education for Home and School* (Crossway, 1984).

6. Margery Williams, *The Velveteen Rabbit* (Heinemann, 1922), 13.

7. Natalie Savage Carlson, *The Family Under the Bridge* (Harper & Row, 1958), 95.

8. Gary D. Schmidt, *Robert McCloskey*, Twayne's United States Author Series (Twayne Publishers, 1990), 149.

9. Schmidt, *Robert McCloskey*, 150.

10. Robert McCloskey, *Time of Wonder* (Viking Press, 1957), 28.

11. Marguerite de Angeli, *The Door in the Wall* (Doubleday & Co., 1949), 76.

12. Carla Hayden and Emma Kantor, "Jason Reynolds Takes Up the Mantle of National Ambassador," *Publishers Weekly*, January 17, 2020, https://www.publishersweekly.com/pw/by-topic/childrens/childrens-authors/article/82196-jason-reynolds-takes-up-the-mantle-of-national-ambassador.html.

13. Marguerite de Angeli, *Bright April* (Doubleday & Co., 1946), 41.

14. De Angeli, *Bright April*, 24.

15. De Angeli, *Bright April*, 26.

16. Noriko Suzuki, "Japanese Democratization and the Little House Books: The Relation Between General Head Quarters and The Long Winter in Japan After World War II," *Children's Literature Association Quarterly* 31, no. 1 (March 2006): 65–86, https://muse.jhu.edu/article/198529.

17. David Brooks, "How to Save a Sad, Lonely, Angry and Mean Society," *New York Times*, January 25, 2024, https://www.nytimes.com/2024/01/25/opinion/art-culture-politics.html.

18. Gregory Boyle, *Tattoos on the Heart: The Power of Boundless Compassion* (Free Press, 2010), 71.

19. Susan Wise Bauer and Jessie Wise, *The Well-Trained Mind: A Guide to Classical Education at Home*, second ed. (Norton and Company, 2004); Sarah McKenzie, *Teaching from Rest: A Homeschooler's Guide to Unshakable Peace* (Classical Academic Press, 2015).

20. Charlotte M. Mason, *An Essay Towards a Philosophy of Education: A Liberal Education for All* (Kegan Paul, Trench, Trübner & Co., Ltd., 1925), 109.

21. Charlotte M. Mason, *Parents and Children*, third ed. (Kegan Paul, Trench, Trübner & Co., Ltd., 1904), 246–47.

22. Mason, *Essay Towards a Philosophy of Education*, 211.

23. James K. A. Smith, *We Are What We Love* (Brazos, 2016), 22.

24. Charlotte M. Mason, *Home Education* (Wilder Publications, 1886), 227.

25. Henry Wadsworth Longfellow, "The Arrow and the Song," in *The Belfry of Bruges and Other Poems* (Little, Brown and Company, 1844). Public domain.

26. Paul David Tripp, *Parenting: 14 Gospel Principles That Can Radically Change Your Family* (Crossway, 2016), 14–15.

27. Gordon Neufeld and Gabor Maté, *Hold On to Your Kids: Why Parents Need to Matter More Than Peers* (Ballantine Books, 2006), 11.

28. Gretchen Rubin, "Secret of Adulthood: The Days Are Long, but the Years Are Short," Gretchen Rubin, September 10, 2014, https://gretchenrubin.com/articles/secret-of-adulthood-the-days-are-long-but-the-years-are-short/.

Chapter 4 The Relationships That Carry Us Through

1. Diana Divecha, "How Alloparents Can Help You Raise a Family," *Greater Good Magazine*, June 16, 2021, https://greatergood.berkeley.edu/article/item/how_alloparents_can_help_you_raise_a_family.

2. Bob Brody, "The Surprising Benefits of Playing with Your Grandkids," Morningstar, November 17, 2023, https://www.morningstar.com/news/marketwatch/20231117202/the-surprising-benefits-of-playing-with-your-grandkids.

3. Isabelle Roskam et al., "Parental Burnout Around the Globe: A 42-Country Study," *Affective Science* 2 (March 2021): 58, https://doi.org/10.1007/s42761-020-00028-4.

4. Hara E. Maran, "The Dangers of Loneliness," *Psychology Today*, July 1, 2003, www.psychologytoday.com/us/articles/200307/the-dangers-loneliness.

5. Adrian F. Ward, Kristen Duke, Ayelet Gneezy, and Maarten W. Bos, "Brain Drain: The Mere Presence of One's Own Smartphone Reduces Available Cognitive Capacity," *Journal of the Association for Consumer Research* 2, no. 2 (2017): 140–54, doi:10.1086/691462.

6. Alan Sroufe and Daniel Siegel, "The Verdict Is In: The Case for Attachment Theory," *Psychotherapy Networker*, March/April 2011, eadn-wc01-10021800.nxedge.io/wp-content/uploads/2020/09/1271-the-verdict-is-in-1.pdf.

7. Marcus Wilder and Chris M. Coursey, *The 4 Habits of Joy-Filled People: 15 Minute Brain Science Hacks to a More Connected and Satisfying Life* (Moody, 2019), 32.

Chapter 5 The Belonging We Crave

1. Jo Jones and William D. Mosher, "Fathers' Involvement with Their Children: United States, 2006–2010," *National Health Statistics Reports*, no. 71 (2013), https://www.cdc.gov/nchs/data/nhsr/nhsr071.pdf.

2. Seth Gershenson et al., "Working Paper 25254: The Long-Run Impacts of Same-Race Teachers," National Bureau of Economic Research, rev. February 2021, https://www.nber.org/papers/w25254.

3. Sharif El-Mekki, "Black Teachers Matter: Why Aren't Schools Trying to Keep Them?" *Word In Black*, May 8, 2024, https://wordinblack.com/2024/05/black-teachers-matter-why-arent-schools-trying-to-keep-them/.

4. National Center for Education Statistics, "Condition of Education: Racial/Ethnic Enrollment in Public Schools," U.S. Department of Education, Institute of Education Sciences, accessed November 20, 2024, https://nces.ed.gov/programs/coe/indicator/cge.

5. "How Many Black Male Teachers Are There in the US?" USA Facts, accessed November 20, 2024, https://usafacts.org/articles/how-many-black-male-teachers-are-there-in-the-us/.

6. Cindy Rollins, *Mere Motherhood: Morning Times, Nursery Rhymes, and My Journey Toward Sanctification* (CiRCE Institute, 2016), 130.

Chapter 6 The Encouragement That Spurs Us Ahead

1. Charlotte M. Mason, *School Education: Developing a Curriculum*, Homeschooler Series, vol. 3 (Tyndale, 1989), 182.

2. Sonya Shafer, "Atmosphere: Core Values of Charlotte Mason," Simply Charlotte Mason, accessed December 2, 2024, https://simplycharlottemason.com/blog/atmosphere-core-values-of-charlotte-mason/.

3. Mason, *Home Education* (1989), 44.

4. Robin Wall Kimmerer, "Skywoman Falling," *Emergence Magazine*, November 5, 2020, https://emergencemagazine.org/op_ed/skywoman-falling/.

5. Elizabeth Goudge, *The Rosemary Tree* (Hendrickson, 2013), 54.

Chapter 7 The Vision Inspiring Our Days

1. As quoted in Sonia Nieto and Patty Bode, *Affirming Diversity: The Sociopolitical Context of Multicultural Education*, fifth ed. (Pearson, 2008), 292.

2. Nieto and Bode, *Affirming Diversity*, 216.

3. Jo Boaler, *Mathematical Mindsets* (John Wiley & Sons, 2015), 2–3.

4. Boaler, *Mathematical Mindsets*, 6.

5. Mason, *Home Education* (2009), 34.

6. Stephanie Bogan, "Silence Those Voices in Your Head," *InvestmentNews*, November 30, 2016, https://www.investmentnews.com/practice-management/opinion/the-limitless-advisor/silence-those-voices-in-your-head-69986.

7. Mason, *Parents and Children* (2009), 46, emphasis added.

8. Mason, *Home Education* (2009), 109, emphasis added.

9. Mason, *Parents and Children* (2009), 201.

10. Mason, *Home Education* (1989), 12.

11. Charlotte M. Mason, *Ourselves: Improving Character and Conscience*, Homeschooler Series, vol. 4 (Tyndale, 1989), 9–10.

12. Mason, *Ourselves*, 11–32.

13. Charlotte M. Mason, *Parents and Children: The Role of the Parent in the Education of the Child*, Homeschooler Series, vol. 2 (Tyndale, 1989), 279.

AMBER O'NEAL JOHNSTON lives in Georgia, nestled among pine trees, hammocks, and zip lines with her husband and their four children. Her happy place is the back porch on a rainy day, preferably with a giant mug of hot tea and a good book. And although she was raised in the air-conditioning, somehow the woods is where she feels most at home these days. Amber is the author of *Soul School* and *A Place to Belong* and is a regular contributor to the Wild + Free and Charlotte Mason homeschooling communities. She writes and speaks about the beauty of an inclusive and culturally and socially conscious home environment, and you can find her sharing literary mirrors and windows at HeritageMom.com and on Instagram @heritagemomblog.

Connect with Amber:

HeritageMom.com

 @HeritageMomBlog

A Note from the Publisher

Dear Reader,

Thank you for selecting a Revell book! We're so happy to be part of your life through this work.

Revell's mission is to publish books that offer hope and help for meeting life's challenges, and that bring comfort and inspiration. We know that the right words at the right time can make all the difference; it is our goal with every title to provide just the words you need.

We believe in building lasting relationships with readers, and we'd love to get to know you better. If you have any feedback, questions, or just want to chat about your experience reading this book, please email us directly at publisher@revellbooks.com. Your insights are incredibly important to us, and it would be our pleasure to hear how we can better serve you.

We look forward to hearing from you and having the chance to enhance your experience with Revell Books.

The Publishing Team at Revell Books
A Division of Baker Publishing Group
publisher@revellbooks.com